SUBJEKTILE

Edited by
Marcus Coelen and Felix Ensslin

Kathrin Thiele

The Thought of Becoming

Gilles Deleuze's Poetics of Life

diaphanes

Dieses Buch wurde gedruckt mit freundlicher Unterstützung von:
Printed with kind support of:
Boehringer Ingelheim Stiftung für Geisteswissenschaften
Johanna und Fritz Buch Gedächtnisstiftung

1. Auflage / First edition
ISBN 978-3-03734-036-3

www.diaphanes.net

Layout: 2edit, Zürich
Druck / Printing: Pustet, Regensburg

Contents

Acknowledgments

This book could not have been written without the support, help, and energy of the many people and institutions accompanying me throughout the time of its creation. First and foremost I would like to thank my advisor, Rodolphe Gasché, for his longstanding support and interest in this project. His continual encouragement was both essential for the completion of the dissertation, and it gave me the confidence to work for this publication. I am also deeply indebted to the other members of my committee at the University of Buffalo: Ewa Płonowska Ziarek, who in her helpful and generous way gave a concrete structure to this project, and Kalliopi Nikolopoulou who in a moment when it was needed most offered her intellectual and professional support. From the many outstanding scholars I was so lucky to benefit from at the University of Buffalo, I would also like to thank Elizabeth Grosz who was the first to teach me Deleuze, and thus gave this project its original impetus.

On the other side of the ocean, I would like to thank the DFG-Graduiertenkolleg *Repräsentation – Rhetorik – Wissen* at the Europa-Universität Viadrina in whose intellectual context I was able to further deepen and extend my research after my studies in Buffalo. Here, I am most of all indebted to Anselm Haverkamp whom I owe so much more than the inspiration to my title. This stimulating intellectual milieu found continuation for me in the DFG-Graduiertenkolleg *Lebensformen und Lebenswissen* at the Universität Potsdam and the Europa-Universität Viadrina, in which as a post-doctoral fellow I have found the right atmosphere to ultimately complete this manuscript. I would like to extend my special gratitude to Katrin Trüstedt, Christoph Menke, Dirk Quadflieg and again Anselm Haverkamp.

Without the financial support from different sides this project would also not have found its way to publication. I would like to thank the *Deutsche Akademische Austauschdienst*, the University of Buffalo, and the *Deutsche Forschungsgemeinschaft* for supporting my studies towards my PhD in both Buffalo and Berlin. Hereafter, I would like to extend my sincerest thankfulness to the *Geschwister Boehringer Ingelheim Stiftung für Geisteswissenschaften* in Ingelheim am Rhein, and the *Johanna und Fritz Buch Gedächtnis-Stiftung*, whose generous financial support made this book publication possible.

I am very honored to be part of a publication series that envisions such theoretical standards and cutting-edge subject matters as Subjektile does. I am thus more than grateful to the editors, Marcus Coelen and Felix Ensslin, for seeing this potential in my work and guiding me through the editing process. In this context I would also like to thank the Verlag *diaphanes*, and especially Michael Heitz and Sabine Schulz.

Last but not least, without the help of friends and family who offered insightful comments and loving reassurance, this project could not have come to fruition. For thought-provoking input on the final version in as much as on earlier drafts I thank specifically Marcus Coelen, Thomas Khurana, Leonard Lawlor and Dirk Setton. To Alastair Hunt and Monika Lanz I am indebted for much more than merely polishing what is not my native language. On the side of my family, I thank Alex, Barbara, and Cornelia Thiele for their wonderful sisterly love, and for their continual support my gratitude goes to Gabriele Lanz, Jürgen Kaiser, and Edith Kaiser. Most of all I thank Birgit Kaiser who not only read and thought through everything with me, but also lived with me through all of this.

While owing everything to this living community, this book is dedicated to the memory of my mother.

I.

Introduction: On Ethics and Poetics

Nothing to be done.
(Beckett, *Waiting for Godot*)

One single question marked the beginning of this project and it pointed out the direction for everything to follow: ›What is wrong with Ethics?‹ This was our first and foremost concern, which, however, in itself is already a double concern. But in saying that much we, before we even have started, announce already a different beginning. We must remain patient for a little while until we can raise the issue of doubling again. First we have to explain how since then, since uttering this statement, we have moved further, maybe even to *somewhere else*. These things happen on a journey, as we all know. And yet, now, after all this time, as we look to adequately introduce what will actually follow here, the issues expressing themselves in this question must still stand at the very beginning. Whatever has *become* must again start with this assertion and we must introduce our undertaking by it. Thus, again — and this first repetition just heralds the many reappearances, reiterations, and returns that will confront us frequently on our itinerary throughout this book: ›What is wrong with Ethics?‹

Here is the alternate beginning, the one that just a moment ago was silenced: the statement at issue, question or claim, harbors in itself a double concern. On the one hand, the expression clearly serves a critical gesture. It takes up the gist of sincere critiques of Ethics that developed over the course of its long history, a history so closely linked to the history of philosophy itself that it, therefore, implicates a critique of ›what philosophy is‹, too. Today this means that the investigation into what is wrong with Ethics speaks the demand to explore the problems and to explicate the shortcomings lying in the presumption of Ethics (and philosophy) to claim for itself the sphere of the Universal, Truth, and Reason — concepts standing for the conditions of philosophical thought as such.

But we move too quickly here. Before we lose the possibility of hearing something else in the statement ›What is wrong with Ethics‹, because too quickly we assure ourselves to know already what it is all about, we must pay closer attention to what happens when we let the statement echo further. Before we slide too easily into a critical dispute over the canon of philosophy, we must ponder the statement so that something else becomes hearable: What is (actually) wrong with Ethics?

All of a sudden the critical claim becomes a question of curiosity, a persisting interest in the ethical that does not disappear no matter which critique of Ethics is articulated. On the other hand, therefore, the expression implicitly also speaks the concern that by unraveling the impasses of canonical ethical thinking, we must not forget about the specificity of the ethical dimension altogether. Thus, the movement that we try to bring across here in the most linear way possible is complicated. And the double—and thus already more than uni-directional—sense is not even the whole story. For as soon as we are about to grasp the doubling further concerns are generated, which can no longer be sufficiently grappled with in a *pro* and *contra* argument. The story to be told in order to prepare the grounds for the book ahead is multifaceted.

And yet the concern that truly stands at the beginning is a critique of what is known as Ethics—as capital ›E‹ Ethics. In considering what is wrong with this kind of Ethics—the Ethics of universal principles, of the Good and the Right, whether in its idealist, utilitarian, communitarian, or liberal version—we can count today on strong allies for interrogating the ›natural‹ equations of the Good with Reason, the Ethical with the Universal, and all of them with the—again capital ›T‹—Truth. In the continental philosophical tradition there is, at least since Søren Kierkegaard's critique of Hegel's philosophy and his thought of Ethics (Kierkegaard 1983), an audible, even if ›minoritarian‹ discourse of a ›decapitated‹ ethics, and thus in the broader sense also of a different kind of philosophy.[1] Jacques Derrida's notion of

---

1 Switching from the capital ›E‹ to the small ›e‹ can be read as a first lesson learned from the critiques of Ethics. In what follows it will be mainly the notion of ›the ethical‹ and at the utmost the minor ›ethics‹, which is of concern to us, both of which precisely do not address an applicable normative system but rather the broadest philosophical approach to ethics, an approach that is expressed in the question of thinking itself as what it is ›to do philosophy‹. And

phallogocentrism (Derrida 1997) maybe expresses best for us how far this critique has penetrated the supposed neutrality and universality of the philosophical tradition up to today. It permeates everything and of course does not stop before the thought of Ethics.[2]

All this immediately comes to mind when we start thinking of Ethics and what *is* wrong with it. In our post-modern times it seems as if it has become our second nature that any conviction in what once was called Enlightenment — the columns of equality, freedom, and fraternity as re-inscriptions of the philosophical concepts of Universalism, Subjectivity, and Reason — is not only lost, but, as if everything needs to be doubled, it is ›lost‹ lost. It is so lost that no further search for any better articulation would be of help. Ethics, once counted as the highest reach for philosophical thought, either becomes a purely academic exercise or it is watered down by too many appropriations into ›applicable‹ approaches. Between total abstraction from daily life and complete immersion of Ethics into every imaginable little niche of society, there seems to be little in-between.[3] And it is this picture

---

since, as the latter part of this introduction will make explicit, our argument strives for a becoming-imperceptible of Ethics to itself, so that a new line of flight for the ethical dimension is opened, we will have to cross over different philosophical registers: from ethics to poetics.

2 To name just one exponent of a whole ›pack‹ of thinkers, in an attempt to give conceptual exactness to the always already directed or biased neutrality and universality of every thought, is of course more than problematic. However, flipping on the other side and pretending to be able to enumerate supposedly all voices is doubtful, too. Acknowledging that one will always remain guilty of having made an (il)legitimate choice, and yet wishing to supplement this selection at least to some degree, let me give some other names that must be thought of when we speak of the critical re-inscription of the Western tradition of Universalism, Reason, and Truth — apart from Gilles Deleuze of course, who will be the singular focus of this book: Michel Foucault's foundational work on *Power* and *Discourse* (c.f. e.g. Foucault 1990), Jacques Lacan's *practice of Psychoanalysis* (cf. e.g. Lacan 1997), Emmanuel Levinas' thought of *Otherwise than Being* (cf. Levinas 1998) and Jean-François Lyotard's *differend* (cf. Lyotard 1999) must be named, as much as Luce Irigaray's work on *Sexual Difference* (cf. e.g. Irigaray 1993), Laclau and Mouffe's thought of *hegemony* (cf. Laclau/Mouffe 1996), and Jacques Rancière's ›*mésentente*‹ (cf. Rancière 1998), all of which are groundbreakers for but also effectuated by feminist, post-colonial, gay & lesbian, and other socio-political movements our societies have witnessed in the decades since WWII.

3 Without being able to elaborate on the diversity of research on Ethics (capital E) undertaken in either academic or other professional contexts, let me at

that makes an engagement with the ethical a somewhat preposterous undertaking, exposed to the cynicism of all those who, from the very constitutive problems of *every* Ethics, maybe even of the mere thought of the ethical as such, draw the conclusion that we must have done with ethics altogether, that because so much hubris goes on under this name, any further investigation into the question of ethics as such is perpetuating at its best a melancholic, at its worst a utopian, but in any case a human-all-too-human endeavor.

It is from this double or even triple dissatisfaction of what seems to be the last word on the ethical today that this project takes its inspiration and asks one more time: but what actually is wrong with ethics? Reading the question in this more curious way admits to the conviction that the ethical is too essential to us, that even when looking outdated it can never be done with. And having begun above to count out allies in regard to an awareness of the ethical, we could also speak of a kind of renaissance of engagement with the ethical. This time reversing the ordinary direction and thus counting from contemporary ›continental‹ thought back to Kierkegaard's caesura with Hegelianism, there are numerous attempts to re-conceptualize ethics in order to inspire philosophy again with a practical dimension, without at the same time falling into the traps of either heightened idealism or mere pedagogical life guidance. In such re-thinking of the question of the ethical the prospect of moving somewhere else with ethics is, however, essential and it is this prospect that the project ahead of us also tries to tackle. In re-investigating the question of the

---

least name the range of it by merely enumerating the most important schools or thought-trains that are generally found as leading in the discussion of this topic. The variety reaches from Neo-Aristotelian and Wittgensteinian analytical philosophy working on a universally valid and applicable (Meta-)Ethics based on Aristotle's life-forms, via the more politically inspired philosophical discussions of Ethics from either a liberal or a communitarian perspective, privileging either the freedom of the Subject or the Good of the community as that which must give measure to such an Ethics, to the newly celebrated Bioethical research whose representatives hope to have found a non-anthropomorphic perspective on the question of what life is, and thus also of what it is all about, perhaps forgetting, however, the anthropocentric baggage they carry along in trusting their ›objective scientific‹ perspective, in as much as it includes all those adjectival Ethics that develop from the most distant societal angles, be it Eco-, Medical or Business Ethics.

ethical I hope not only to show a way out of certain deadlocks every Ethics necessarily experiences, but also to carefully circumnavigate any simplistic appropriation of ›this world‹, the reference of which must, however, not be avoided in a discussion of the ethical.

But in saying this, yet another beginning suggests itself, and one more issue must be addressed at this beginning because it instigated this project in its specific orientation. Why ethics at all? one might ask. Why not finally leave behind this philosophically abstract realm of prescriptions, principles, and rules, and move on — especially since there is it seems another notion much better suited to do the job in these ultimately secularized times? We are of course alluding to the notion of politics, or to say it in a less substantive way, the dimension of the political, both of which are today the much more common references when it comes to an engagement with *this* world. A thorough elaboration of the point in question, that is the relation between ethics and politics, their interrelation as the ethico-political dimension but also their differentiation in regard to how each of them addresses and intervenes into this world, would be most desirable. However, precisely out of the *structural* interrelatedness of the two dimensions, such categorical analysis is most difficult to achieve. And at this point this question must remain insufficiently answered and has to be postponed to another time. But what I can say and hope to raise at least through my investigation into the specific question of ethics — and this precisely out of concern for the political — is an awareness in regard to all too unproblematic deployments and substitutive usages of these two terms in too many of our contemporary discussions. While the progressive substitution of politics for ethics in the last century might have been an emancipatory move away from all *a priori* fixation of the world and thus a tool for the multiplication of lives we live, our contemporary political conditions also make us feel the political ambivalences of both a proceeding moralization of politics and a politicization of nearly every single aspect of our lives. This investigation purposefully chose the dimension of the ethical, and although it remains focused on this element alone, in what follows I do hope to address today's *Zeitgeist* effectively when claiming that for the sake of both areas — ethics *and* politics — we must re-learn to a certain degree to differentiate between the two.

After these extended beginnings, it does not come as a great surprise that the project at stake here is not interested in a controversy between specific aspects of an already established frame for Ethics. Rather, my thought is still caught up in the question of the ethical itself, of how to approach and where to locate it philosophically, and thus this book pursues first and foremost the demanding question of *how to think the ethical.* In choosing such an approach to the question of ethics we must leave aside all actual discussions of Ethics, which are always already concerned with the ›best‹ way to articulate the ethical, arguing about the one principle on which to found it. It is as Nietzsche once formulated:

> As strange as it may sound, the problem of morality itself has been *missing* from every ›science of morals‹ so far: there was no suspicion that anything was really a problem. Viewed properly, the ›grounding of morals‹ (as philosophers called it, as they demanded it of themselves) was only an erudite form of good *faith* in the dominant morality, a new way of *expressing* it; as such, it was itself already situated within the terms of a certain morality. (BGE #186)

In appreciation of Nietzsche's unsurpassed rigor in thought, the distinction between different possible Ethics or moralities on the one side, and re-thinking the *question of the ethical* as such on the other side, i.e. the *problem of morality* that gives orientation to my discussion here, goes back to his critique. In order to truly move somewhere else with the ethical, a move that will have effects on and be already effectuated by a different philosophical thought, we must un-ground the grounding itself. It is as easy (or difficult — depending on the perspective —) as that: we have to think differently!

To start with the question of thinking, of how to think the ethical, is then also the reason why the project will enter what seem to be the remotest and most outdated areas of philosophy: metaphysics and ontology, and the debate between transcendence and immanence placed at the heart of these philosophical regions. Only here, however, does the question of thinking become the question of philosophy proper, of what it means ›to do philosophy‹. And it is thus that the question of ethics is related to, if not transformed into, the controversy of how we think the world, which is also the question of how we approach ›this world, as it is‹. Our first claim is thus that that which can be read easily as an exaggerated complication of things is, to the contrary, the very condition of any a/effective discussion of the ethical. It is the conflict between a thought of transcendence *versus* one of immanence that determines from the very beginning where to go with the ethical, and it will be one of my major concerns in the following discussion to explicate in adequate detail how and why this is the case. In engaging with the philosophical terminology of transcendence and immanence it may seem as if this project is placed on a level too high to master, especially when claiming at the same time that to engage with *this* world is the reason for raising the question of the ethical at all. However, and this is our second claim, only in treating the issue on this level will we face adequately what the argument presented here — starting with the question of what is wrong with Ethics — sees as the fundamental problem in the tradition of Ethics: *transcendence.* It is this transcendental heritage seemingly glued to every thought of ethics, our post-metaphysical times notwithstanding, which will find problematization in the argument pursued here. And while such claim — to announce transcendence to be blamed for the impasses ethical thought finds itself in — appears as a crude and dangerous assertion of the ultimate reduction of thought to the realm of immanence, known to us only as either brute materialism or utter *Diesseitigkeit,* in such pre-judging we might make the most common and yet fatal mistake: not to move at the right speed and thus to judge too quickly. It might be that in rejecting this claim we simply do not yet know *what immanence is capable of,* because so far we only ever have thought immanence in the name or representation of ›Otherness‹, i.e. as the Other of transcendence and thus never dared to think *immanence in itself.* On a closer look then we will have to acknowledge that we are so caught up in the dualism of transcendence *versus* immanence that we are unable to see that there might be a different thought altogether — preceding this distinction in as much as being prior to any dualistically structured code of thinking itself.

Having said all this, we can propose our thesis: What is wrong with Ethics — this is what the following argument wants to explicate — is the seemingly natural belief that *either* one finds the ultimate principles that govern our way of life — *eternal* values, *universal* scope, and the one *Truth* — giving not only guarantee and meaning to this world but establishing also ›what ought to be‹, *or* one cannot but join into the victory of a relativism that again divides itself into either mere pseudo-arguments of ›freedom of speech‹ and a discourse of ›political correctness‹ or the elimination of all specificity to the constitutive ethical dimension of thought, both of which lead to cleansing thought of all its ethical potential and to shuffling the whole set of problems surrounding the ethical into the sphere of the political.

The discussion presented here will argue that a thought structured by such an *either/or* is the inescapable consequence of the logic of transcendence or, to say the same in different terms, of the logic of Being, that is ontology in the classical sense. While both of these ›logics‹ — as we want to call them — need, of course, to be handled carefully and must not be conflated, since they speak of this world according to different matrices, for our purposes they must be put together for what they fundamentally share: a belief (however concealed) in something ideal — something that is and has to be made present — behind the world such as it is lived and experienced; a belief that generates an image of this world as ›given‹ and is in consequence unable to avoid the common dead end streets of dualism: mind or matter, soul or body, true or false, good or evil. It is such belief in the real not as something to be produced and constructed — which is not at all the same as an ›anything goes‹ mentality — but as a (however complex and intriguing) ready-made out there, to be found and grasped correctly, which in a step further sets forth the ethical conviction that we first of all need the category of the Good in order to give orientation to our lives; and when then the high heavens of the Good fail, it seems that only Evil is left…

If, however, we dare to move somewhere else with the question of ethics, towards an ethics ›beyond Good and Evil‹ (a thought, of course, much more complicated than any simple stepping beyond), if we dare to think otherwise, as my discussion will more than once demand from the reader, we have to approach the ethical in a radically different manner — and the notion of ›radical‹ here is no hyperbolic addition. What the argument will show is that if we want to succeed in this thought we have to approach the ethical from a *radically immanent* perspective, venturing to take away everything that has become so natural to us when we think of Ethics. And to begin right at this moment, at the very start of the book: more than anything else we must rid ourselves from the belief that as a system of objective norms Ethics tells us ›what ought to be‹ and ›who we are‹. We must reject both Idealism and Subjectivism. Furthermore, what else is needed is that we must strip Ethics of everything that makes it a solution or an applicable conduct rather than a problem awaiting an always precarious response, *whensoever* and *wheresoever*. Ultimately, then, this means to make Ethics *imperceptible* as Ethics, and to redirect its discourse towards a more *indirect* way of thinking such as our move from the optical and present-oriented logic of Ethics to the latent proceedings of a poetics will suggest, a move that takes seriously what Michel Foucault once envisioned in his early article on Maurice Blanchot's »Thought of the Outside«. There Foucault claims that instead of thinking merely the truth, such a thought — a thought that is urgently needed for the possibility of any real future — rather thinks through ›fiction‹ (Foucault, 1998c: 149). It consists, he concludes, not »in showing the invisible, but in showing *the extent to which the invisibility of the visible is invisible*« (Foucault, 1998c: 153). Thus, when speaking of ›moving somewhere else‹ with ethics, we have to keep in mind such a primary refusal of the demand for presence and visibility in order to adequately understand what is at stake in the ethical claim proposed here.

Such an approach brings us to the philosophy of Gilles Deleuze. Deleuze, who never explicitly wrote on ethics, but whose major concern in all of his works was nonetheless to think differently, to produce a new thought — hopefully for a better future, one might add in a Nietzschean manner. His is also the project of reversing and finding a line of flight from what in his own terms is called ›majoritarian‹ philosophy, which from the perspective of modern philosophy — as Giorgio Agamben draws out in one of his articles on Deleuze — is the tradition of transcendental philosophy.[4]

---

4 See Agamben's two different trajectories of modern philosophy: »a line of immanence and a line of transcendence« (Agamben 1999: 239). According to this map the line of transcendence moves from Kant through Husserl and Heidegger and arrives at Levinas and Derrida, while the line of immanence begins with Spinoza, moves then to Nietzsche, crosses over to Heidegger, and leads into Deleuze and Foucault. While such categorizations always generalize something that is of course more complicated, distinguishing these two lines of philosophy is helpful when approaching the history of philosophy from a point of view that investigates how different ways of thinking end up approaching the same questions in significantly different manners. For very clarifying and

In his work, there are only very few passages in which Deleuze explicitly touches the question of ethics. This absence — an absence so striking that one cannot but pay attention to it — calls for further investigation. And it seems to be even more significant because of the irritating fact that most common criticisms issued against Deleuze point simultaneously to his lack of attention to the question of morality and normativity, and — contradicting this very first charge — to his provocative over-politicization of philosophy, especially, as is said, in his collaborations with Félix Guattari. The lack of any pure ethical concern in his philosophy together with the contamination of the order of thought with the impurity of social and political affairs seem to be the major accusations against Deleuze, which up to now do not make him a very common reference in the field of ethics. Again, however, such judgment comes too hastily. It is the aim of this work not only to demonstrate that one of Deleuze's major concerns in his *œuvre* is an attempt to re-formulate the relation that philosophy carries to ethico-political and other non-philosophical issues, but also to show that Deleuze's response to one of philosophy's main questions, the question of what it means ›to think‹, is a response with *inherent* ethical potential. However implicitly, Deleuze's whole work expresses an ethicality inherently linked to thought, and *vice versa* his whole work expresses a thought inherently linked to practice. And while the notions of practice and ethics cannot and should not be used in an undifferentiated manner, and we do need to acknowledge a certain distance between the practical and the ethical dimension, what we will see is that when it comes to Deleuze both notions become interrelated in such a manner that the one is always already in the vicinity of the other, which thus allows for the suggestion of a kind of reciprocal relation between the two.[5]

—

helpful discussions of the difference between the two most famous contemporary philosophers of difference, Derrida and Deleuze, especially in regard to the question of transcendence and immanence, cf. also Smith 2003, and Lawlor 2003b.

5 To state it thus implies the refutation of criticisms which claim that Deleuze defies all true ethicality both because of his affirmed Nietzschean heritage (against the much more cautious thought of the negative) and his conviction that in view of the many human and other catastrophes which this world is witnessing, it is only a thought of radical immanence that can lead a way out of a thought without force (*puissance*). Vincent Descombes (cf. Descombes 1980)

But again we have to slow down in order not to lose what is of significance here. Let me therefore explicate in a bit more detail here where such claim in regard to Deleuze's thought comes from.

At a historical moment in the philosophical field when it was rather difficult to touch the so called ›big issues‹, because it was believed that the question of transcendence vs. immanence was either long decided or, if this was not the case, would never find any conclusion, since such tension is constitutive of philosophy itself, Deleuze not only stressed the problem over and over in nearly every work that he completed, but went as far as claiming that a philosophy of radical immanence is both needed and possible. In continuation of a specific tradition in philosophy, a tradition that our discussion will trace in appropriate detail, his claim remained that we must dare a different thought — however impossible and futile it might seem at first. For no other reason did Michel Foucault in »Theatrum Philosophicum« speak of Deleuze's work as demanding a new thought, »thought without contradiction, without dialectics, without negation...« (Foucault 1998b: 358). And Foucault continues:

> Far from being the still incomplete and blurred image of an Idea that would, from on high and for all time, hold the answer, the problem lies in the idea itself, or rather the Idea exists only in the form of a problem: a distinctive plurality whose obscurity is nevertheless insistent, and in which the question ceaselessly stirs. (Ibid)

In the very same essay, which is devoted to Deleuze's major philosophical works *Difference and Repetition* and *The Logic of Sense*, Foucault concludes that such »new thought is possible« and »thought is again possible« (Foucault 1998b: 367).

> This thought does not lie in the future, promised by the most distant of new beginnings. It is present in Deleuze's texts — springing forth, dancing before us, in our midst; genital thought, intensive thought, affirma-

---

is of course to be named first in judging thus on *French Modern Philosophy* in general and on Deleuze in particular, but for a more recent replication of this claim, cf. Nick Nesbitt's »The Expulsion of the Negative: Deleuze, Adorno, and the Ethics of Internal Difference« (Nesbitt 2005).

tive thought, acategorical thought—each of these an unrecognizable face, a mask we have never seen before. (Ibid)

Taking this considerably enthusiastic statement of one intellectual towards another as yet a further point of departure, it is with Deleuze that I want to approach the ethical in a radically immanent manner. His outspoken project of immanence, an immanence immanent only to itself, or (to say the same in the language of ontology) his thought of becoming that moves further than the ontological difference of Being/being, will be read as a new line of flight for ethics itself. Thus, rather than interpreting the absence of an explicit discussion of the ethical as a shortcoming or lack, the intention of this project is to show that the ethical concern in Deleuze's philosophy is *everywhere*. Reading this Deleuzian ›empirical conversion‹ precisely as a new turn on practical philosophy, this book investigates a strange formula that structures Deleuze's philosophy at its most fundamental level:

ontology = ethics

Ontology as the thought of radical immanence contains always already an *ethical* attitude towards the world *in as much as* ethics ›is‹ always already a *constructive* rather than a prescriptive endeavor—such is the statement. While in a moment we will have to explain the complex character of this equation in order not to be perceived wrongly, let us look at this formula first in the way it presents itself to us, for the far-reaching consequences become identifiable instantaneously. Not only does such an approach strip ethics of everything that normally belongs to it—of all principles, norms, and judgments, which have always distinguished themselves precisely in *not being* (≠) ›what this world is‹ (ontology in the traditional sense)—but in this formula ethics also all of a sudden *becomes* philosophy, that is, it is *becoming-imperceptible* to itself and thus moves somewhere else. If, however, we imagine that positing such an equation affects only one side, we have not yet understood the logic of equation at stake here. The equation overseeing my project must be read as always already moving in at least two directions: ontology ›is‹ ethics in as much as ethics ›is‹ also ontology. Thus, while ethics will change its face so that it no longer represents any closed system of normative claims on top of ›what the world is‹, and rather becomes inherently linked to the question of thinking, i.e. constructing this world itself, such thought—ontology or metaphysics as the thought to think the world—also undergoes a radical transformation. Instead of being merely an accurate description of what the world is supposed to be, ontology in being related to ethics in this immediate and non-hierarchical way must itself transform into a practice, a creative practice or an active thought as we will call it. Taking up Deleuze's impetus to think a philosophy of immanence, a philosophy of *Difference and Repetition*, I will follow his grammar of thinking, which is a *grammar of becoming* writing a new ontology as a practical approach to *this* world. The equational sense proposed here leads to a different attitude towards this world, to what it means to live this world. In such understanding, ontology stays no longer as the thought of ›what is‹, but it becomes the thought of what ›*this world is capable of*‹—always already more than what it seems to be, always already a question of attitude, of *how* to create this world, and thus always already an *ethical* approach. That such an approach is, however, no simple utopianism caught up in the progressive logic of thought which it precisely claims to avoid, is exemplified in two most significant statements that Deleuze made on the ethical and that are of singular importance for our undertaking. Both of these statements distinguish Deleuze's thought from both ineffective extra-worldliness and the all too easy and straightforward appropriation into political activisms, two directions that are frequently chosen in Deleuze's more recent reception.[6]

Not surprisingly, the statements we are building on come in disguise. The first one we find in a book which rather than having anything ethical in mind asks the question *What is Philosophy?*. Here, in

---

6 For the claim of ›extra-worldliness‹ cf. esp. Alain Badiou's criticisms of vitalism, empiricism, and a mystical tendency issued against Deleuze at different occasions (e.g. Badiou 2000 and 2007), and Peter Hallward's *Out of This World. Deleuze and the Philosophy of Creation* (2006), who as a strong Badiouian thinker shares the former's opinion. For an in my opinion (and here I agree with both Badiou and Hallward) over-activist interpretation of Deleuze's philosophy, cf. Michael Hardt's and Antonio Negri's *Empire* and *Multitude. War and Democracy in the Age of Empire* (Hardt/Negri 2000 and 2004); for a ›mixed‹ reception into a *messianic politics*, cf. Giorgio Agamben's work on *bare life, form-of-life*, and, more recently, on *Profanations*, which he acknowledges was inspired by Deleuze (cf. Agamben 1998 and 2007).

his last collaboration with Guattari, »late in life« when this question can be spoken of again »concretely« instead of being asked »too indirectly or obliquely« (WPH: 1), they claim the following:

> It may be that believing in this world, in this life, becomes our most difficult task, or the task of a mode of existence still to be discovered on our plane of immanence today. This is the empiricist conversion (we have so many reasons not to believe in the human world; we have lost this world, worse than a fiancée or a god). The problem has indeed changed. (WPH: 75)[7]

And, at a very different time, right at the very beginning of his philosophical career in *The Logic of Sense*, of which Foucault said that it »could also have as a subtitle: *What Is Thinking?*« (Foucault 1998b: 354), Deleuze quite directly already tells us in the ›Twenty-First Series of the Event‹:

> Either ethics makes no sense at all, or this is what it means and has nothing else to say: not to be unworthy of what happens to us... Nothing more can be said and no more has ever been said: to become worthy of what happens to us, and thus to will and release the event... To become the offspring of one's event and not of one's actions, for the action is itself produced by the offspring of the event. (LS: 149–150)

Like the equation ›ontology = ethics‹, these two statements keep watch over and give structure to the project ahead of us, whose first and foremost aim it is to adequately understand both Deleuze's equational or serial thought, and to draw out comprehensibly what follows from it for the discussion of the ethical. It is our aim to take the exemplary character of these scattered statements on ethics not as

---

7 As we will see later on in this book, Deleuze speaks again and in yet another mask, this time in his writing on cinema, of the necessity to restore the belief in this world — »the world, as it is«, as he significantly adds there (cf. C2: 171–172). It is no accident that this thinker refers to the ethical twice in the guise of something else, be it cinema or philosophy. We already see that his approach to the ethical always has to speak from somewhere else in order not to reduce it to any applicable morality.

markers of a lack of attention by its author, but precisely as his singular way of approaching the ethical.

At this moment, however, still right at the beginning of this book, such announcement cannot but remain abstract. As is essential to our argument here, the transformative relation between ethics and ontology cannot be explained on the purely conceptual or definitional level but it must be performed in its movement itself. Thus, before we come back to the further description of our project, we should turn our attention to the movement at stake, the singular movement of the equation, which becomes productive for our purpose only when we actually understand how to read it.

Ontology = ethics. This is, as we clarified before, to state that while ontology ›is‹ ethics, ethics also ›is‹ ontology. There is never just one movement but always already a doubling at stake that cannot be brought to a halt. Instead of aiming at an ascending movement of normative claims that are built coherently and will find an endpoint, in my presentation of the equation ›ontology = ethics‹ which follows from Deleuze's thought of becoming I hope to create an encounter that ›flattens‹ and thus equalizes what before was always taken as a hierarchical relation.[8] In such a serial logic nothing is cancelled out. Rather, as Deleuze says:

> The two heterogeneous series converge toward a paradoxical element, which is their ›differentiator‹. This is the principle of the emission of singularities. The element belongs to no series; or rather, it belongs to both series at once and never ceases to circulate throughout them. (LS: 51)

In a serial encounter something will always be generated and produced, opening the series to infinite movement. However, the infinity

---

8 Instead of putting both on equal levels, ethics has mostly been seen to be second throughout the history of philosophy, after what is supposed to be philosophy proper. Even Kant's *Critique of Practical Reason* comes second and is built on his first *Critique of Pure Reason*, although Kant might be seen as one philosopher who gave ›Morality‹ a fundamental position in his thought. It is against the backdrop of this commonly supposed secondary character of ethics, as merely one special field of philosophy, that Emmanuel Levinas' claim that ethics comes first, even before ontology, is still a claim of great significance (cf. Levinas 1998 and 2000).

we speak of here remains on but one plane (this is the difference from all kinds of dialectical thinking). The closest mathematical sign to visualize such a *mapping*, as I would like to call it, is a proliferating ›=‹. It is neither the causal ›→‹, nor the hyphen ›—‹, a sign otherwise well suited to express serial effects of infinite proliferation. The equation as it is suggested in Deleuze's thought, however, does not merely link its elements in a chain that can be extended *ad infinitum*. If read as an *eternally insisting* movement rather than the mere substitution of one element by another, the ›=‹ is not simply equating two things (in the sense of making them the same or the copy of each other, that is, relating them in terms of resemblance). Rather equational thinking becomes a means of cartography, creating in a singular movement a (virtual) n-dimensional map, which never ›is‹ as presence but always only ever ›becomes‹ in the expression of something else. It expresses a movement of becoming that never bridges the difference that is its very condition. While causal thinking of course aims at precisely such an overcoming of difference, the hyphen in its one-dimensional quality also misses the movement at stake here: an infinitely immanent movement, moving in both directions at once without ever leaving the plane for a position outside of it, which would produce a movement immanent to something else instead of being immanent only to itself. In such an *affective* equation that can be read and dealt with from either side, the equals sign ›in the middle‹ stands for the movement itself. It is not merely equalizing ontology to ethics, or *vice versa*. Rather, it is the fold in-between two sides that not only opens the equation to infinite movement (multi*pli*city) but that makes each side also necessarily face the other—even if so only ever in disguise. Precisely with a concern for ethics as an engagement with *this* world, what I hope to show in my argument is that bringing the ethical onto the level of ontology does not equal (≠) an ultimate elimination of the possibility for something new, such as the statement ethics ›is‹ nothing but ›what is‹ at first seems to suggest. In bringing both in relation to each other so that they only ever come to life through each other, I want to show in what sense Deleuze's thought of becoming changes what we think of as ethics, but also what we think thought to be. Both must undergo a major transformation. Therefore, instead of seeing thought as mere theoretical reflection on practice, and thus continuing the theory/praxis divide that is another of philosophy's ›natural‹ assumptions, Deleuze approaches thought as much as a practice as any other practice it is supposed to reflect on. Again in an encounter with Foucault in which both discuss the question of »Intellectuals and Power«, Deleuze states very clearly what is essential for an adequate understanding of his thought. Explicating the shortcomings of the theory/practice divide as following from a perspective that understands their relationship in terms of »a process of totalization«, for him »the question is seen in a different light« (Foucault 1996: 74). Rather than understanding theory as complementing practice in a process to reach ultimate truth, for Deleuze,

> [t]he relationship which holds in the application of a theory is never one of resemblance. Moreover, from the moment a theory moves into its proper domain, it begins to encounter obstacles, walls, and blockages which require its relay by another type of discourse (ibid).

With such an understanding of the relation between theory and practice, an understanding, in which theory is »a relay from one practice to another« (ibid), Deleuze can conclude his opening statement to the discussion by arguing that because of such a relation of multiplication rather than separation, the theorizing intellectual or the thinker if you want »is no longer a subject, a representing or representative consciousness« (Foucault 1996: 75). To the contrary, Deleuze claims:

> Who speaks and acts? It is always a multiplicity, even within the person who speaks and acts... Representation no longer exists; there's only action—theoretical action and practical action which serve as relays and form networks. (ibid)

However, in as much as theory is practice what is called practice is also transformed and becomes »a set of relays from one theoretical point to another« (Foucault 1996: 74). Theory and practice are on but one level, on but one plane, which is the plane of immanence. From its character of application or unreflective behavior, practice, by becoming equal to thought, receives the character of a *task*; a task, however, which no longer finds legitimacy outside its own infinite practices but which has to face up to its inherent demand at any moment. This gives practice a new significance altogether: to be responsible before and for itself with no safety line at hand that always already predetermines ›what has to be done‹. As Deleuze points out in his essay »Michel Tournier and the World without Others«, there is no ›Other‹ available any longer, such as a safe transcendental structure that »assures the margins and the transitions in the world« (LS: 305). There is only immanence, an immanence that exposes us *radically* to the question of what happens when the Other »is missing from the structure of the world« (LS: 306). That such ›Otherlessness‹ in Deleuze does, however, in no way speak for a self-centered or even more rigid identitarian discourse, but rather claims a thought of ›waiting, following, and carrying‹, all notions inherently expressing the task for relation, will hopefully be brought across by our presentation from the very start.[9]

The equation of ›ontology = ethics‹ has to be seen as a re-formulation of the equational map that Deleuze draws out in his discussion of theory/thought and practice. In giving this equation the weight it deserves, in the course of the book we will develop the following claims: 1) in the affirmation of theory/thought as practice, ontology becomes a practical question, a task ›to create‹, while ethics becomes the affirmation of the world, as it is (radical immanent ethics) instead of the idealist rejection of this world; 2) Deleuze's ontology of becoming is, therefore, always already an active thought, which on the other side of the equation leads to the transformation of Ethics into the *ethos of becoming* that is best understood as a *poet(h)ics of life* as our argument will show; and 3) this leads to nothing but the re-formulation of the ethical question itself, which instead of being concerned with the essence of the world and its subjects — expressed in the imperative ›What ought to be‹ — can only ever expose itself to the most difficult task of ›What is to be done next‹.

Bringing to the fore these dimensions in Deleuze's thought is the aim of the discussion ahead. In such a *practical* understanding of the

---

9 The circumscription of thought as waiting, following, and carrying, I take from Leonard Lawlor's Derridian reference to Paul Celan's »Die Welt ist fort, ich muss dich tragen« in his newest book *This is not Sufficient. An Essay on Animality and Human Nature in Derrida*. Here, Lawlor states right at the beginning: »[B]ut thought, I am going to claim, amounts to three things: waiting, following, and carrying. I must wait for what arrives — yet in the most desperate urgency; I must follow — yet without any program; I must carry you — yet or because the world has gone away« (Lawlor 2007: 10).

philosophy of becoming I see a new line of flight both for thinking and theorizing and for the conceptualization of the ethical itself. As my concern lies precisely with a different *thought* of the ethical, it is Deleuze's re-writing of ontology that first and foremost has to find appropriate explanation. Only by understanding the transformation that thought undergoes in its reversal from a thought of Being into one of becoming will we also see how the question of the ethical changes, and how both thought and ethics are liberated from their traditional image, such as it stands as Deleuze's project in all of his works but most of all in his discussion of the ›Image of Thought‹ in *Difference and Repetition*.

The main part of the book ahead will focus on what I want to call Deleuze's plane of thought, and it aims at the re-construction (which is never a question of simple reproduction) of the questions of immanence, difference, and repetition, as characterizing his thought of becoming. While in each chapter we approach Deleuze's thought via the thought of someone else, or better via Deleuze's own thinking on someone else's thought, the aim of each of these chapters is no truthful representation of any of these different philosophical influences. By approaching Deleuze by way of *his* Spinoza, *his* Bergson, and *his* Nietzsche, we rather hope to show in what sense these three vectors give force to Deleuze's thought of immanence as a philosophy of difference and repetition. It is only in *following* Deleuze's thought in its movement of thinking, a movement that is always a zigzagging through diverse media and different thinkers, and among them most of all Spinoza, Bergson, and Nietzsche, that I hope to *map* his thought.

While the following chapter draws out a first diagram of the thought of immanence via Deleuze's Spinozism, the subsequent chapters will differen*t/c*iate this first picture that we get from this plane of immanence in two fundamental ways. Chapter III investigates Deleuze's Bergsonism through which his plane of thought gains its differential and thus dynamic character, a dynamism that alone is fitting a thought of becoming. Chapter IV differentiates this thought of difference in itself as a selective thought, so that it truly is difference and not sameness that the movement of becoming speaks of—a dimension so fundamental to an a/effective ethical thought. It is this movement of an active thought of affirmation that will be exemplified with Deleuze's Nietzscheanism.

Only after having re-constructed Deleuze's plane of thought as a radically immanent philosophy of difference and repetition, a philosophy of becoming, will we be able to return both to our equation of ›ontology = ethics‹ and to the ethical statements cited briefly earlier in this introduction. It is only via the detour of an adequate understanding of the ontology of becoming as Deleuze develops it in his philosophical texts that we can move to the other side of the equation and think about both the location of the ethical in this thought and what to make of the figure of becoming as *ethos*. Once more in the turn of three moves chapter V exemplifies Deleuze's poetical imperative of the creation of *a life...* as the expression of restoring ›a belief in the world, as it is‹ and as the demanding practice ›of becoming worthy of what happens to us‹.[10] However impossible such *ethos* may sound for as long as we force ourselves to approach it *directly*, arguing in a purely theoretical way and looking for principles to guide, I hope that by cautiously following the multi-layered movements drawn out in this book, the reader may find new inspiration on how to approach the ethical question, and thus the subject of how to live this world.

---

10 However estranging it may seem for some to relate Deleuze's philosophy to a terminology of poetical thinking and to a poetics, in this project I hope to successfully show that it is precisely via the exposition of different thought-registers to each other that we not only best approach the highly demanding thought-universe of Deleuze, but in this encounter of philosophy with literary thinking in its widest sense also develop a new way of thinking the ethical question. For an interpretation of Deleuze's work as always already implicated in and exposed to literature and literary thinking, cf. for example Daniel W. Smith's ›Introduction‹ to the English translation of Deleuze's *Critique et Clinique*, in which Smith begins his introductory remark with the following statement: »Although *Essays Critical and Clinical* is the only book written by Gilles Deleuze that is devoted primarily to literature, literary references are present everywhere in his work, running almost parallel to the philosophical references« (Smith 1997: xi). For further support of this claim for a strong relation between poetical and ethical thinking in Deleuze, we should also think of the first essay in precisely this project of *Essays Critical and Clinical*, that carries no other title but ›Literature and Life‹ (Deleuze 1997b).

II.

»To Express!« or the Thought of Immanence: *Spinoza*

> There has only ever been one ontological proposition: Being is univocal.
> (Deleuze, *Difference and Repetition*)

What is philosophy? While Gilles Deleuze poses this question explicitly only at the end of his lifetime, the matters of why, how, and what kind of philosophy drive him throughout his entire philosophical life. A member of the extraordinary generation of thinkers that France has been witnessing after World War II — a generation that maybe not for the first time but at a right time found a way to effectively question an overconfident rationalist and positivist philosophical tradition — Deleuze nonetheless distinguishes himself from most of his fellows in regard to the strategies chosen to produce a *different* philosophical thought. Rather unfashionable amongst his generation, if not even problematic at this turning point in the 20th century after the catastrophe of the shoah, his strategy is to remain affirmative of the so-called ›big issues‹ of philosophy, and to remain affirmative of the questions of ontology and metaphysics itself. As he himself once phrased it, he never felt much guilt »about ›doing philosophy‹« (Deleuze 1995: 89). Thus, unlike many of his contemporaries he decides not to leave the highly problematic areas of thought to others, be it the analytical philosophical tradition or Heideggerianism, on the one hand, or the newly emerging life sciences, on the other hand. In taking into account what has happened,[1] he means to produce a new thought of ontology, one that might be understood as a re-

---

1 While in this study, out of reasons that were shortly mentioned in our introductory chapter, Deleuze's clearly *political* impetus ›to do philosophy‹ may only serve in the background, we should not forget that the issues of totalitarianism, Fascism and the increasing ›controlling‹ of nearly all aspects of life in our societies must be seen as primary questions underlying and driving Deleuze's whole philosophical endeavor towards a non-dogmatic, open and critical way of thinking, such as this book will exemplify.

formulation of Heidegger's question ›what it means to think‹ as the central philosophical question today, even as it is developed in a direction most distant from the latter. Calling himself »perhaps... the most naïve philosopher of our generation« (Deleuze 1995: 88), he claims as the philosopher's unique task the *creation of concepts*. Right at the beginning of his last collaboration with Félix Guattari *What is Philosophy?*, the philosopher is defined as the concept's friend:

> The philosopher is the concept's friend; he is potentiality of the concept. That is, philosophy is not a simple art of forming, inventing, or fabricating concepts, because concepts are not necessarily forms, discoveries, or product. More rigorously, philosophy is the discipline that involves *creating* concepts. (WPH: 5)

Alain Badiou, who, as we will see later on, in his book *Deleuze. The Clamour of Being* is wrong about many aspects central to Deleuze's philosophy, nevertheless shows absolutely the right attunement when he argues that the all too common and easy (mis-)readings of Deleuze's work as one of pure anarchy, aiming at the destruction of the philosophical tradition in general, overlook the sobriety and lucidity with which this thinker confronts the tradition head on. »One misses everything«, Badiou writes,

> if one disregards such explicit declarations as ›Philosophy merges with ontology‹..., or from ›Parmenides to Heidegger it is the same voice which is taken up... A single voice raises the clamour of being‹... The historical unifier of philosophy, as the voice of thought, as the clamour of the utterable, is Being itself. From this point of view, Deleuze's philosophy is in no way a critical philosophy. Not only is it possible to think Being, but there is thought only insofar as Being simultaneously formulates and pronounces itself therein (Badiou 2000: 20).

And another ›apprentice‹ characterizes Deleuze's singular method in very similar terms:

> Although he denies any preconstituted structure of being or any teleological order of existence, Deleuze still operates on the highest planes of ontological speculation... Deleuze insists... on alternatives within the ontological tradition. (Hardt 1995: xiii)

For Deleuze, thought as a positive—not positivist—productive force of life is possible. As we have already heard above, Michel Foucault expressed this active affirmation of thought in his famous essay »Theatrum Philosophicum« on Deleuze's main works *Difference and Repetition* and *The Logic of Sense*, the two books that appeared only a year apart in 1968 and 1969.[2] And it is one of the main goals of this book to work towards an adequate understanding of the kind of thought we are speaking of here. Seen from such perspective, Deleuze's philosophy is philosophy in the traditional sense, dealing with the issues of ontology and metaphysics in a constructive rather than a deconstructive sense. If, however, I succeed in my task of bringing Deleuze's fidelity to philosophy to expression, it will emerge that we did not yet know what could become of ontology and metaphysics—what could become of philosophy itself.

Therefore before starting with the re-construction of Deleuze's plane of thought via the three major philosophical influences that can be named as *his* tradition, I would like to give a preliminary list of characterizations that Deleuze himself at different times uses to describe his philosophical project: a reversal of Platonism; a bottomless and incorporeal materialism overcoming any idealist subjectivism; a refutation of all dialectical negation especially Hegelian dialectics; a construction of ontology without the ›return to Being‹; and a superior empiricism, that is, a *transcendental empiricism* in which »[i]mmanence is immanent only to itself« (WPH: 45). Such enormous scope in a philosopher's area of engagement reveals the difficulty of the project ahead of us. Any attempt at a complete, systematic, or simple reconstruction of Deleuze's system of thought is bound to fail. It simply cannot be done. The good news, however, about this impossibility is that it is the abundance and immodesty of his thought that means Deleuze leaves it to his readers to decide where to start from in order to *construct* a plane of thought worthy of this philosophy. In Deleuze's thought multiple lines cross, connect in new ways, transform each other, and produce a very singular structure of relations and theoretical positions. He forces his read-

---

2 It is here that Foucault also writes his today so well-known sentence that »perhaps one day, this century will be known as Deleuzian« (Foucault, 1998b: 343).

ers to *select* and to *invent* new strategies when moving through his thought. He insists not only theoretically but also practically — in a practice of thought and thinking — on always *producing* and *creating.*[3] Such a *becoming-thought* is, therefore, already on this very elementary level more than just theory: as theory, it is a practice of (un)becoming, a (re)construction and a (re)creation. Deleuze »sets down that philosophy is a practice and that it is ›no more abstract than its objects‹«, Badiou writes (2000: 15). It is this demand on philosophy that both makes it sometimes hard to keep one's bearings within Deleuze's system of thought and points towards its inherently creative and transformative power. Deleuze's thought never confines itself to just one plane of ideas. Rather it always develops in the combination, multiplication, and intensification, of many philosophical and non-philosophical planes.

The question of where to start then in this labyrinthine universe of thought, has just one answer: it demands from us to find our own way in. We have to leap into the unknown and start in the middle. We have to leap, and as if this move were not enough, we also need to affirm this leap — actively — so that, as Deleuze says, we »learn to swim«.[4]

---

3 For a detailed discussion on the centrality of the *creation* of concepts for philosophy, cf. WPH, especially »Introduction« and chapter 1 »What is a concept?«. It is important to emphasize here that while such vocabulary cannot totally escape what Peter Hallward in his book on Deleuze calls ›extra-worldliness‹, I do not agree with the latter's conclusion that Deleuze is »most appropriately read as a spiritual, redemptive, or subtractive thinker« (Hallward, 2006: 3). Instead of understanding ›creation‹ in an overly spiritual sense, it must be linked to Deleuze's empiricist, pragmatist, and constructive heritage, a ›productive‹ logic of thought that Deleuze precisely shares with his friend Michel Foucault, and that is completely missing in Hallward's reading of Deleuze's philosophy.

4 Such description of the twofold procedure at work in Deleuze contains already everything that I try to unfold slowly and step by step for the question of thinking itself: (re)investigation, (re)formulation, or (re)construction, never mean something simple, a repetition in the base sense as we will learn later on. Rather, the extraordinary emphasis on the prefix *re-* wants to draw attention to the complex and highly demanding task that such a repetitive undertaking always already is — leaping *and* affirming. For Deleuze's analysis of the process of learning as ›leaping into the unknown‹, rather than resembling or copying, cf. DR: 23 and 165. ›To start by way of the middle‹ is an expression by Deleuze that he uses in the context of his take on the question of »Spinoza and Us«:

* * *

Considering the purpose of our investigation, it is best to start with Deleuze's insistence on radical immanence. For understanding this concept is crucial if we are to grasp the powerful implications of Deleuze's philosophical thought.

At first sight, it might not seem so extraordinary to stress immanence in the field of philosophy. The ›post-metaphysical‹ attitude we have acquired as a kind of second nature makes the claim of immanence initially appear to be the very characteristic of all philosophy. Moreover, it is this claim to immanence that always counts as the defining interest and that distinguishes philosophy from both religion and *doxa*—those two orders against which modern philosophical thought first of all positions itself.

Yet the immense risk of confusion whenever it comes to the conceptualization of immanence is the reason why Deleuze and Guattari, again in *What is Philosophy?*, stress that »[i]mmanence can be said to be the burning issue of all philosophy« (WPH: 45). Always a highly debated affair in the long history of philosophy, immanence was and is rarely thought in itself, and thus is taken as *immanent to* something else—»a ›dative‹, Matter or Mind« (WPH: 44), as they say. Since its early, even pre-modern beginnings, philosophy has subordinated immanence to something else, be it Form and Idea (Plato), the Cogito (Descartes), the Subject (Kant), or in the more recent phenomenological tradition Spirit (Hegel) and consciousness (Husserl), all of which serve as containers of immanence. In providing such ›locations‹ that for themselves remain beyond and above the realm of immanence, philosophy puts immanence in a hierarchical relation to transcendence; it hands it over to transcendence and the confusion between philosophy and religion has still not ended. »Whenever there is transcendence«, Deleuze and Guattari say, »vertical Being, imperial State in the sky or on earth, there is religion; and there is philosophy whenever there is immanence« (WPH: 43).

Directing philosophy itself to the issue of immanence, and starting again with this burning question of immanence, the two thinkers

---

»[T]his phrase could mean many things«, he writes, »but among other things it means ›us in the middle of Spinoza‹. To try to perceive and to understand Spinoza by way of the middle« (Deleuze 1992: 625).

argue that philosophy must not think immanence as immanent ›to‹ something. Rather immanence must be taken as »immanent only to itself«, so that it »captures everything, absorbs All-One, and leaves nothing remaining to which it could be immanent« (WPH: 45). Such total absorption that can perhaps be best imagined as a *flattening* of thought,[5] is precisely Deleuze's philosophical project. For us it is here that we find our first step moving towards what I will call a new ontology, and a new image of thought: to think immanence not as immanent to something else, but as immanent only to itself! Not, however, in order merely to simplify the problem and end up with a brute materialism or even a strengthened positivism. What such new folding strives for is to tackle what remains of the experience of the struggle between transcendence and immanence, an ongoing struggle, as we have heard.

In our modern moment, Deleuze and Guattari therefore explain, »we are no longer satisfied with thinking immanence as immanent to a transcendent; *we want to think transcendence within the immanent, and it is from immanence that a breach is expected*« (WPH: 47). Contrary, however, to any profound existence-philosophical claim, such as e.g. Karl Jasper's notion of ›Encompassing‹ (*das Umgreifende*), which once more hands immanence over to transcendence, and also Jean-Paul Sartre's transcendental field that is still determined as the field of a consciousness, what is asked from us in a true thought of immanence is that the movement of the infinite—immanence in itself—*must not* be stopped. »Transcendence enters as soon as movement of the infinite is stopped. It takes advantage of the interruption to reemerge, revive, and spring forth again.« (Ibid) Thus, to think transcendence within the immanent without again handing over im-

---

5 A ›flattening‹ gesture in thought will have to be developed, however, without falling back to a ›before‹ of the Heideggerian ›ontological difference‹, which, as Deleuze in one of the rare and directly affirmative engagements with Heidegger shows, must remain fundamental to all philosophical questioning, i.e. stand at its very beginning: »We regard as fundamental this ›correspondence‹ between difference and questioning, between ontological difference and the being of the question.« (DR: 66) If in this work we use the notion of flattening, of absorption into but one level, it is to further radicalize this Heideggerian understanding of difference that »is not ›between‹ in the ordinary sense of the word. It is the Fold, *Zwiefalt*« (DR: 65). For a (re)construction of Deleuze's thought as producing a ›flat ontology‹, cf. also DeLanda 2002.

manence to transcendence, that is, to let immanence be all ›there is‹ without reducing it to an impoverished category cut off from what before was called transcendence—this is the movement of thought demanded by a mature philosophy of immanence, understood in the sense given by Deleuze and Guattari in *What is Philosophy?*. Only this way is thought freed from any given form, in particular from the dominating influence of a Judeo-Christian tradition in philosophy, and thereby making it possible to speak of a *plane of immanence*.

That such a way of positioning oneself in the philosophical tradition, in turn, has radical consequences for the philosophical project itself, is the claim this chapter will try to develop in appropriate detail. For now it is enough to know that what it will lead to is a de-subjectified, a de-centered philosophy. That this does, however, not mean nothingness, no movement, no change, no ›agency‹ whatsoever, is essential to emphasize straight away. Instead, we will have to face a *nomadic* thought whose infinite movement is immanence alone. We will have to put an end to the illusion of ever being saved from this immanence. We will have to work against the philosophical prejudice that sees immanence as a prison from which we would have to be saved by transcendence.[6] And all this means that we will have to *begin* differently.

For Deleuze, who takes »the thinking of thought« to be »philosophy's unique object«, as again Badiou accurately states (Badiou 2000: 20), the question of where to begin is the crux to a true thought of immanence.[7] To start with an already formed notion of conscious-

---

6 I find the following statement, with which Elizabeth Grosz introduces her philosophical project in her book *The Nick of Time*, to be relevant for all thought-projects, and thus suitable to be cited at this point: »We have forgotten where we come from. This is a double forgetting: of the elements through which all living things are born and live, a cosmological element; and of the specific body, indeed a chain of bodies, from which we come, a genealogical or maternal element«. A little further on she continues that »[w]e need to return to, or perhaps to invent anew, the concepts of nature, matter, and life, the most elementary concerns of the cosmological and the ontological, if we want to develop alternative models to the inscriptive and constructivist discourses that currently dominate the humanities and social sciences« (Grosz 2004: 2–3).

7 Rodolphe Gasché comes to a very similar assessment of Deleuze in his essay »Thinking within Thought«, cf. Gasché 2007, where he emphasizes that Deleuze's philosophical project is one that attempts to liberate thought from »a single Image in general« (DR: 132) in order to make ›thinking‹ possible again.

ness, subject, or idea, cannot be a solution. The problem of beginning must start from somewhere else. We must avoid the return to transcendence, the comfortable blind spot of philosophical discourses that safeguards thought by seemingly providing us with a universal standpoint. While, as Deleuze in his central discussion of »The Image of Thought« in *Difference and Repetition* shows, modern philosophy has managed at its beginning to eliminate objective presuppositions such as Plato's eternal realm of Ideas or the notion of God in Scholasticism and negative theology, it still all too often maintains and forcefully defends an implicit universal point of view of subjectivity or pure consciousness, from which it seems *natural* to begin. By still taking for granted what both *thinking* and *being* mean, as much as always already postulating a place from where to speak, philosophy today continues the transcendent heritage. It still most often starts from the implicitness of an ›Everybody knows…‹:

> Everybody knows, in a pre-philosophical and pre-conceptual manner… everybody knows what it means to think and to be… As a result, when the philosopher says ›I think therefore I am‹, he can assume that the universality of his premises—namely what it means to be and to think…— will be implicitly understood, and that no one can deny that to doubt is to think, and to think is to be.… *Everybody knows, no one can deny.* (DR: 129–130)

It is this ›everybody knows, no one can deny…‹-image of thought, the naturalization of the equation of to think = to be, in which the › = ‹ remains unnoticed, for ›we all *know* what it means‹, that, according to Deleuze, has to be fundamentally stopped. He calls it not only a »dogmatic« but also a »moral« image of thought (DR: 131) which, in basing thought on the implicit assumption of a Subject that possesses the capacity to think as a natural faculty of good will striving for eternal truth, domesticates the true force of thought. It moralizes the question of thinking by giving it the form that is most useful to us. The traditional or »natural image of thought« (ibid) not only ascribes a specific ›place‹ to thought—consciousness as its most recent name[8]—but also already decides what it actually means to think. It

---

8 »Beginning with Descartes, and then with Kant and Husserl, the cogito

says again and again to think = to want the true.

> In this sense, conceptual philosophical thought has as its implicit presupposition a pre-philosophical and natural Image [sic] of thought, borrowed from the pure element of common sense. According to this image, thought has an affinity with the true; it formally possesses the true and materially wants the true. It is *in terms of* this image that everybody knows and is presumed to know what it means to think. Thereafter it matters little whether philosophy begins with the object or the subject, with Being or with beings, as long as thought remains subject to this Image [sic] which already prejudges everything: the distribution of the object and the subject as well as that of Being and beings. (DR: 131)

In strong opposition to a naturalized image of thought that has become an impasse for thinking itself, Deleuze's philosophical undertaking is to re-open the space of thought. Real thought, according to Deleuze, is not reproduction in the sense of describing most accurately what is already there — imagined as eternal truth. Rather, thinking implies an *encounter*, a clash, something comes from the outside and forces us to follow. And by following this encounter not only do we enter »*terra incognita*« (DR: 136), but such a following always also means a radical transformation of what thinking itself is. Instead of describing, genuine thinking brings something new into our structure. This is the reason why Deleuze concludes as follows: »›Everybody‹ knows very well that in fact men think rarely, and more often under the impulse of a shock than in the excitement of a taste for thinking« (DR: 132). Thinking, thus, never comes *from* a subject. Subjectivity is but one possible effect of the movements of thought itself.[9] In order not to fall prey to subjectivism and to avoid the rein-

---

makes it possible to treat the plane of immanence as a field of consciousness. Immanence is supposed to be immanent to a pure consciousness, to a thinking subject.« (WPH: 46)

9 In his essay on »The Vertigo of Immanence: Deleuze's Spinozism«, Miguel de Beistegui approaches the question of thinking in Deleuze in a very similar manner. He also takes Deleuze's thought of radical immanence as bringing about again the question of ›What does it mean to think?‹, but he also characterizes Deleuze's image of thought by a twofold trait which explicates something in my discussion that so far has remained implicit. This is what he says about Deleuze and the question of thought: »First, thought is external to what

troduction of transcendence above immanence (metaphysics in the onto-theological sense), philosophy, for Deleuze, is asked to engage with immanence prior to anything else. This means to think immanence as immanent only to itself, so that the construction of a true plane of immanence is possible. It means to write a new ontology.

1. Ontology vs. Analogy

If we look at the history of philosophy, there are only very few thinkers who have conceived of ontology based on *radical* immanence as their explicit project. While—as we will make clear in this book—there is more than one occasion in this history of thought at which such a rigorous way of thinking immanence as immanent only to itself, has emerged, for Deleuze, there still is only one event that remains singular in all of philosophy's time. This event is called *Spinoza*! The attribution of singularity to Spinoza recurs throughout Deleuze's whole work. Continuing our discussion from *What is Philosophy?*, we can refer to the statement which directly follows after the problem of transcendence in the history of philosophy has been spelled out. Deleuze and Guattari then state that »Spinoza was the philosopher who knew full well that immanence was only immanent to itself and therefore that it was a plane traversed by movements of the infinite, filled with intensive ordinates. He therefore is the prince of philosophy« (WPH: 48). But Deleuze said the same in a seminar-session at the University of Vincennes in his course on Spinoza in the winter 1980/1981:

> There has never been but a single ontology. There is only Spinoza who has managed to pull off an ontology. If one takes ontology in an extremely rigorous sense, I see only one case where a philosophy

---

it thinks... Thought happens as a result of an *encounter* with the outside. It is a response—a creative response—to something that has taken hold of us... At the same time, thought is said to be entirely *immanent* to what it thinks, immanent to the real that provokes it, and not, as is often the case, the other way around: it is not the real that is immanent to thought... The difficulty—and I believe, the singularity—of Deleuze's thought lies in having to uphold this double axiom that constitute its image: exteriority *and* immanence« (Beistegui 2005: 85).

has realized itself as ontology, and that's Spinoza. (Deleuze, Seminar 03/24/1981)[10]

While we do not necessarily have to subscribe to the exclusivity that Deleuze himself ascribes to this event, what we need to do in order to find a way into Deleuze's plane of thought is to follow the movement announced here and to draw out the lines that a radical thought of immanence according to him implies.

Heretical Times

Expressionism in Philosophy: Spinoza, the second, ›minor‹ thesis that Deleuze composed for his doctorat in 1968, is definitely his most elaborate discussion of Spinoza. However, both the diverse smaller texts on Spinoza that Deleuze wrote later in his lifetime and the seminars that he held at Vincennes from 1978 to 1981 represent an invaluable additional source for an understanding of the significant role Deleuze assigns to Spinoza.[11] There, on November 25, 1980, he begins his first semester-session on Spinoza with the following remark:

> It's quite curious to what extent philosophy, up to the end of the 17th century, ultimately speaks to us, all the time of God. And after all, Spinoza, excommunicated Jew, is not the last to speak to us of God... And from all of them, whether it's Descartes, Malebranche, Leibniz, we get the impression that the boundary between philosophy and theology is extremely vague... Why is philosophy so compromised with God? (Deleuze, Seminar 11/25/1980)

The issue of transcendence vs. immanence as *the* question of philosophy is right here, standing at the beginning of Deleuze's teaching of Spinoza's thought: What happened in the 17th century? Why does all philosophy speak to us of God? And in Deleuze's response, a rather extraordinary formula indicates the direction in which he wants to take both his students and the thinker under consideration.

---

10 Deleuze's seminar sessions on Spinoza at the University of Vincennes are published at www.webdeleuze.com.

11 To name just the most important collection of texts on Spinoza other than the *Expressionism*-book, cf. *Spinoza: Practical Philosophy* (Deleuze, 1988), originally published in 1970, with an enlarged edition followed in 1981.

He says: »With God, everything is permitted« (ibid).

The counter-intuitive statement, inverting Dostoyevsky's famous formulation from *The Brothers Karamazov,*[12] brings us to the heart of the issue that preoccupied 17th century thought and to that which Deleuze wants us to draw from it: instead of lamenting the influence religion and the Church had at the time (the most obvious critique from a perspective of immanence), Deleuze argues that it is in this century that ›God‹ — or better, ›the speaking of God‹ —, becomes an emancipatory force for philosophy, liberating thought from merely being »the simple representation of things« (ibid). Drawing a comparison with what determines the field of painting at the very same time, Deleuze again, instead of emphasizing how restricted painters were back then because of clerical influence, sees these constraints — (ab)used in the hands of extraordinary painters — as productive factors which alone made the emancipation of colors and the unleashing of forms possible, methods and forms that would have been unimaginable, ›out of the picture‹, without such a constrained discursivity.

> ›...el Greco...‹ This creation could only be achieved on the basis of Christian figures... It's true that there are constraints from the Church which operate on the painter, but there is a transformation of constraints into means of creation. They make use of God in order to achieve a liberation of forms, to push the forms to the point where the forms have nothing to do with an illustration. The forms are unleashed *[se déchaînent]*. (Ibid)

If we return this gesture to philosophy, we recognize that, although there is, of course, no question that up to the 18th century philosophy is compromised by the demands of the Church, it is — thinking of philosophers such as Descartes, Spinoza, Leibniz — precisely during the proliferating 17th century that concepts are pushed to their limits, that they are no longer defined by the task of representing something, but rather encountered as things themselves — the condition »to allow the possibility of thinking and living otherwise, to allow the very possibility of philosophy as a *critical* way of thinking« (Goodchild 2001:

---

12 Dostoyevsky's statement is »If God does not exist, everything is permissible« (quoted in Smith 2001: 167).

157, my emphasis). The 17th century for Deleuze counts as one of the richest and most inventive eras of philosophy in its characteristic and specific *task* »to create concepts«, precisely because, within its narrow framework, »God, in philosophy, functions as a transcendental ideal which incites us to take thought beyond the limits of possible experience« (Goodchild 2001: 156). For modern philosophy (as for art) it becomes the time of the break or hiatus away from religion which for the first time made a truly immanent thought — that is a »pure ontology« — possible (Deleuze, Seminar 12/12/1980).

And yet, according to Deleuze, it is only Spinoza who comes out as ›the prince of philosophy‹, as we heard above. He is the one who alone went far enough. So far, in fact (and as we know *too far* for his own lifetime), that he not only pushed the question constituting philosophy itself — the question of transcendence and immanence — to its limits, but, as Deleuze says, »[he] wants to *make* something else« (Deleuze, Seminar 11/25/1980, my emphasis). This is what Deleuze learns from Spinoza. Only Spinoza arrives at a pure ontology because, for Deleuze, he did not compromise the thought of immanence. Only he had the courage to push through the thought of the *immanent cause* in all its radicality.

> Spinoza arrives. He was preceded no doubt by all those who had been more or less audacious concerning the immanent cause, that is to say this cause that's quite bizarre in that not only does it remain in itself in order to produce, but what it produces remains in it. God is in the world, the world is in God. (Ibid)

Spinoza's (Anti-)Cartesianism

But let us set up the stage properly. If we want to understand Deleuze's privileging of Spinoza over others at this significant moment in the history of philosophy (that is in particular over both Descartes and Leibniz), we have to follow the lines of demarcation inscribed in the 17th century. We have to articulate the antagonism of a thought of ontology *versus* a thought of analogy — or, to ›personify‹ the conflict, of Spinoza *versus* the negative theology of Thomism, and Descartes as the latter's philosophical inheritor.

Spinoza's anti-Cartesian path is the condition of possibility for a thought of immanence as radical as that which Deleuze tries to unfold both in regard to Spinoza and himself. In *Expressionism in Philosophy*, he exemplifies the debate between Descartes and Spinoza first of all as a disagreement concerning the *methodological* level: the method at stake, however, is no minor tool, but nothing less than the method of how to think as such, that is, of how to actually arrive at a thought of Being. To say this in the language of the 17th century, it is the philosophical and theological problem of proving the existence of God.

In his image of God as *infinite perfection*, Descartes continues a tradition according to which thought can only ever be of an analogical nature, it never reaches ›reality‹ itself. It can, thus, never touch on the divine. Thinking can only ever strive for God's most correct, that is, its *legitimate* representation. This path was set up by the Greeks starting with Plato, and it was followed too by most scholastic traditions (negative theology) preceding Descartes. God as absolute cause is absolute incomprehensibility from the always imperfect viewpoint of the human world. The quest of seeking knowledge of God—heretic immodesty is in the air—is modestly transformed here into a question of non-contradictory knowledge, which at least ensures an »*upright nature on the part of thought*« (DR: 131). These are the words Deleuze finds for this theoretical move in his discussion of the predominant image of thought in philosophy.

Now, that every effect is linked to a cause is not the issue at stake in the debate between Descartes and Spinoza. Neither is it that knowledge always will remain of the level of effects. The issue of dispute is precisely which form we give to this relation, i.e. in what ways we relate the two terms in question, namely, cause and effect or God and the knowledge we gain from him. Descartes' technique of the elimination of doubt—based on the unbridgeable division of cause (infinity) and effect (finitude)—never arrives at direct knowledge.[13] Rather, what is possible is only perfectibility of the understanding of an effect (being) so that we gain a legitimate disposition from which we can draw conclusions about the nature of Being itself.

---

13 Although this short discussion can in no way do justice to Descartes' complex argumentation, both the *Discourse on Method* (1637) and *Meditations on First Philosophy* (1641) exclusively favor a knowledge that is gained step by step, but that remains always of an analogical nature. Up until today this is shown in the Cartesian heritage of epistemology.

Perceiving the relation of cause and effect, of the One and being, in this way, Descartes' philosophy continues the classical and scholastic triad of *equivocation, eminence,* and *analogy*. Deleuze gives the following definition of these three terms in *Expressionism in Philosophy*:

> *[E]quivocation* (God is cause of himself, but in an other sense than that in which he is the efficient cause of the things he creates…); *eminence* (God thus contains all reality, but eminently, in a form other than that of the things he creates); and *analogy* (God as cause of himself is not, then, grasped as he is in himself, but by analogy…). (EP: 162–163)

According to this logic, human understanding is never able to reach a thought of Being — knowledge of the cause — ›in itself‹, because it always lacks perfection. Between imperfection and perfection there is the abyss of two different orders that divide the universe: eternity on the side of perfection, and change and discontinuity on the side of imperfection. This was already the solution Christian theology found for the problem of causality. Its argument is that, if God or the One is (to be thought as) omnipotent, absolute will, and highest understanding, he himself must be of a different order than the very things he creates.[14] Otherwise we would be unable to draw clear distinctions between the divine order and its human ›application‹. God cannot be the cause of himself in the same way as he is cause of everything else. While within him all reality is contained, he must contain it in a different form — a form clearly distinguished from all forms of being. God and his creations cannot be of the same order; they cannot share the same world.

The consequences which follow from the Cartesian conceptualization of thought become significant for the whole tradition of modern philosophy. But Descartes' solution to the problem he faced as a philosopher in a time of great religious influence is ultimately a momentous trick. He reformulates the question of knowing the cause itself, a question that with Christianity receives the scent of immodesty, into

---

14 We again might want to refer to *Meditation III »Concerning God: That He Exists«* (Descartes 1993) in which Descartes builds his proof of the existence of God on the presuppositions of equivocation and eminence, which leads into the conclusion that knowledge of God can ever only be one of analogy.

one of *truthful* knowledge about it. Knowledge based on the distinction between true and false, however, remains relative to the cause itself whose infinite perfection it lacks. In conceptualizing God as absolute will and the highest form of understanding, whatever knowledge we — as effects and creatures — might ever be able to gain, it does not endanger the distribution of positions in this knowledge-contest. Philosophical knowledge remains of analogical nature. That is to say, it is conceptualized as a kind of knowledge which mirrors the unsurpassable gap between creator and creation that structures everything. Such is the *modesty* that we could make out in Descartes' solution to the problem of knowledge. If we look closer, however, as Spinoza has done, we also see a form of knowledge that from the viewpoint of lesser perfection, i.e. from the viewpoint of creatures, nonetheless arrives at conclusions by claiming *congruence of proportion or proportionality*. It is thus that it shows that God must necessarily exist, and that he must do so in even greater perfection.[15] The Cartesian method strives for clear and distinct ideas of an effect. Taking this rational framing of clear and distinct ideas of an effect as both the legitimate ground and model on which to move towards conclusions that go beyond this realm of lived experience (a beyond to which we have no access whatsoever, according to this method), shows not only the affinity between Descartes and scholasticism but also the sneaking in of anthropomorphism precisely where, for reasons of ›modesty‹, one set out to avoid it.

Relating the Cartesian argumentative sequence to yet another debate, Deleuze sees in Descartes a preference for analysis over synthesis that aims at overcoming the impasses classical Aristotelianism left us with. Descartes' *analytical* method is »a method of inference or implication« (EP: 156), he states. It is directed against Aristotle's claim of *synthesis* — the claim that in principle we are able to acquire *real*

---

15 Deleuze states the problem in the following way in his discussion of the differences between Cartesianism and scholasticism on the one side, and Spinozism on the other: »An analogical method sets out explicitly to avoid anthropomorphism: according to Aquinas, qualities attributed to God imply no community of form between divine substance and creature, but only an analogy, a ›congruence‹ of proportion or proportionality... The significance of Spinozism may here be judged by the way he inverts the problem. Whenever we proceed by analogy we borrow from creatures certain characteristics in order to attribute them to God either equivocally or eminently.« (EP: 46)

knowledge of the cause — a method which, as Deleuze reminds us, for Descartes must have »an exaggerated ambition, and gives us no means of knowing real causes« (EP: 159). As imperfect creatures we cannot know in itself; such a method can only »advance to abstractions which are wrongly presented to us as causes, and so, despite its pretensions, merely examines causes through their effects« (ibid).

For Spinoza, however, things are different. As pointed out earlier, his quarrel was not with the assumption that an effect is related to a cause, and that, thus, knowledge will always — necessarily — start from the level of effects. Nothing actually seems to be more Spinozian than the claim that every effect must have a cause, that cause and effect are indispensably interrelated.[16] However, as Deleuze shows in his discussion, the issue of disagreement between Spinoza and Descartes was what consequences to draw from this dependency of the effect on its cause. It is here that one position is antipodal to the other. Spinoza's criticism against the analytical method is unambiguous according to Deleuze:

> Spinoza says: It is possible to start from a clear knowledge of an effect, but from it we will arrive only at a clear knowledge of its cause, we will know nothing of the cause beyond what we consider in its effect, and will never obtain *adequate* knowledge. (EP: 156, my emphasis)

Descartes moves too quickly, this is Spinoza's critique.[17] The Cartesian claim that with the reformulation of the question of knowledge into one of ›clear and distinct ideas‹ the existence of God can and actually does gain sufficient proof, so that *real* knowledge is possible, confuses — in Spinoza's terms — *property (proprium)* and *essence (natura)*; it confuses the relative with the absolute. According to Spinoza, infinite perfection in the way in which we described it above — the Cartesian as much as the scholastic definition of

---

16 Cf. one of the first claims in Spinoza's *Ethics*: »From a given determinate cause there necessarily follows an effect; conversely, if no determinate cause exists, it is impossible that an effect should follow.« (EIA3)

17 That Descartes has moved too quickly is a common criticism leveled against Descartes, of which Gottfried Wilhelm Leibniz was probably the most forceful proponent. Cf. Deleuze's discussion in EP: 83ff.

God — cannot be an *adequate*, that is, a *real* and *sufficient* idea of God, since it does not *express essence* but draws only an *analogy* to it. Rather than grasping essence, analogical knowledge reduces essence to one property. »The property [however] tells us nothing of the nature of the being to which it belongs, and does not suffice to prove that such a being involves no contradiction« (EP: 73), Deleuze says in taking up Spinoza's distinction between essence and property. Spinoza's claim is that God is not to be *conceptualized* as infinite perfection, he *is* absolute infinity. For as long as such knowledge does not find expression, the clearest and most distinct idea of all cannot suffice to prove this existence. For Spinoza, there is more to be done. For a real understanding of the cause one must advance to a different modus of knowledge: instead of clear and distinct ideas — *abstractions* as we have to call them according to Spinoza (and Deleuze, as Spinoza's reader here) — we need *adequate ideas*. In distinction from Cartesianism, *adequacy* is not asserted by showing only nominally (that is by way of analogy) in what sense an effect depends on its cause. Rather, one must also show how *the very knowledge of the effect itself depends on knowing its cause* (cf. EP: 157). Only this way do we gain *real* knowledge of both cause and effect, and do not end up in abstraction. While we are unable to discuss all the implications in appropriate detail here, what is so important for us in this discussion between the Cartesian approach to the world on the one hand and Spinoza's on the other, is twofold: while at first the formulation that we are capable of knowing the cause itself, that thought of Being is possible, seems so outrageously ›immodest‹, it is actually Descartes' declared modest‹ of thought which ultimately not only presupposes a miraculous know-how of proportionality between effects and cause, but as both Deleuze and Spinoza would hold, out of necessity ends up in formulating the infinite in terms of the finite, and thus reducing both sides to something smaller than they actually are. Such a thought does not think transcendence but always already only the distinction between the transcendent and the immanent in which both sides are suffocated.

Pure Ontology

In his *Ethics* — the book which significantly he did not entitle *Ontology* — one of Spinoza's most important claims is precisely that the confusion of the relative with the absolute that comes with the supposed difference in kind between the finite and the infinite, must be untangled in order to be able to think the absolute in a new, and that means in a truly immanent, way. This argument of the right disentanglement is also what Spinoza strives for when he speaks of the necessity — and this means for him the real possibility — of overcoming our passions in Books III and IV of the *Ethics*. Suffering from passions is nothing but suffering from inadequate knowledge, i.e. having only knowledge of an effect of which we do not know its cause (either knowledge of the first or second kind, with Cartesian universality in its abstract truth reaching ever only the second level). This condition must be transformed into adequate knowledge, i.e. into actions instead of passions. We have to move towards *adequate* knowledge of the cause itself, towards knowledge of the third kind, as Spinoza calls it. This knowledge not only ultimately reaches expression of essence itself but, as such, is pure joy: »Whatever we understand by the third kind of knowledge we are pleased with, and this is accompanied by the idea of God as its cause«, Spinoza concludes in the last book of his *Ethics* (EvP32). And Deleuze summarizes:

> Until one gives a real definition, bearing on the essence of a thing rather than on *propria*, one remains among the vagaries of what is merely conceived, without relation to the reality of the thing as it is outside of our understanding. (EP: 73–74)

Real definition of a thing, that is, a concept exposing itself to the thing itself and not reducing it to the limited categories of our understanding, must and ultimately can be achieved. This claim does, of course, rely on Aristotle. Deleuze emphasizes the philosophical affinity between Aristotle and Spinoza in demarcation from Descartes, a demarcation — we can say — between the possibility of synthesis/ontology on the one hand, and analysis/analogy on the other hand:

> On all these points Spinoza stands as Aristotelian against Descartes... Aristotle showed how scientific knowledge was to be had through causes. He didn't just say that knowledge must discover causes, reach the cause on which a known effect depends; he said that an effect is not known, except to the extent that its cause is already, and better, known. (EP: 157)

And the *Ethics* carries this *task* of producing a knowledge that is no longer content with merely reaching the most appropriate analogy already in its title which reads in its entirety »Ethics, Demonstrated in Geometrical Order«. Rather than understanding itself as a truthful representation of any eternal idea of the world, and from there leading us to knowledge of what the right conduct is, the *Ethics* wants to be understood as a *construction* of the world, as must be implied by producing a knowledge on the level of cause.[18] The *Ethics* is a genetic rather than an analytical tool in as much as geometry in mathematics counts as constructive and genetic in its procedure of proofs (definitions, axioms, propositions, scholia, etc.), however fictitious mathematics at the same time may be.[19] It is thus that the philosophical gesture of the first propositions in the *Ethics* must be understood, not as merely explicative and representative statements, but rather as an attempt at construction itself. All that is said of attributes, modes, their expressive relation to substance, and the expressiveness of substance itself, is proposed in a way that both conceives of each in its absolute singularity, and yet, in this as sharing something with each other and as remaining inherently related to the other. In this complex relation—expression—of which we will have to speak in more detail later on, each aspect must not be taken merely as representing something that is already there as ›given‹, but also as constructing that which it conceives of. Deleuze writes:

> Expression does not relate to substance or attributes in general, in the abstract. When substance is absolutely infinite, when it has an infinity of attributes, then, and only then, are its attributes said to express its essence, for only then does substance express itself in its attributes. It

---

18 In a moment we will see that this understanding, which can be called constructivist rather than representational, becomes Spinoza's solution to the impasses of both Neo-Platonism and Aristotelianism, which although both demand for a knowledge of the cause itself still keep absolute separate the order of cause and effect, thus leaving untouched the notion of knowledge as *finding the Truth* rather than *generating a world*.

19 »We have an adequate ides to the extent that, from a thing, some of whose properties we conceive clearly, we give a *genetic* definition, from which follow all of its known properties (and still others that we do not know). It has often been noted that the only role of mathematics in Spinoza is to provide such a genetic process.« (EP: 135)

would be wrong to invoke Definitions 3 and 4 in order to deduce directly from them the relation between substance and attribute in God, because God himself ›transforms‹ their relation, rendering it absolute. (EP: 20)

Making each aspect irreducible to any other (singularity) while ascribing to all dimensions a *community in form*, Spinoza flattens the top-down model of his predecessors, according to which we have to keep the separation of two different realms that can only ever be bridged via analogy, mimesis, or imitation. In thinking relation as expression, Spinoza arrives at an interrelatedness by which the substance that is formed, and the thought or knowledge of it, really approximate each other on the same plane. Instead of knowledge of probabilities high up in the heavens, God is *real*.[20] And while the specific relationality between cause and effect will have to be followed through in more detail below, we already glimpse the revolutionary conclusion that Spinozism is able to draw from here: »God is in the world, the world is in God« (Deleuze, Seminar 11/25/1980). A unique *parallelism* — the flattening of thought as I called it before — is what Spinoza sets both against Cartesian analogy and ancient naturalism (and here also ends Spinoza's affinity with Aristotle).

It would indeed be surprising if analytic and synthetic methods implied the same conception of being. Spinoza's ontology is dominated by notions of a *cause of itself*, *in itself* and *through itself*. These terms are to be found in Descartes himself; but the difficulties he encountered in their use should teach us something about the incompatibilities of Cartesianism and Spinozism. (EP: 162)

---

20 In commenting on Definition 6 in Book I of the *Ethics* which reads »By God I understand an absolutely infinite entity, that is, a substance consisting of an infinity of attributes, each of which expresses an eternal and infinite essence«, Deleuze writes: »The definition takes up the terms ›substance‹ and ›attribute‹ and gives them the status of realities« (EP: 75).

2. Univocity vs. Equivocation

›Cause of itself, in itself and through itself‹ — here we arrive at an even older debate helping us to deepen our understanding of Spinoza's thought of Being as radical immanence: the debate of *univocity* vs. *equivocation* in the philosophical-theological discourses of the Middle Ages, mirrored also in the Neo-Platonic debate of the ›problem of participation‹.

It was the philosophical school around Duns Scotus in the 13th century which in its struggle against Thomism had introduced the concept of univocity into philosophy. This school, of which not that much is known, represents for Deleuze the first source of a thought of immanence whose goal it was to liberate the thought of Being from theology. Its attempt is to re-establish »the firm separation of philosophy from theology by making metaphysics the science of being as such, separable from the One and all other ›transcendentals‹«, as Philip Goodchild explains in one of the few discussions that pay more attention to this specific medieval heritage of Deleuze's Spinozism (Goodchild 2001: 159). Instead of a world of *equivocation* — the hierarchical division of the world into two, ›One‹ always unreachable for the forms life takes, tainting the latter with the stain of failure and lack (model of analogy) — the world according to the perspective of *univocity* »is an essentially anti-hierarchical world«; it is »the world of immanence« (Deleuze, Seminar 12/12/1980). In contrast to ›equivocation‹, in a thought of univocity the notion of ›equality‹ is emphasized:

> They [the school of Duns Scotus, KT] say all the time that being is fundamentally equal. That doesn't mean that existing things, or beings [étants], are equal. *But being is equal for all*, which means, in a certain way, that *all beings are in being*. (Ibid)

Duns Scotus is the first to posit such a thought of Being in which the community of form between God and creatures is stressed rather than that the world is taken to be based on a dichotomy which requires an above or beyond. Instead of separating essence from existence, such as is required by the Cartesian continuation of the Thomist tradition, the univocity of Being that is said only in a single sense, as Goodchild says, »involves a refusal to distinguish between

›the knowledge of whether a thing is and what it is‹«. It is »a metaphysics beyond the dichotomy of essence and existence« (Goodchild 2001: 159).

Essence = Existence

Much more than these remarks could be made of this highly interesting theologico-political event taking place in 13th century philosophy. However, what has to interest us at this point is how it is taken up again by Spinoza's philosophy. And we only have to look at Definition 1 of the *Ethics* itself, which sets as its beginning this important shift away from the separation of essence and existence to their equation constitutive of univocal thought: »1. By cause of itself I understand that *whose essence involves existence*, or, that whose nature cannot be conceived except as existing« (EID1, my emphasis). Thinking through the question of causality in a radically immanent way, that is, daring the thought of the univocity of Being, the hierarchical and unbridgeable dichotomy of essence and existence disappears. What is cause of itself has to possess existence as its very nature. Everything else—and here we realize the significant difference to the rationalist tradition we spoke of above—would be impotence on the side of infinite substance, that is, God.[21] Such an argument, however, in turn also arrives at the opposite conclusions for the side of finitude: instead of stigmatizing the latter with a structural lack, here everything which exists always necessarily expresses essence, that is, it ›is‹ (in) substance. »Whatever exists exists in God, and nothing can exist or be conceived without God« (EIP15). And the *Demonstration* further explicates:

> No substance exists or can be conceived besides God... that is... a thing which is in itself and is conceived through itself. But modes... can neither exist nor be conceived without substance; therefore they can exist

---

21 This is the opposite of what the majoritarian tradition in philosophy has taken to be the case. According to Spinoza, existence, rather than being only a possibility of essence, is the condition of essence. Herein lies his much more than simply ›clever‹ argument against the accusation of hereticism. Proposition 7 of his *Ethics* states: »It belongs to the nature of substance to exist« (EIP7), and the explication of it we find in the alternative proof in Proposition 11: »To be able not to exist is a lack of power, and on the other hand to be able to exist is a power (as is self-evident).« (EIP11)

solely in the divine nature. And can be conceived through that nature alone. But nothing exists besides substances and modes... Therefore, nothing can exist or be conceived without God. QED. (Ibid)[22]

According to Spinoza, we cannot argue differently. As soon as we re-open the gap between the finite and the infinite as one of two different orders, we are led into the impasses that scholasticism and negative theology, as much as Cartesianism, could not avoid. We fall back into what Deleuze calls a philosophy that conceives itself in terms of resemblance, identity, opposition, and analogy (cf. DR: 29).

In the thought of univocity substance always ›is‹, and everything ›is‹ (in) substance (though in different degrees—this is a question of power as we will see later on). Because of this, there is but one substance, a substance, however, of and as absolute infinity. Nothing besides, above, or beyond: immanence, radical immanence. This is Spinoza's grand statement structuring his system of thought. It is this seemingly simple yet most forceful *equation* (as non-teleological complication) that is the formula of univocity: Essence = Existence.[23] Everything else will follow and find its place from here.

Three centuries after the Scotist school then, Spinoza in his *Ethics* gives the thought of univocity *reality*. Deleuze shows that up to Spinoza's revival of the notion of univocal Being, the thought of absolute infinity could not yet get rid of its abstractness and remoteness. Only with Spinoza, he says, does univocity become »an object of pure affirmation« (DR: 40).[24] This is the reason why for him Spi-

---

22 We can see that in this equation essence = existence lies already a first hint for our equation ›ontology = ethics‹.

23 For yet another occasion of this equation in Spinoza's *Ethics*, cf. EIP20: »God's existence and his essence are one and the same.« In what follows, we have to investigate this equation in more detail, we have to pay close attention to the › = ‹ in its particular functioning for this equation.

24 Cf. also Goodchild 2001: 160: »The potential for developing the concept of God as immanent cause was not developed by Scotus. Deleuze regards Spinoza's ontology as considerable advance over that of Scotus: being becomes an object of pure affirmation... so Scotus' metaphysical concepts are substantives, such as ›causality‹, the ›producible‹, and ›haecceity‹. With Spinoza, ›univocal being becomes identical with the unique... and infinite substance: it is proposed as *Deus sive Natura*‹.«

noza occupies the extraordinary place in the history of a thought of immanence of which we were speaking before. For Deleuze, Spinoza manages to synthesize knowledge and Being in a way that enables us to move away from the repetition of dogmatic dichotomies, be it between God and creatures, the One and the all, or between mind and body. His formula *Deus sive Natura* (a formula so different from the one Descartes put forward with its upwardly pointing *ergo* in the formula *Cogito ergo sum*) is an equation that moves — at once — on both its sides, without, however, collapsing one side into the other. It, thus, does not compromise immanence but gives it the complexity it deserves. Univocity is no totality, nor does it resemble one. Spinoza's philosophy ›parallelizes‹, or better, it interweaves transcendence (*Deus*) and immanence (*Natura*) rather than pressing the two in a vertical order. In saying that univocity in no way collapses transcendence into immanence means that it also does not constitute a relation of parts and whole in the way a concept of unity would presuppose. Unity, in opposition to what we will see univocity to be, propagates itself as a One that stands in opposition to its parts. It wills a One of identity eliminating difference and multiplicity. In contrast, univocity does not refer to anything outside its expressions and thus remains exposed to all inherent difference and multiplicity. By employing the concept of univocity, Spinoza moves away from the perspective of two separated realms that cannot but create a hierarchical structure in which one order is handed over to be judged by the other. He moves towards a plane of but one substance — a substance, however, of and as *absolute infinity*; a substance, thus, that always already is a *multiplicity*.

Immanent Cause

While Scotus is one angle from which it seems fruitful to investigate Spinoza's thought of univocity, the debate between a thought of transcendence and one of immanence is already ongoing in the ancient debate of the ›problem of participation‹. In order, thus, to get a firmer grip on the issues that are at stake in this argument between univocity and equivocity, it is important to move still further backwards in time and relate Spinoza's formula of the *immanent* cause — ›God or Nature‹, where both sides of the equation express essence *and* existence at once, the One *and* the all — to ancient philosophy's most famous (Neo-)Platonic solution to the problem of participation: *ema-*

nation. While the significant difference (between *immanence* and *emanation*) is visible from the outset, moving to the debate of the problem of participation, one of the most originary problems of philosophy (if we take philosophy to have originated in ›Greece‹), will enable us to specify what the concept of the immanent cause really implies, and how in Spinoza's return to the Ancients—and in protest against his own Christianized time—this thinker developed a distinct understanding of what could be learnt from this philosophy.

Therefore, to start at the beginning: »Everything may, it seems, be traced back to the Platonic problem of participation« (EP: 169), Deleuze says. Plato, creator of the thought of distinction, divides the universe into, on the one hand, the (transcendent) Ideas high up in the heavens, and, on the other hand, their representations, faithful imitations or demonic distortions, here on earth. The way in which Plato sets out the problem of participation is that to participate is, at best, to rank second. Here begins the degradation of being in comparison to Being, which will accompany the history of Western philosophy. In Plato's idealization or dialectics, the modern conceptualization of God as infinite perfection is on the horizon.[25] The perspective on being as precisely lacking this perfection announces itself. Plato only looks at the side of what participates—i.e. he treats the question of Being as one of legitimacy—and ignores the problem of the logic of causality itself. His question is how to decide which of the things that exist ›participate‹ in the Ideas, because they are legitimate copies, and which ones do not, and thus have to be *morally* rejected as distortions or mere simulacra. The problem of Platonism is the following as Deleuze extrapolates in his appendix to *The Logic of Sense* on »The Simulacrum and Ancient Philosophy«: because Plato's concern with this division is rather »to distinguish pretenders; to distinguish the pure from the impure, the authentic from the inauthentic... to distinguish the true from the false one« (LS: 254), the problem of how participation in itself has to be thought, remains literally untouched. It does not become problematized in itself. And already in *Expressionism in Philosophy* Deleuze has said that

25 »Platonism thus founds the entire domain that philosophy will later recognize as its own.« (LS: 259)

> the principle of participation was always sought by Plato on the side of what participates… It usually appears as an accident supervening on what is participated from outside, as a violence suffered by what is participated. If participation consists in being a part, it is difficult to see how what is participated suffers no division or separation. If to participate is to imitate, there must be some external artist who takes the Idea as his model (EP: 169).

As happens with Cartesianism later on, because the problem of participation — the problem of causality — is addressed purely as an issue on one side — namely on the side of what participates — the whole question at stake is transformed into a question of *morality*, of the good vs. the evil copies, that no longer touches the question of participation itself but only ever strives for a most *legitimate* representation. What follows is an image of thought conceptualized as analogy rather than as a reality in the sense we spoke of above (real knowledge as construction). The world is divided in two separate realms which become and remain unsurpassable to each other.

Spinoza reacts to this ›too easy‹ solution in a twofold manner. On the one hand, he employs the philosophy of Ancient Greece in questioning his own Christianized time by reviving the Neo-Platonist and Aristotelian criticisms of Plato's *moral* image of thought that became dominant in the history of modern philosophy. On the other hand, however, in taking up this tradition Spinoza both flattens the Neo-Platonist perspective from a cause of emanation that still remains — though less abstract — beyond and above its effects, and he also takes away the inherent distinction between cause and effect that gives Aristotelian naturalism its ever-lasting stability.

In a manner different from all of these traditions, Spinoza moves to a radically immanent cause that ›is‹ (only ever in) its effects as much as its effects ›are‹ (always already in) the cause itself without any measure left to this relation that could claim an external objectity.[26] This thought ›is‹ radical constructivism. Instead of exclusively

---

26 Such is the result of a thought that not only thinks the problem of causality to its limit but pushes it so far as to think an immanent cause immanent only to itself. The accusation of hereticism issued against Spinoza does after this not really come as a surprise. Why? »Because this was undoubtedly the most dangerous theme. Treating God as an emanative cause can fit because there is

approaching the question of how the one ›is part of‹ an All, or how all ›are part of‹ the One from the side of what participates — the ›accident‹ which in a logic of imitation does violence to the One in dividing it in two — Spinoza demands that we reverse the approach. The formula God *or* Nature, the *One-All* as Deleuze and Guattari call it in *What is Philosophy?* as we will see in a moment, in Spinoza can never be taken apart. God and Nature — substance in its double movement — ›are the same‹ so to speak, but ›the same‹ only in their difference, in their eternally differing from each other. This is exemplified in Definition 6 of Book I in the *Ethics*: »By God I understand an absolutely *infinite entity*, that is a substance consisting of *infinite attributes*, each of which *expresses* eternal and *infinite essence*« (EɪD6). It is one substance for both *each* and *all* attributes. »[T]here is [not] only one substance for each attribute, but… there is only one substance for all attributes.« (EP: 34) All and One are linked internally — for the very first time. All attributes express the one ›infinite essence‹, and the essence of this substance is expressed in every single ›one‹ attribute.

The One-All

As was said above, such an approach to the One as univocal Being has to be distinguished from all Neo-Platonist (and Aristotelian) emanation which still (though implicitly) maintains the difference in form between the cause and its effect, and the One and the All, that Plato had established as an external relation.

Spinoza emphasizes the logical necessity of an indivisible One,[27] which, while in permanent differentiation, does not lose its very oneness. Infinite substance is, thus, already a One of multiplicity. Only this way do we truly manage to think immanence, and only this way do we avoid the anthropomorphism into which analogical thought with its dichotomy of infinite perfection and finite imperfection inevitably falls. It is one of the merits of Deleuze's interpretation to show that Spinoza pushes parallelism so far that a necessary *co-existence* of both dimensions — the One and the All — with one being *expres-*

---

still the distinction between cause and effect. But as immanent cause, such that we no longer know very well how to distinguish cause and effect, that is to say treating God and the creature the same, that becomes much more difficult.« (Deleuze, Seminar 11/25/1980)

27 EɪP13: »An absolutely infinite substance is indivisible.«

sion of the essence of the other becomes possible. Both directions have to be thought at the same time; this is the sense of the equation essence = existence. Spinoza wants us to think a simultaneity that unlike identity or imitation relies purely on difference. Only in such a *paradoxical gesture* do we achieve an account of real and infinite differences that a One of multiplicity expresses.

To collapse the divine back into the mundane and to re-introduce hierarchies, this time only the other way around, is not the gesture we are speaking of here. This is not enough for the hard-line rationalist Spinoza. What is necessary in order not to reduce or simplify, is that we have to—radically—reconsider the relation of the One and the Multiple/All. What we have to reconsider is what a One ›is capable of‹. This is what the concept of univocity implies: against the view that what is One must eliminate all difference within it, a *univocal One* lives all the differences that ›are‹ the expression of its essence; a One, in fact, that remains ›alive‹ only by propagating difference. Univocity is the concept for a One-ness that because of its indivisibility (*absolute infinity*) is nothing but its own process of differentiation. There is no eminent cause which *emanates* out of itself and yet ›must‹ remain above and beyond its effects, i.e. on an extra terrain. This is still the *moral* image of thought of which Deleuze speaks when he refers to Plato's ›pretenders‹. Spinoza's, on the contrary, is a radically different thought: no superiority of the One above being, but a non-hierarchical *equality of Being*. Deleuze counts this as one of the most significant events in the history of philosophy, and this claim on *univocity* becomes his very own ontological *credo*:

> Being is univocal. There has only ever been one ontology… which gave being a single voice… from Parmenides to Heidegger it is the same voice which is taken up, in an echo which itself forms the whole deployment of the univocal. A single voice raises the clamour of being… [But Being] is nevertheless not a genus… We must add that being, this common designated, in so far as it expresses itself, is said in turn *in a single and same sense* of all the numerically distinct designators and expressors. (DR: 35)

Being is univocal, there is but one voice raising ›the clamour of being‹. This one voice, however, the One-All is ›not a genus‹; it is no classificatory system describing a closed totality outside and above its modes or expressions. Rather, what is fundamental to the thought of the One-All is that ›in so far as it expresses itself, [Being] is said in turn *in a single and same sense of all* the numerically distinct designators and expressors‹. Instead of thinking the relation of the One to the All either as one of parts (all) to whole (One as unity), or as one of the particular (one) to the general (All as universality), i.e. as an *external* relation, the One-All has to be thought as a relation in which both sides inherently belong to each other—they are linked *internally*. The two sides cannot be taken apart, and yet they remain differentiated. Both have to be thought *at once* without homogenizing the double movement to a linear one-directionality.

What is important is not only that Being is said *in a single and same sense*, but that it is said in a single and same sense »*of all* its individuating differences and intrinsic modalities« (DR: 36). Such an *equality* does not lead to infinite regress. Rather, as Deleuze says, it »allows [Spinoza] immediately to reconcile the ontological unity of substance with the qualitative plurality of its attributes« (EP: 182). Instead of an emanative cause, eminent and above being, Spinoza's *immanent cause*[28] inherently links all elements in this relation without pressing them into a previous totality or unity, and thus without stopping its constitutive infinity. Although the distinctions of essences are not done away with in Spinoza, what for Deleuze is so fascinating is that one nonetheless has to think both as inherently related. Substance, attribute, and modes are *equal* in the sense that attributes and modes (as modifications of attributes) equally *express* the essence of substance which in itself ›is‹ nothing but these infinite expressions. Substance expresses itself in attributes, which in their turn both express the essence of substance, and express themselves in modes which are thus—again—nothing but expressions of the essence of substance. For Deleuze, and this will be our focus for the last part of our discussion, the significance of Spinozism is that

---

28 Cf. EIP18: »God is the immanent but not the transitive cause of all things.« As immanent cause has to be understood a cause that produces an effect within itself, as transitive has to be understood a cause that produces an effect outside of itself (cf. Parkinson 2003: 29).

it asserts immanence as a principle and frees expression from any subordination to emanative or exemplary causality. *Expression itself no longer emanates, no longer resembles anything.* And such a result can be obtained only within a perspective of univocity. (EP: 180)

Every part in this relation shares in a community of form, this is univocity of Being. It is to misinterpret Spinoza if one collapses his logic of expression into one of emanation, precisely because of the deconstruction of hierarchies that characterizes expressionism. While emanative thought cannot avoid re-introducing a realm *above* emanation in order to begin the movement of differentiation of the One, expressionism is capable of imagining a movement of differentiation that happens in multiple directions at once, without looking for reference in any previous ›whole‹ that resides above the procedure itself. While Neo-Platonist emanation keeps a superior cause that »produces through what it gives, but is beyond what it gives« (EP: 172), immanence is immanent only to itself when »its effect is ›immanate‹ in the cause, rather than emanating from it« (ibid). God's existence and his essence are one and the same; substance cannot but express itself in infinite attributes—it ›is not‹ apart or aside from this expression. This is the multiplying ›infinite‹ movement that from the analogical structure of idealized divine heights together with the corresponding human depths returns to the *inhuman* surface of immanence. Like the surface of the sea, it is a surface of multiplicity, a One not of *already constituted* units, but a One that only ever *becomes* in its very expression(s).

3. Expression vs. Representation

These conclusions drawn from the debate between analogical vs. ontological, and equivocal vs. univocal thought, lead us finally to the one significant notion that from the very start structures Deleuze's Spinozism: *expression*, or better the *logic of expression*, which, as Deleuze wonders in the introduction to *Expressionism in Philosophy*, has not really been taken into account by most of Spinoza's commentators:

> [W]hy have the most respected commentators taken so little, if any, account of this notion in Spinoza's philosophy? Some completely ignore it. Others give it a certain indirect significance, seeing in it another name for some deeper principle. (EP: 17)

As Deleuze shows us in his interpretation of Spinoza, there is, however, no deeper principle behind expression. For him, as was already mentioned, this *is* the Spinozist revolution: expression, or better the logic of expression, always remains on but one plane. If we think of the term itself and the relation it unfolds, every expression remains internally related to *what it expresses* and yet it *does express it*, that is, it is not reducible to or merely identical with what it expresses. Expressionism, thus, describes a movement that without referring to any other level is able to produce movement and thus difference. It is what we earlier called a surface-movement spreading in infinite ways, not above or below, but everywhere else — infinitely.

Expressionism

Spinoza conceives a most immanent relation of substance, attributes, and modes. The attributes — never external to substance — *express*, as Deleuze says, the very infinite essence of substance:

> [E]ssence, insofar as it has existence, has no existence outside the attribute in which it is expressed; and yet, as essence, it relates only to substance. An essence is expressed by each attribute, but this as an essence of substance itself. (EP: 27)

And modes are nothing but *modifications* of attributes. They are variations which in their turn express these attributes in qualitatively infinite ways. Being defined thus, they are directly related to the essence = existence of substance. As Spinoza says, modes are »affections of substance«.[29] While taking the notion of expression from Spi-

---

29 »By mode I understand the affections of substance, or, that which is in something else, through which it is also conceived.« (EɪD3–5) Cf. also EɪP23: »Every modus which exists both necessarily and as infinite must necessarily have followed either from the absolute nature of some attribute of God, or from some attribute modified by a modification which exists both necessarily and as infinite.«

noza, it is Deleuze who truly grasps the potential movement at stake in Spinoza's language of expression, and unfolds for us the one — but only one — plane on which all this happens:

> This notion of expression is essentially triadic: we must distinguish what expresses itself, the expression itself and what is expressed. The paradox is that ›what is expressed‹ *has no existence* outside its expression, yet bears no resemblance to it, but relates *essentially* to what expresses itself as distinct from the expression itself. (EP: 333)

The triad of the logic of representation (equivocation, eminence, and analogy) is transferred in the logic of expression into but one plane differing *in-between* itself. An expression is neither representation of nor identification with something external, outside, or beyond the process of expression. We have to avoid perceiving of the relation in the mode of a representational ›as if‹, such that we again assume the intellect ascribing attributes to a reality that in itself is without attributes (the anthropomorphist trap). We must be careful to distinguish the movement we are after here from the model of imitation working with mirrors and resemblances, ›as if‹ there is something pre-existing to be mirrored or to be resembled. Misunderstanding expression as resemblance, we remain ignorant of the immense difference that the infinitesimal turn of perspective effectuates. What is asked from us is not to fold back the relation at stake here into the Platonic universe of an eternally given original and temporarily existing (true or false) copies. With Spinoza, we have to deal with the *affective* equation that moves — at once — on both sides, and in which attributes *are* substance (cf. Parkinson 2003: 18), so that they *express* the *essence* of substance. An adequate understanding of expressionism shows that in the equation essence = existence, neither side can exist on its own; both only gain ›Being‹ in the very process of expression.

Implicare/Explicare

Expressionism is Deleuze's Spinozism; it is what he himself takes from Spinoza which in Deleuze's case also implies that it might be more than Spinoza himself is able to give. From expressionism, Deleuze starts conceptualizing his plane of immanence: there are not two realms, one always privileged over the other, but only ever one.

A One, however, so immanent that it is immanent only to itself. It is not a One above or beyond difference and multiplicity, but a *One-All* that »takes what is expressed as involved, *implicit*, wound up, in its expression... or... *explicates*, unwinds expression so as to restore what is expressed« (EP: 333). Radical immanence, for Deleuze, is this *affective* movement of expression which shows concurrence with the Medieval and Renaissance couple of *implicare/explicare*.

> Implication and explication, involution and evolution: terms inherited from a long philosophical tradition, always subject to the charge of pantheism. Precisely because the two concepts are not opposed to one another, they imply a principle of synthesis: *complication*. (EP: 16)

Rather than opposing or bouncing off each other, the logic of implication/explication is the production of more, it produces an excess and thus moves somewhere else. It never ›is‹ but it ›becomes‹. It creates something that at the same time was always already its most inner principle: this is what a thought of complication speaks of. To reduce Spinoza's expressive substance merely to the side of explication, such as it happens in the critique of post-Kantian philosophy and most famously in Hegel's criticism of Spinoza, therefore, means again missing the point. While for Hegel »to be a follower of Spinoza is the essential commencement of all Philosophy... [because w]hen man begins to philosophize, the soul must commence by bathing in this ether of the One Substance« (Hegel 1995: 257), substance with Spinoza, according to him, »is not yet determined as in itself concrete« (Hegel 1995: 258). Acknowledging in Spinoza's conceptualization of substance the genetic movement of self-development that he himself is after, but taking the movement of ›explication‹ — a substance explicating itself in infinite attributes and modes — as the only movement at stake here, Hegel accuses Spinoza of a lifeless and abstract substance, i.e. a One of traditional monism. As Deleuze says: »Spinoza's substance seemed to [Hegel] lifeless, his expression intellectual and abstract, his attributes ›attributed‹ to substance by an understanding that was itself ›explicative‹« (EP: 18). This Hegelian accusation against Spinoza claims that because substance cannot account for the side of the individual, i.e. the experience of subjectivity, because of its (literal) *one*-sidedness, the whole system remains abstract and thus without true reality.[30] In his article »Hegel, Pantheism and Spinoza«, Parkinson summarizes the Hegelian criticism as follows:

> Relying exclusively on the categories of understanding, Spinoza emphasized abstract, not spiritual unity, and his system remains stuck in metaphysical abstraction… it is essential that true reality (*das Wahre*) shall be grasped, not as substance, but also as subject. (Parkinson 1977: 453)

While Hegel applauds Spinoza for emphasizing that all determination is negation, he absolutely disagrees with what he believes to be Spinoza's conclusion: that the world is nothing but »mere phenomenon«, that is, that it is not genuinely real (cf. Parkinson 1977: 451). For Hegel, this is the conclusion which must follow from the ultimate prioritization of substance as ›absolute affirmation of itself‹ (substance as *causa sui*), in which »God alone is the positive, the affirmative… [and] all other things, on the contrary are only modifications of this substance, and are nothing in and for themselves« (Hegel 1995: 286). What for Hegel is missing in Spinoza's focus on substance is the very movement that is necessary for getting out of the trap of mere abstraction. What is missing is the movement that produces concreteness, i.e. true reality of the world itself, and this is for Hegel of course the development of self-consciousness.[31] This is why Hegel's claim of ›the negation of negation‹ (sublation) is introduced, which alone produces this self-development—»a movement that starts from itself and returns to itself« (Parkinson 1977: 452).[32]

Hegel's perspective, however, as readers such as Parkinson and Deleuze show, might misunderstand what is revolutionary about the generative power of Spinoza's concept of immanence. Earlier we dis-

---

30 »[A]bsolute substance is the truth, but it is not the whole truth; in order to be this it must also be thought of as in itself active and living, and by that very means it must determine itself as mind.« (Hegel 1995: 257)

31 Hegel thus again reverses Spinoza's criticism of Platonism, and puts forth a philosophy that focuses on the side of what participates (logic of representation) instead of the question of participation itself (pure ontology).

32 Cf. also Hegel 1995: 286.

cussed the logic of expression as a genetic movement on but one level. With Parkinson we emphasized that, instead of merely resembling or mirroring a fixed and total substance, attributes *are* substance, in the sense of Deleuze's ›they *express* infinite substance‹. It is one-sided to state that substance *explicates* itself into attributes. What must always be implied is that attributes *are* substance *explicated* in the way that they, as Parkinson says, »constitut[e] its essence« (Parkinson 1977: 454). Substance *is* nothing but attributes and modes *implicated*. However, when substance itself is grasped as absolutely infinite, i.e. constituted only in these very expressions, we speak of a relation of *complication* or *synthesis* in which both sides — *affect* and *affection* — are accounted for. This movement expresses at least two directions ›at once‹. And while such a theoretical move seems absolutely impossible because it is paradoxical, it is the movement that is at stake in a radically immanent thought, or as we will call it at the end of our argument, in a *thought of becoming*. There is no beginning or end but only *complicated relationality*.[33] »So that God must be defined as identical to Nature *complicative*, and Nature as identical to God *explicative*« (EP: 176), as Deleuze writes. Contrary to what Hegel suggests, it is not by the movement of negation that we overcome abstraction. This solution only throws up the new problem of a system that is even more ›total‹, ›unitary‹, and reliant on a conception of the One. On the contrary, a *vital Spinozism*, as we might call Deleuze's approach, *internally* links the thought of substance to every expression of it as the only existence substance itself possesses, and this means, the only essence it ever has. There is no ›One‹ prior to expressions, ›all‹ is happening at once. What we speak of here is a *plane of consistency or composition*, in the way Deleuze and Guattari characterize it in *A Thousand Plateaus*:

> Here, there are no longer any forms or developments of forms... There are only relations of movement and rest, speed and slowness between unformed elements... There are only haecceities, affects, subjectless in-

---

33 To help us grasp such a movement, we should also think of how Deleuze chooses to conceptualize this relationality at another time. He then speaks of the figure of the *fold* with its two dimensions of enfolding/enveloping and unfolding/developing. He develops this logic of the fold both in *The Fold* (Deleuze 1993) and in his book *Foucault* (Deleuze 1998).

> dividuations that constitute collective assemblages. Nothing develops, but things arrive late or early, and form this or that assemblage depending on their composition of speed... We call this plane, which knows only longitudes and latitudes, speeds and haecceities, the plane of consistency and composition... It is necessarily a plane of immanence and univocality. (TP: 266)

Linking our discussion of Spinoza's pure ontology to the conception of the One-All as plane of immanence developed by Deleuze and Guattari, we are transferring a 17th century thought into the late 20th century. However, while their thought, of course, introduces modifications and is couched in a different linguistic idiom, it fully speaks the Spinozist revolution. In Spinoza, as Deleuze already has shown in *Expressionism in Philosophy*, »[God] cannot understand himself without producing an infinity of things, and without also understanding all that he produces« (EP: 185). In order to reach an understanding of itself — i.e. in order to ›express itself to itself‹ — Spinoza's substance *has to* explicate itself in infinite attributes and modes which in their turn *essentially express*, that is, *constitute* substance. Essence, which in Spinoza always implies an adequate idea of the cause itself, is expression, which itself is nothing else but endless production or composition. Such a productive and constructive perspective is also the reason why Spinoza argues against a notion of God as ›absolute free will‹. »God does not operate by means of freedom of will« (EIP32C1), he states thereby irritating most of his contemporaries. However, according to Spinoza's logic, such argument is the only coherent one. It is not by transcendent judgment — by a ›wise choice‹ — that Spinoza's God operates, since such a conceptualization of omnipotence is already modeled according to *human* spirit, an omnipotence that interposes distance and reflection between itself and the things produced. Against any such anthropomorphist reductions Spinoza's God *is* nothing but Nature complicated, independent from both subjectivist and representational models. He is One *and* All, he is a *One-All*; a One-ness that is no longer the opposite of multiplicity but — in countering the thought of a One that can only be One by excluding all difference — a One-ness of that which infinitely differs (univocal Being).[34] Such a conception of the One as multiplicity allows ontology to move away from the image of an already constituted space (Being) in which—secondarily—things (beings) become distributed, which then, in turn, are categorized, hierarchized, and compared to each other in order to make sense of them. The logic of expression enables us to think the plane of immanence as space producing itself only through its very infinite expressions—expressions *distributing* space itself—a *nomad nomos* no longer immanent to something else but immanent only to itself.

The Plane of Immanence

In *Difference and Repetition*, Deleuze points us to this very crucial difference between the two ways of imagining the plane of immanence:

> We must first of all distinguish a type of distribution which implies a dividing up of that which is distributed: it is a matter of dividing up the distributed as such... A distribution of this type proceeds by fixed and proportional determinations which may be assimilated to ›properties‹ or limited territories within representation. (DR: 36)

This type of distribution represents—if we substitute ›distribution‹ with ›participation‹—the Platonic conceptualization of the relation of the One and the All, and it is what in *A Thousand Plateaus*, Deleuze and Guattari call »as much a *plan(e) of organization* as of *development*« (TP: 265, my emphases). It is a *plan(e)* organized according to the logic of parts and whole: the tree is already given in the seed, everything is already ›present‹ in the origin from which everything else follows. »*Even if it is said to be immanent*«, Deleuze and Guattari say, »it is so only by absence, analogically (metaphorically, metonymically, etc.)« (TP: 266).

If we move on, however, and see how the citation from *Difference*

---

34 We have to be careful here not to fold back Deleuze into Hegelianism. Again, while Deleuze's intention certainly can be said to bear similarity to Hegel's, it was made clear in our discussion before that there is a crucial difference—a difference in kind—between the Spinozist ›univocity‹ (in Deleuze's terms a One-All) that requires a thought of difference ›in itself‹ and Hegel's All-One in which difference ultimately is replaced by the highest form of identity.

and Repetition in which Deleuze distinguishes the two types of distribution continues, we learn that

> [t]hen there is a completely other distribution which must be called nomadic, a nomad *nomos*, without property, enclosure or measure. Here, there is no longer a division of that which is distributed but rather a division among those who distribute *themselves* in an open space—a space which is unlimited, or at least without precise limits... To fill a space, to be distributed within it, is very different from distributing the space (DR: 36).

Expressionism—an operative logic *at once* unfolding in more than one direction—precisely enables us to think ›infinity‹, or, as we heard, a space which ›is at least without precise limits‹, without the introduction of another level, without a level either higher up or prior to the operation of its own expression. In pushing the thought of Being to its limits, this logic is able to conceive an immanence no longer stopped by anything but immanence itself. It is able to think immanence infinitely, an immanence from which a breach is expected but which does not transfer back immanence to transcendence. When we began our discussion with the quote from *What is Philosophy?* we could not yet see how such a thought may be more than a paradoxical construction leading to a theoretical cul-de-sac. Nearing the end of our discussion now, however, it has become clear that in order to arrive at an adequate understanding of the problem of immanence, we must confront this paradox of an immanence immanent only to itself which nonetheless allows for more than what we usually have thought of immanence to be. The thought of the univocity of Being—the expression Deleuze gave to Spinoza—is indispensable for a *pure ontology* which thinks of immanence as only immanent to itself and nothing outside, beyond, above, or below it. It was only Spinoza, according to Deleuze, who was able to »pull off« such an ontology, because it is only with him that »[t]here is an interiority of essences and that does not mean that they merge. One arrives at *a system of intrinsic distinctions*« (Deleuze, Seminar 03/24/1981, my emphasis). Only when these are adequately understood does thought become *real, singular*, and *concrete*.

In concluding this first chapter then we have to summarize what is important for us to remember when we turn to our next investigation of the thought-lines that constitute Deleuze's philosophy of becoming. Two aspects of Deleuze's Spinozism are of major significance for his philosophical project. First, the notion of expression, which, as was said, up until Deleuze rarely made it into the center of attention in interpretations of Spinoza's philosophy.[35] It is, however, precisely an adequate understanding of this *logic of expression* that Deleuze develops in his reading of Spinoza and that is fundamental to the distinction of the thought of *univocity* from the tradition of the concept of *unity*. As I have shown in my presentation, we must not confuse expressionism with the traditional ›optical‹ model of representation that is linked to the notions of mirroring or of the dualism of original and copy, be it finite or infinite, subjectivist or objectivist. Expressionism also must not be misunderstood as either the Neo-Platonic emanative cause or the mere explicative substance that Post-Kantian philosophy made of it. Rather, in Deleuze's re-construction, Spinoza goes further than all these approaches. His crucial contribution to and specification of the thought of univocity is the emphasis on the *equality of Being* without equalizing and leveling the inherent differences. In contrast to theories reliant on an untouchable realm that serves as the model or ground from which everything else receives its form, expressionism — adequately understood — does not only do away with these hierarchies (›every being is equal‹), but it also manages to produces a wholly different understanding of Being itself. Rather than delimiting the space of distribution in advance, in not having an *objective* measurement left according to which things can be categorized, compared, and ranked, expressionism reaches a different way of thinking, in which equality no longer equalizes differences, but a thinking able to ›live‹ the equality of everything unequal.

---

35 Exceptional cases prove the rule (instead of undermining it). An exception to the omission of expressionism in Spinoza criticism is G.H.R. Parkinson who already in his essay from 1977 has stressed the notion of ›expression‹ in Spinoza's way of thinking (cf. Parkinson 1977: 455). In his recent translation of Spinoza's *Ethics* for the series *Oxford Philosophical Texts* (Parkinson 2003) he pays meticulous attention to the Latin ›exprimere‹.

> The words ›everything is equal‹ may therefore resound joyfully, on condition that they are said of that which is not equal in this equal, univocal Being: equal being is immediately present in everything, without mediation or intermediary, even though things reside unequally in this equal being. (DR: 37)

Here, we touch on the second important aspect of Deleuze's Spinozism that will have to be kept in mind as our text unfolds. Contrary to the usual interpretation of Spinoza's system as traditional *monism* — one static system in which substance is first and attributes or modes only ever ›explicate‹ it — Deleuze complicates these systemic movements and thus *dynamizes* Spinoza's system. Attributes are not merely explicating substance, as we heard, they *are the expression of the essence* of substance; they *are* — in expression — constitutive of substance itself. Since existence and essence are *inseparable*, the process of expression is a process of production, and in this sense this process is *infinite movement*. Instead of an eternal substance that explicates itself into attributes and modes, Spinoza internally — that is necessarily and essentially — links the existence of substance to its expressions in attributes and modes. In doing so, he tears away monism from ›given-ness‹, and thinks a Moebius strip-like relation between attributes, modes, and substance, in which each ›is‹ the other — only seen from the other side. Substance no longer describes a One that is a totality, the outlines of which — even if only ideally — have to be presupposed in order to think its expressions. Again, this would be the anthropomorphist — and later on the subjectivist — trap into which even Leibniz, who in all other regards is so close to Spinoza, fell.[36] For Deleuze, it is only with Spinoza that it is possible to think a

---

36 This accusation of anthropomorphism in Leibniz, in my opinion, still holds, although Deleuze changes his assessment of this philosophy in his later work *The Fold*. Leibniz's world remains based on an image of God as absolute reason, ›having chosen the best of all possible worlds‹. According to the Deleuze of *Expressionism in Philosophy*, Spinoza's expressionism has to be distinguished from the Leibnizian one, which Deleuze puts on the side of equivocity, creation, and emanation, all notions unacceptable for Spinoza's claim on radical univocity and immanence. In the appendix »The Theory of Expression in Leibniz and Spinoza. Expressionism in Philosophy«, Deleuze writes: »Far from expression being, in Spinoza, consistent with creation and emanation, it rather excludes these, relegates them to the order of inadequate signs or

substance which ›is‹ only its expressions without in return collapsing their *differences in kind*. The simple equation of univocity (essence = existence), thus, remains the easy formula; and yet, it should not be taken in any reductive way, ›as if‹ everything becomes indistinguishable. The two sides of the equation do ›express‹ the same, and yet, expression is never enacted or actualized without variation. Something always (has to) happen(s) in an expression—necessarily—and it is such deferral and production without end, that characterizes the process of expression and leaves a structural openness to this oneness. The one-ness of substance becomes—on the other side of the equation—a plurality. This is the thought of the One-All as multiplicity, which is so fundamental to a real thought of becoming, that is a thought, which concens *this* world, and which we now have to investigate further.

---

equivocal language. Spinoza accepts the truly philosophical ›danger‹ of immanence and pantheism implicit in the notion of expression. Indeed he throws in his lot with that danger. In Spinoza *the whole theory of expression supports univocity*... Here, I feel, lies the real opposition between Spinoza and Leibniz: *the theory of univocal expression in the one should be opposed to the theory of equivocal expressions in the other.*« (EP: 333)

III.

»To Endure!« or the Thought of Difference: *Bergson*

> There lies the whole Bergsonian dimension of the formula proposed by Deleuze — pluralism = monism — …
> (Alliez, *The Signature of the World*)
> … the possibility of a new *monism*
> (Deleuze, *Bergson*)

A leap into pure ontology — daring the thought of immanence as immanence immanent only to itself — is what we have learned from our first approach to Deleuze's thought via Spinoza. In this discussion, ontology as the thought of univocity — Being as univocal — was understood in terms of expression rather than analogy or emanation, providing us with »an idea of expressive immanence« (EP: 169), an *affective* immanence with no need for external causation. In our presentation of both the problem of causation according to the 17th century and the Ancient and Medieval problem of participation, we saw the hidden anthropomorphism (the confusion of property and essence) at work in *analogical* thought, which, according to Deleuze, Spinoza alone manages to escape in order to construct a real plane of immanence. This, according to Deleuze, is the true Spinozist revolution: overcoming analogy by a radical logic of expression.

> Analogy cannot do without equivocation or eminence, and hence contains a subtle anthropomorphism, just as dangerous as the naive variety… The analogical method denies that there are forms common to God and to creatures but, far from escaping the mistake it denounces, it constantly confuses the essence of creatures with the essence of God. In some cases it does away with the essence of particular things, reducing qualities to determinations that can belong intrinsically only to God, in some cases it does away with the essence of God, lending to him eminently what creatures possess formally. Spinoza, on the other hand, insists on the identity of form between creatures and God, while permitting no confusion of essence. (EP: 46–47)

Though in a certain sense one could argue that Deleuze's own philosophical project unfolds in a discussion and interpretation of *his* Spinoza, in my opinion this would be a conclusion drawn too quickly. If we look closely the strong Deleuzian postulation of Spinoza's claim of ›the identity of form‹ on the one hand with yet ›no confusion of essence‹ on the other hand, still must bother us. For we realize at this point that what lies in the task ›to think‹ nothing less than the paradox of both a community of form and absolute difference of essences, is not only the crux of what we call a real thought of immanence — an immanence from which a breach can be expected without handing over immanence to transcendence at the very same time — but it also displays the limit to the Spinozist heritage. A limit, of course, which Deleuze in his thinking another's thought manages to overcome, but only because his dealing with thought shows a special virtue that we have to mention explicitly here and about which he himself is very clear. In a »Letter to a Harsh Critic« from 1977, a piece of writing that should be taken as a telling example on more than one level regarding the manner in which Deleuze counters accusations against his way of *doing* philosophy, he describes his philosophical practice in the following way:

> I suppose the main way I coped with [the repressing role that the history of philosophy plays in philosophy, KT] was to see the history of philosophy as a sort of buggery or (it comes to the same thing) immaculate conception. I saw myself as taking an author from behind and giving him a child that would be his own offspring, yet monstrous. It is really important for it to be his own child, because the author had to actually say all I had him saying. But the child was bound to be monstrous too, because it resulted from all sorts of shifting, slipping, dislocations, and hidden emissions that I really enjoyed. (Deleuze 1995: 6)

The philosophical practice of *reading* — if it is worthy of its name — must not only out of necessity accept but actively affirm that it ›moves somewhere else‹, that it produces difference in correspondence with the text, that reading always means reading alongside ›at least one other series,‹ which creates encounters and crossovers, and that in the interstices something new is able to emerge — at its best. That this spontaneity and openness to new meanings so characteristic of Deleuze's writing, can, at times, also be misleading, does not really come as a surprise.[1] If, however, we want to grasp his thought, we cannot expect linearity but must follow this zigzagging, the resonances, and correspondences. As he shows so lucidly in this very same letter: no, he is not trapped or stuck; there is nothing to admit (»I'm not admitting anything« (Deleuze 1995: 5)), it is on us to learn to *read* him!

Since what we are after here is precisely what could be called Deleuze's thought-map, it is important at this moment, when we could draw the conclusions too quickly, that we do not opt for such a possibility, but rather follow the different routes carefully. We must construct the kind of series Deleuze himself creates. It is necessary to pause and find out how, in the particular lineage this book suggests, Deleuze's Spinozism draws inspiration from somewhere else.

Let us recapitulate for a moment: the paradoxical construction of univocal substance (God *or* Nature), of which we have spoken in the preceding chapter, the community of form between cause and effect without the confusion of their essences, does not really find its concepts in Spinoza himself. Rather, both the notion of univocity and its corresponding logic of expression (instead of representation) are what Deleuze ›literally‹ gives to Spinoza, and he develops them conceptually in *Expressionism in Philosophy: Spinoza*. In this discussion, the stating of the equation of essence = existence *becomes* the construction of an all-absorbing One-All that is caused only by itself and independent of all its expressions, but—at once—›is‹ also only in its very expressions in attributes and modes. What we have here is the double trait of a logic that implies pure relationality and a Oneness that claims absolute indivisibility. While Spinoza—the radical 17th century thinker—still emphasizes that substance is first, that it precedes its attributes and modes, Deleuze in thinking the thought of univocity to its end (and attributing this thought to Spinoza him-

---

1 Calling Deleuze's philosophical practice a *reading* is justified only in the present context in which he, and thus we speak about his engagement with the history of philosophy. In no way do I want to approximate Deleuze too closely to what we today know as Jacques Derrida's ›method‹ of deconstruction. However, an ›indirect‹ linking seems legitimate in as much as it is with Derrida's critical reflections on how we read texts that the philosophical tradition became aware again of the contingency (which is not arbitrariness) that every (textual) *Auseinandersetzung* harbors.

self) shows that this substance, this One-All, cannot be anything outside—that is above or beyond—its expression(s). Something, thus, happens between or in the interval of these two thinkers, and in pursuing this route further, because of what we are after in this work, we both have to acknowledge the difference between Spinoza and Deleuze and, thus, shall learn to understand the productive paradox that Deleuze sees inherent in Spinoza's thought.

It is precisely the concurrence of equality of being and inequality of essence, as Deleuze called it in the citation from *Expressionism in Philosophy*, which is of specific interest to us and our purpose of learning how to read Deleuze. What is at stake in this concurrence is that while maintaining the distinction between what in Spinoza receives the names of *natura naturans* and *natura naturata*, these essences are neither ascribed to two separate realms nor related in any hierarchical manner. According to Spinoza, it is such an argument alone that enables a rigorous thought of immanence and that saves us from sacrificing immanence to either sheer positivism or the eminent cause.[2] While in Spinoza, we thus find a *parallelism* of One-All, with the relation between them implicitly assumed rather than clearly thought through, it is only in Deleuze's focus on the notion of expression that this parallelism is brought to the surface as *the* operative Spinozist logic, which in flattening without collapsing differences into identity drives the thought of immanence. It is the

---

2 We have not discussed explicitly Spinoza's conceptual coupling of *natura naturans* and *natura naturata*. However, since they are expressions of the very same problem that occupied us throughout our discussion of Spinoza, I hope that in simply mentioning them the reference is still clear. Spinoza introduced these scholastic terms in the first part of his *Ethics*, cf. EɪP29. The editor's explanation of this conceptual couple, its context, and its *adequate* understanding is again extremely helpful, and thus shall be quoted in its entirety here: »*Natura naturans, Natura naturata*. These terms have a long history, going back to the medieval Scholastics, and were still discussed in Spinoza's time. For example, the German Cartesian philosopher Johannes Clauberg (1622–1665) pointed out that the Scholastics divided Nature into *Natura naturans*, or God, and *Natura naturata*, or the universe of things. The distinction, he added, was superfluous—the terms ›God‹ and ›creatures‹ were enough. (...) Spinoza, for his part, gives the terms a pantheistic slant: both God, and what is commonly thought of as God's creation, may be thought of as two kinds of ›Nature‹.« (Spinoza 2000: 328 n58) In this distinction from the Scholastic tradition, we not only see again the difference between Descartes' and Spinoza's conceptualization of causality but also the (mis)reading Hegel fell for in his interpretation of Spinoza.

logic of expressionism, its *triadic* division into that which expresses itself, the expression, and what is expressed (cf. EP: 333), that for Deleuze is the key to Spinoza's philosophy. This triadic division allows Deleuze to tear away Spinoza's ultimate monism (substance is first) from its status quo, and to *dynamize* what otherwise would remain too close to a logic of static presence (such as already Hegel feared). Through the formula of expression, Deleuze manages not only ›to bring to expression‹ the (im)possible thought of infinite immanence without recourse to a ›beyond‹, but also to adequately enact this thought. Instead of resolving the paradox once and for all, in bringing it to expression he rather (un)folds and, thus, productively repeats it. Enduring the paradox in this way, he gives something to Spinoza that latently already structures this thought without being truly his own. What, then, emerges from the encounter of these two thinkers—in their interval—is a true offspring, which also might be called an offspring of *time*: time both in the sense of a time that has passed between the 17th and the 20th century, and of a thought of time itself. It is *time as endurance*, i.e. the singular time of movement, which helps Deleuze to understand the texture of Spinoza's substance differently.

For the source of this thought of time he, however, has to turn to someone else than Spinoza himself. It is the right moment, then, to introduce the second *conceptual persona*[3] for Deleuze's plane of

---

3 As Deleuze and Guattari explain in *What is Philosophy?*, »concepts need conceptual personae« (WPH: 2). In their chapter on »Conceptual Personae«, they inherently link the plane of immanence to conceptual personae that »carry out the movements that describe the author's plane of immanence, and... play a part in the very creation of the author's concepts« (WPH: 63). While Deleuze and Guattari speak of conceptual personae such as Socrates in Platonism, or the Idiot in Descartes, and most of all of Nietzsche's many conceptual personae—Dionysus, Zarathustra as the sympathetic ones, Christ, the Priest as the antipathetic ones—as inherently needed for the articulation of thought, we would like to read *Spinoza*, *Bergson*, and *Nietzsche* as Deleuze's conceptual personae when we approach him via *his* plane of immanence. Deleuze and Guattari continue their definition of the conceptual personae by saying that they are »not the philosopher's representative but, rather, the reverse: the philosopher is only the envelope of his principal conceptual persona and of all the other personae who are the intercessors, the real subjects of his philosophy... I am no longer myself but thought's aptitude for finding itself and spreading across a plane that passes through me at several places« (WPH: 64).

thought, Henri Bergson, who stands for yet another turning point in Deleuze, and must be seen as the supplementing source for his thought of immanence (the ›somewhere else‹) inspired by Spinoza.[4] It is with this »last of the great metaphysicians«, as Elizabeth Grosz calls Henri Bergson, this perhaps »last unselfconscious, nonironic affirmation of the place of metaphysics« (Grosz 2004: 155), that we will further clarify how the thought of the univocity of Being has to be pictured, so that it appears neither as a monism of the One nor a relativist pluralism of the many, but — as the epigraph to this section showed — a new *monism*; a pluralism sidestepping the boundaries of the One and Many in favor for a logic of *multiplicity*.[5]

---

4 The notion of ›turning point‹ should not be read as any intention to define different phases for Deleuze's thought, i.e. first Spinozist, then Bergsonian, and at last Nietzschean. Deleuze's first publication on one of these thinkers was actually an article on »Bergson, 1859–1941« (1956) and, thus, one could make the claim that Deleuze was first and foremost a disciple of Bergsonian thought; after his book on Hume, the thought-relation our project does not further reflect on. However, I want to emphasize the multiplicity, the zigzagging between specific individual thinkers that become ›coordinates‹ in Deleuze's philosophy rather then linear chronologies. Instead of turns that slice time into a before and after, in this project Deleuze should be pictured as entering into serial relations with his three reference points ›all at once‹. For one thing, however, Bergson seems to be a turning point in the more common sense meaning of the word. As I hope to show in the following discussion, it is with Bergson that Deleuze seems to be able to articulate both the limits of traditional Metaphysics and Ontology, and to cross into a truly new territory — on precisely the level of Metaphysics and Ontology. Neither Spinoza (out of reasons that concern his specific condition in and the context of the 17th century) nor Nietzsche (because of his radical style, his refusal to ›explicate‹ systematically) is able to provide us with an explicit philosophical alternative such as Bergson dares to articulate. Neither Spinoza nor Nietzsche pinpoint the kernel of all philosophical systems in the clarity Bergson does in his refutation of ›space‹ as the primary category of thought and his rigorous move towards a pure thought of time. It is only through such an emphasis, however, that we will be led to a new approach of ontology itself. For a very helpful discussion of this particular Bergsonian philosophical heritage, cf. Grosz 2004. That there is of course a great recognition of the issue of time in modern philosophy as such is in no way disputed here. Most famously — and nearly contemporaneous to Bergson — the philosophy of Martin Heidegger, whose rather estranging critique of Bergson in one famous footnote of *Sein und Zeit*, shows, however, the irritation which Bergson's philosophy produced in its readers — contemporary in as much as future readers (cf. Heidegger 2001: 432–433).

5 For the crisscrossing of thought-lines between Spinoza and Bergson in Deleuze, cf. Pearson 2002: 112: »A radical reading of Spinoza would be one that

* * *

Reading Bergson's thought as a philosophy of multiplicity, Deleuze claims that for as long as we perceive the problem of ›grounding‹ and ›beginning‹ of thought in terms of the One and the Many (or the Multiple as it is according to philosophical strands using set theory), we will remain within the dualistic impasse we find the philosophical tradition to be in. Thus, he states in his study of the philosopher in question here:

> A very important aspect of the notion of multiplicity is the way in which it is distinguished from a theory of the One and the Multiple. The notion of multiplicity saves us from thinking in terms of ›One and Multiple‹. There are many theories in philosophy that combine the one and the multiple. They share the characteristic of claiming to reconstruct the real with general ideas. We are told that the Self is one (thesis) and it is multiple (antithesis), then it is the unity of the multiple (synthesis). (B: 44)

Rather than thinking *relationality in itself*, that is, the *singular movement* structuring the relation or the (invisible) *in-between*, the mostly dialectical history of philosophy from Plato to Hegel remains stuck in the counter-posing reflection of the terms constituting it. The problem of relationality is approached from the opposition of the two terms instead of paying attention to what happens in the interstices of the relation itself. Instead of series thinking the singular, there is negation thinking the general. Rather than affirming a productive repetition of it, pushing it to its limit, and ›expressing‹ this relation in its essential multiplicity, relationality is still conceived as a problem to be resolved, to be eliminated, and ultimately to be *sublated* into something else.

For Deleuze it is the philosophy of Henri Bergson that, against any definitive resolutions of paradoxical relationality, offers a new perspective, a perspective that maneuvers itself through the dangers of both simplification and abstraction, and that avoids the »baggy

---

took its inspiration from Bergsonism, and this is what Deleuze in effect does in his major study.« See also Pearson's earlier commentary on the linkage of Spinoza and Bergson within Deleuze's thought in Pearson 1999: 11f.

clothes, [which] are much too big. The One in general, the multiple in general, nonbeing in general... In such cases the real is recomposed with abstracts« (B: 44). Bergson, and Deleuze in following him, is rejecting all abstract resolutions referring to the general for their »false movement« (ibid). Dialectics, according to *Bergsonism*, is »a movement of the *abstract* concept, which goes from one opposite to the other only by means of *imprecision*« (ibid, my emphases). Equating dialectics with abstraction and, therefore, with philosophical imprecision, and reformulating the task for philosophy again as *precise thinking*, which for Bergson means striving for a thought of the singular rather than the universal, exemplifies the provocation Bergson's thought represents to the tradition.[6]

It is the aim of this chapter to draw out the very serious challenges to the question of thinking that Bergson poses in his philosophical work, and to follow his inspiration in pushing thought to its limits once more, making it explore new directions: from a thought based on totality—a spatial construction of the One that cannot rid itself of the image of completeness—towards a plane of time, which ›is‹ nothing but flow. This means to move from the image of a substance still too much conceptualized as given essence, and thus still too dependent on the eternal Ideas—a presence totally present to itself because it has no time to itself—towards a plane of duration, the *virtual* which is always already in motion and as such never present, yet absolutely *real*. It means to think a thought that brings an end to the mystification of the theories of the One and Many (or Multiple) by thinking multiplicity itself,[7] a thought of »the One of pluralism«

---

6 Such provocation is at least one explanation for the alienation the majority of contemporary philosophy still feels towards Bergson. The distancing attitude towards Bergson's philosophy—the winner of the Noble Prize in Literature in 1927—is, however, about to change, and that this is the case must also be attributed to Deleuze's long lasting rehabilitation, starting at a time when nearly everyone wanted to escape the long shadow of Bergson (Deleuze's first engagement dates back to 1956, his major study on Bergson *Bergsonism* was published for the first time in 1966, and in Deleuze's later books on cinema Bergson again takes a privileged place (1983/1985)). Today, we can even speak of a kind of renaissance of Bergsonism in many areas of the Humanities, including philosophy, literature, film theory, and psychoanalysis.

7 »It is the category of multiplicity, with the difference in kind between two types that it involves, which enables us to condemn the mystification of a thought that operates in terms of the One and the Multiple.« (B: 47)

as Pearson calls it in *Philosophy and the Adventure of the Virtual* (Pearson 2002: 105). By interrogating the opposition of the One and the Multiple and approaching a thought of multiplicity itself, we will return to the One of pluralism as a new *monism*.

1. Intuition vs. Analysis

One of Bergson's most important contributions to philosophy, noticeable already in the specific way he names many of his works, is to rethink what it means to be a dualist. The preface to the seventh printing of Bergson's most famous work today *Matter and Memory* from 1910 begins with the following words: »This book affirms the reality of spirit and the reality of matter, and tries to determine the relation of the one to the other by the study of a definite example, that of memory. It is, then, frankly dualistic« (MM: 9). However, in pushing dualism to its very limits, which means, as we will see, to endure the relation rather than sublating the encounter of the ›at least two‹ terms in question, he finds a way out of opposition: *serialization*.[8]

Critically continuing the Spinozist tradition, Bergson too maintains that there is but one substance — life — and not two separate worlds. There is not the sensible, filled with bodies and matter — Nature on one side, and on the other, opposed to it, the intelligible, the world of mind and reason, the Divine in the classical sense.[9] Emphasizing a *complicated* ›One-ness‹ does, however, not mean that there is but one reality, or one experience, of it. This is just — as Spinoza would have

---

8 In *The Logic of Sense* Deleuze says in regard to the »minimal conditions for a *structure* in general« (LS: 50) there are »always at least two heterogeneous series,« which converge towards a paradoxical element. The ›at least two‹ series do not stand in a hierarchical relation but encounter each other on equal levels. This is the condition in which something else — difference, the new — is able to emerge. Among the dual series that Bergson has established, see also *Duration and Simultaneity*, and *The Two Sources of Morality and Religion*. Deleuze seems to re-enact this strategy. He, too, creates serial relations in the titles of his works, see e.g. *Difference and Repetition*, *Nietzsche and Philosophy*, *Proust and Signs*, or as in the subtitle of his collaboration with Guattari in *Anti-Oedipus: Capitalism and Schizophrenia*.

9 For Bergson's critical acknowledgement of Spinoza as one of his ›predecessors‹, cf. CE: 347–354.

called it—›not to know, what a body can do‹.[10] In all of his books Bergson works towards a new and *differential* thought which, without reducing the different terms in relation to each other, nonetheless lets them be of the same ›stuff‹. In saying this, we use an expression of the pragmatist philosopher William James, who around the time when the younger Bergson has met him for the very first time wrote that in order to escape the philosophical impasses »we [have to] start with the supposition that there is only one primal stuff or material in the world, a stuff of which everything is composed« (James 2003: 2). Bergson, thus, does not think relationality from its constitutive endpoints but from within and as the movement itself. Deleuze, in his very early essay »Bergson, 1859–1941« from 1956 states the issue in the following way:

> In distinguishing the two worlds, Bergson replaced them by the distinction of two movements, two directions of one and the same movement, spirit and matter, two times in the same duration, the past and the present, which he knew how to conceive as coexistent precisely because they were in the same duration. (Deleuze 2004a: 24)

Instead of two different substances, spatially conceptualized and separated—one high above the other (which then lacks in (moral) height)—Bergson thinks two movements in time. To be precise: not even two separate movements but only *two directions of one and the same movement* (paradoxical movement). The name of this movement that becomes all ›there is‹ is *duration*. Spirit and matter are nothing but *two times in the same duration*—one anchoring us in

---

10 In the *Ethics*, this is Spinoza's materialist formula, claiming that mind *and* body parallel and yet in absolute singular ways express the essence of substance »conceived now under the attribute of thought and now under the attribute of extension« (EIIIP2S). He continues: »However, although the situation is such that no reason for doubt remains, I find it hard to believe that men can be led to weigh these things calmly in their mind, unless I confirm the matter by experience—so firmly are they persuaded that the body now moves and now is at rest simply at the command of the mind, and that it does very many things that depend solely on the mind's will and ingenuity. For no one has so far determined *what the body can do*...« (ibid, my emphasis). Deleuze's interpretation of Spinoza takes a lot of inspiration from this formula, both in what concerns the logic of expression and the ethical dimension as radical constructivism. Cf. the section ›What Can a Body Do?‹ in EP: 217–234.

where we come from, the other opening us out onto a radically uncertain future. And at the intersection or the encounter of the two directions, there is the creation of a contingent yet singular (enduring) present.

We have to pause. All concepts normally constituting safe philosophical coordinates seem to dissolve with this citation. No substance left — are we now left with *nothing*? And what to make of this movement of paradoxical direction? How to think such impossibility? For a philosopher of purity such as Bergson, these are questions which only an ›intellect‹ can pose. While more lies in this response than what at this moment we are able to address, we see already that Bergson's challenge to philosophical thought is nothing less than a radical challenge to the common tendency to equate our seemingly *natural* form of intellectual thinking aligned as it is with space, matter, the motionless, and a fixing in eternal presence, with philosophical thinking in its truest form. In *Matter and Memory*, Bergson writes:

> Accustomed to seek its fulcrum in a world of ready-made motionless images, of which the apparent fixity is hardly anything else but the outward reflection of the stability of our lower needs, [our intellect] cannot help believing that rest is anterior to motion, cannot avoid taking rest as its point of reference and its abiding place. (MM: 217)

What Bergson here implies is that because of the way our intellectual imagination works, it is nearly impossible for us to think ›in motion‹, or to imagine a ›One of pluralism‹ — a One of multiplicity — that ›is‹ only in enduring. Our intellect works by dividing things into separable blocks. It can settle itself only by dividing duration into such separable things, i.e. comprehensible ›stills‹. These things — or better these categorized things — are, however, only the cut-outs of an otherwise *continuous* real. To grasp this continuity that does not have its opposite in any discontinuity, because the latter remains just one possible form of continuity — its constant interruptions and turnings, detours or complications — is, as Bergson shows, nearly impossible for the human intellect as it developed throughout its evolution. And yet, to approach a thought of the flux itself must be the task of philosophy. Bergson, thus, continues:

> But let us, on the contrary, banish all preconceived idea of interpreting or measuring, let us place ourselves face-to-face with immediate reality: *at once* we find that there is no impassable barrier, no essential difference, no real distinction even, between perception and the thing perceived, between quality and movement. (MM: 218, my emphasis)

For Bergson, the task of philosophy proper is to arrive at a thought that changes the image of the ›texture‹ and ›consistency‹ of thought itself, so that the One—*life* in the terms of Bergson—is *at once* »a unity that is multiple and a multiplicity that is one« (CE: 258), such as it ›is‹ in its reality.

Bergsonian Method

As soon as we formulate this task of philosophy or thought, we realize that if we want to succeed in such an (im)possible way of thinking, it is not just a question of ontology but it is one of its very articulation, too. The problem again implicates the epistemological level, the level of knowledge and method—the question of *how* to think and approach such a thought. In the introduction of his project in *Creative Evolution*, Bergson pays tribute to this double directionality; an attentiveness, which for Deleuze is one of Bergson's »inestimable contribution[s] to a philosophy of difference« (Deleuze 2004b: 32). Bergson, thus, says of the linkage of ontology and epistemology:

> This amounts to saying that *theory of knowledge* and *theory of life* seem to us inseparable. A theory of life that is not accompanied by a criticism of knowledge is obliged to accept, as they stand, the concepts which the understanding puts at its disposal... On the other hand, a theory of knowledge which does not replace the intellect in the general evolution of life will teach us neither how the frames of knowledge have been constructed nor how we can enlarge or go beyond them. It is necessary that these two inquiries, theory of knowledge and theory of life, should join each other, and, by a circular process, push each other on unceasingly. (CE: xiii)

For thinking differently, we need a different ›method of thinking‹, Bergson claims. In this very same introduction, he continues that only together may the two strands »solve by a method more sure, brought nearer to experience, the great problems that philosophy poses« (ibid). Now, the method that Bergson suggests, which pays tribute to this double obligation, is *intuition*; a notion of intuition, however, that has nothing in common with what we usually mean when we speak of it, and relate it to a feeling or an inspiration. For Bergson, on the contrary, intuition describes »a fully developed method« as Deleuze writes. »It has its strict rules, constituting that which Bergson calls ›precision‹ in philosophy« (B: 13).[11]

In the words of the young Deleuze, the task for Bergson in his philosophical work is »to ›return‹ to the things themselves, to account for them without reducing them to something other than what they are, to grasp them in their being« (Deleuze 2004b: 32). In this intention, similar to Husserlian phenomenology, Bergson searches for a new solution of the seemingly (im)possible ›third‹ in the old philosophical conflict between idealism on the one hand and realism or materialism on the other hand.[12] The famous Bergsonian concept of ›image‹ from

---

11 It is in this sense that this ›method‹ is already more than what we are used to understand by a methodological concern in general. In his book on Nietzsche, which will be in our focus in the chapter following this one, Deleuze, in view of this ›more‹, delimits the usual understanding of philosophical methods, still relying on the distinction of truth and error, from what the Greeks have called *paideia*, that is, a formation or culture in the sense of education, training, or ›molded‹ to the ideal. »Thought does not need a method but a paideia«, he writes, »a formation, a culture. Method in general is a means by which we avoid going to a particular place, or by which we maintain the option of escaping from it.« (NP: 110) We should keep in mind that Bergson's method of intuition is precisely taking up the issue of a new ›culture of thinking‹, one that moves far beyond that which methods usually are supposed to put forth.

12 While Bergson's philosophy of duration must be seen in proximity to the Husserlian phenomenology, not only because both share a similar impetus to overcome the two dominating traditions of philosophy (Rationalism on the one hand and (Hegelian) dialectics on the other hand), but also because especially Husserl directly acknowledges the work of Bergson, the differences between the two thinkers are immense and touch precisely the issue of method or what is implied in the claim to ›return to the things themselves‹. While with Bergson, as we will see, we have to imagine a beyond of the human condition—putting ourselves into the duration of life (the impersonal) itself—in Husserl, on the contrary, the *epoché* ultimately means the bracketing of consciousness. With regard to the same concern, Bergson—as Deleuze again rightly points out—seems to reverse the philosophical problem of immediacy vs. mediation while Husserl remains faithful to the Cartesian legacy beginning with a given immediacy (sensible things) in order to arrive at constructed mediation (mind). In contrast to this in »Bergson, 1859–1941« Deleuze writes that for Bergson »[w]e are separated from things; the immediate given is therefore not immedi-

Matter and Memory, by which is meant »a certain existence which is more than that which the idealist calls a representation, but less than that which the realist calls a thing — an existence placed halfway between the ›thing‹ and the ›representation‹« (MM: 9) — makes explicit this difficult philosophical position. While the validity of the Bergsonian concept of image is of less interest to us here, what is of major significance in our context is this: what does such an alternative tell us in regard to the method of thinking itself? That is, how do we arrive at such a different creation of concepts? Bergson in his approach to the question distinguishes two different types of knowing a thing. There is a knowledge or theoretical approach to the world that remains external to what it wants to know. This kind of knowledge sets up the thing as *Gegen-stand*, and in a process of objectification arrives at the subject/object divide that determines most philosophical debates and our day-to-day perception of life, too. What Bergson sets against such an externality is a kind of knowledge that, in distinction to circling around that which it wants to know, ›enters into‹ the thing, and, thus, begins to *think* instead of merely gaining valid information of what is in front of it. While such a description of ›entering the thing‹ might irritate our ears in certain justified ways, we should wait and see in what sense this ›entering‹ leads to the very opposite of any master signifier. A thinking that ›enters into the thing‹ is the definition Bergson himself gives in his acclaimed essay »Introduction

---

ately given. But we cannot be separated by a simple accident, by a mediation that would come from us, that would concern only us. The movement that changes the nature of things must be founded in things themselves; things must begin by losing themselves in order for us to end up losing them« (Deleuze 2004a: 23). Lastly, and this will implicitly run through our discussion here, Bergson's method for a new way to approach the relation of subject and object is one that strives for ›entering‹ into the things themselves so that we are able to think an inner relation and overcome the subject/object divide, while Husserl's ›bracketing‹ ultimately *accepts*, as Bergson would say, that ›we as intellects‹ will always only know ›externally‹, so that his method strives rather for the truest knowledge and, thus, the accurate recognition of the division between the subject and the object. While I hope that the claims on the Bergsonian side will become clear throughout the discussion in this chapter, two of the most central texts for learning about Husserl's Cartesianism and the phenomenological *epoché* are his *Cartesian Meditations* (1931) and his essay »Die Philosophie in der Krisis der europäischen Menschheit«, presented in Vienna in 1935, and published as *Die Krisis der europäischen Wissenschaften und die transzendentale Phänomenologie* (1936).

to Metaphysics«, in which he introduces the method of intuition as a proper philosophical method of thinking:

> If we compare the various ways of defining metaphysics and of conceiving the absolute, we shall find, despite apparent discrepancies, that philosophers agree in making a deep distinction between two ways of knowing a thing. The first implies going all around it, the second *entering into it*. (CM: 159, my emphasis)[13]

While with the first mode we approach the thing by way of *analysis*, seeing and speaking from a supposedly universal viewpoint, going all around the thing but always remaining ›outside‹ of it, and, thus, producing a knowledge *relative* to the thing, the second method of ›entering into the thing‹ approaches it, according to Bergson, by way of *intuition*, reaching for the *absolute* knowledge of the thing. Bergson, then, continues:

> And what I feel will depend neither on the point of view I adopt toward the object, since I am in the object itself, nor on symbols by which I translate it, since I have renounced all translation in order to possess the original. (Ibid)

While it seems so legitimate to question not only the theoretical attitude (›possess the original‹) but also the serene confidence of such a philosophical project, such a self-assured definition of what it means to think, maybe we have to slow down and first of all remember again the long tradition that such a thought builds on, a tradition that we have already encountered in our last chapter. In Bergson we see the same philosophical purity that we found in Spinoza's claim that *adequate*, i.e. *real* knowledge—knowing not just by analogy, but also in absoluteness—is possible. Instead of logical deduction, i.e. analysis, we need *adequacy*, Spinoza's philosophy claims; adequate ideas which for this thinker are not of any other world but precisely the task of philosophy in this world.

---

13 »Introduction to Metaphysics« was published in Bergson's last collection of essays *The Creative Mind* that appeared in 1934. While we will always indicate which of the texts in this collection we are speaking of, reference will be made only to the whole collection.

In the discussion that follows, we should bear this issue of adequacy and reality in Spinoza in mind so as to ensure that we do understand the Bergsonian method of intuition adequately. Following both thinkers along the way we then might not only learn what Spinoza ›is capable of‹, but also realize what strong philosophical heritage lies dormant in the concept of intuition.

The Problem of Immediacy

For Bergson, only the second mode of thinking—intuition—truly defines a philosophically proper relation to the world: a return to the things by putting oneself into the life of the object itself, ›entering into duration itself‹, and thus breaking open the supposedly given dualistic structure of subject and object.[14] Inversing the philosophical problem of immediacy, the immediate, for Bergson, is precisely not immediately given. To the contrary, we always already lose the things by being—*naturally*, so to speak, this is our condition—placed in impure mixtures in which we always already form composites, and are nothing but composites ourselves. What philosophy, however, must achieve is to get a hold of the absolute again and, thus, to move beyond the subject/object opposition which separates into motionless blocks what in reality is in a relation of one flux. In his lecture »Philosophical Intuition« given at the Philosophical Congress in Bologna in 1911, Bergson speaks of the recent tendency to draw metaphysics closer to life, a direction that he thinks of as »correct« (CM: 107). However, as his argument develops, such closer *attachment to life* for philosophy must mean at the same time *detachment from life* as it is indispensably lived by us, that is, as directed towards action and unable to follow the moving reality—duration—itself. Thus, Bergson's *credo* of a philosophy worthy its name: »Undo what they have done, bring our perception back to its origins, and we shall have a new kind of knowledge without having been obliged to have recourse to new faculties.« (CM: 128)

---

14 This is what we claim: intuition can no longer be called ›knowledge‹ in the way ›analysis‹ gains knowledge of a thing. Rather, as this chapter tries to unfold and thus relates *Bergson* back to *Spinoza*, intuition is a way of *thinking* as *act*, which is needed for an adequate thought of radical immanence, and thus for the investigation of Deleuze's plane of thought.

In Bergsonian terms such a claim has to do neither with philosophical immodesty nor with the introduction of a kind of mysticism into philosophy. Rather, for him such a claim is the only way »to establish philosophy as an absolutely ›precise‹ discipline, as precise in *its* field, as capable of being prolonged and transmitted as science itself«, as Deleuze says (B: 14). In the section »The Method of Philosophy« in *Creative Evolution* Bergson himself, thus, emphasizes a *modesty* of his philosophical undertaking: instead of »the exaggerated confidence of philosophy in the powers of the individual mind... more modest, and also alone capable of being completed and perfected, is the philosophy we advocate« (CE: 191). Such attitude is even further underlined by Bergson's claim that his can only be a first attempt at such a philosophy, as no »individual work of a man of genius« (CE: xiv) is able to completely achieve it.[15] It is the failure of most philosophical traditions, be they mechanism or finalism (*Creative Evolution*), realism, materialism, or idealism (*Matter and Memory*), to reduce the issue of what it means to think to the categories of the human intellect alone, i.e. to but one *property* of life, and one that works by reducing movement to stasis, duration to essence, and time to space. A metaphysics deserving its name as philosophy proper, has to expose itself again — such is the claim of ›entering into the thing‹. It has to plunge into the world of things, enlarge what is called consciousness, and this, according to Bergson, is to go *beyond the human condition*. Only beyond »the decisive *turn*« as Bergson calls it in *Matter and Memory* (MM: 184), will we gain access to the concreteness of reality, avoiding the problems of representational thinking, whether analogical, dialectical, or critical (in the Kantian sense).

> If there exists a means of possessing a reality absolutely, instead of knowing it relatively, of placing oneself within it instead of adopting points of view toward it, of having the intuition of it instead of making

---

15 The whole passage reads: »But a philosophy of this kind will not be made in a day. Unlike the philosophical systems properly so called, each of which was the individual work of a man of genius and sprang up as a whole, to be taken or left, it will only be built up by the collective and progressive effort of many thinkers, of many observers also, completing, correcting and improving one another. So the present essay does not aim at resolving at once the greatest problems. It simply desires to define the method and to permit a glimpse, on some essential points, of the possibility of its application« (CE: xiv).

the analysis of it, in short, of grasping it over and above all expression, translation or symbolical representation, metaphysics is that very means. (CM: 162)

While our last chapter was thus an attempt to rehabilitate ontology, in this chapter we move to yet another »dirty word« of today's philosophy: metaphysics.[16] Metaphysics, according to Bergson, is not to be understood as the logic of a transcendent framework that holds our world together, like the ›eminent cause‹ in the classical sense or the ›infinite perfection‹ that we find in Descartes. Here Bergson joins the side of Kant, who as Bergson says already recognized that if metaphysics were possible,

> one could only penetrate into the beyond by a vision... That is what Kant brought out so clearly and that, it seems to me, is the greatest service he rendered to speculative philosophy. He definitely established that, if metaphysics is possible, it can be so only through an effort of intuition (CM: 139–140).

Kant himself, however, continues to picture such a vision as absolutely beyond our faculties, which for Bergson means that »[t]hey all believe that to break away from practical life was to turn one's back upon it« (CM: 140). In departing from this long philosophical misconceptualization, taken in the practical or realist way Bergson himself suggests, metaphysics becomes simply ›another mode‹ of grasping this world, *in difference to* the physical, biological, i.e. scientific modes, which are doomed to cut life into isolated moments with no movement left to it.[17] Countering the spatializing tendencies of our

---

16 A helpful discussion of Deleuze's return to ontological speculation and metaphysical realism, of which we also borrowed the expression of ›dirty words‹, is Murphy's article »Quantum Ontology. A Virtual Mechanics of Becoming« (Murphy 1998: 211–229).

17 The relevance of such a claim can be shown when we look to the so called life sciences themselves, which both originate in this spatializing mode of our mind and further it through ever more exact data and instruments. Marie François Xavier Bichat, who counts as the father of histology and pathology, demonstrates in the invention of new methods for the medical tradition how every pursuit of life is possible only through death. This is also taken up by Michel Foucault in his study of *The Birth of the Clinic* in which he follows

intellects and science as such, metaphysics for Bergson remains

> our only mode of access to that which the sciences, and intelligence itself, cannot address: the continuity of duration, the indivisible interpenetration of life and matter, the intervals between things, states, and properties — in short the analogue continuity that marks material reality (Grosz 2004: 155).

Philosophy = Meta-Physics

Written at the turn of the 20th century, that is, at a time when the scientific turn overtakes nearly every aspect of life, not only in the intellectual discourses but also in daily life itself, Bergson's philosophy distinguishes itself in two very important dimensions: while as a philosopher he was never afraid of engaging with scientific discourses, and indeed acknowledges them as relevant for his own philosophy, in such an engagement he never downplays the absolute difference of the access to the world they provide for us.[18] While he is looking for a useful and productive connection between science and philosophy, his work argues against any subsumption of philosophy under the domain of science, and *vice versa* (cf. CM: 123f). Without deny-

---

the scientific fact that it is impossible to look at life, that is, at movement itself: »[D]eath was the only possibility of giving life a positive truth« (Foucault 1994a: 144–145). In all of Foucault's philosophical engagement with life, there is both agreement with and differentiation from what Bergson claims. He is agreeing in as much as it is precisely Bergson's project to show the inescapable limits of scientific observation in regard to life. However, Bergson — in distinction to Foucault, as I would say, but this would have to be proven in a much more detailed investigation — believes in a different engagement with life that is possible ›in life‹ itself, and this is a metaphysical, i.e. philosophical engagement with the world, tearing the question of life away from a bio-political milieu and returning it, so to speak, to a very particular — but pure — philosophy of spirit (*esprit*). For a helpful discussion of this notion of spirit as it is developed by Bergson throughout *Matter and Memory* and in his discussion of intuition, cf. Lawlor 2003a, esp. 116–125.

18 This exposure even led Bergson to a public encounter with Albert Einstein in Paris in 1921, the reflections of this discussion being published in *Duration and Simultaneity, with Reference to Einstein's Theory* (Bergson 1999). In more general terms, Bergson's thinking is informed in all of his works by non-philosophical discourses, be it psychology and medicine (MM), the life sciences (CE), or literature, anthropology, or mysticism (Bergson 2002).

ing the value of scientific knowledge and discovery, he argues for the indispensability of a uniquely philosophical approach to this world, if we want to *experience* it instead of merely *using* it. Only philosophy, which for Bergson in its truest sense is metaphysics, can avoid reducing life to the artificiality of a closed system on which every scientific perception must inevitably be based.[19] What Bergson stresses is that life is first and foremost a continuous flow, and change is all there ›is‹.

> A thousand incidents arise, which seem to be cut off from those which precede them, and to be disconnected from those which follow... Our attention fixes on them because they interest it more, but each of them is borne by the fluid mass of our whole psychical existence. Each is only the best illuminated point of a moving zone which comprises all that we feel or will—all, in short, that we are at any given moment. It is this entire zone which in reality makes up our state. Now, states thus defined cannot be regarded as distinct elements. They continue each other in an endless flow. (CE: 3)

If for a short moment we return to the two different modes of knowing of which we spoke above, we now understand that (mis)taking the scientific mode of knowing—the scientific ›snapshot‹-method or analysis of the object—for reality itself is like assuming that »by multiplying photographs of an object in a thousand different aspects, you will reproduce the object itself« (CE: 31). Approaching the object as *Gegen-stand*, we surely get to know the object, but through such an analysis we will never reach the object's own reality, this absolute knowledge of its ›inner being‹ which requires—as Bergson says—»that I am in harmony with these states and enter into them by an effort of imagination« (CM: 159). *Reality* has to be understood in its movement, its duration itself, and it is only philosophy as meta-

---

19 »Science is the auxiliary of action. And action aims at a result. The scientific intelligence asks itself therefore what will have to be done in order that a certain desired result be attained, or more generally, what conditions should obtain in order that a certain phenomenon take place. It goes from an arrangement of things to a re-arrangement, from a simultaneity to a simultaneity. Of necessity it neglects what happens in the interval... it cannot follow the moving reality, adopt the becoming which is the life of things. This last task belongs to philosophy.« (CM: 125–126)

physics that—at its best—is able to access this duration by *leaping* into it. Instead of being the end of any specifically philosophical mode of thinking, the encounter Bergson initiates between science and philosophy allows for a new way of looking at the philosophical field itself: to think otherwise than science, »to think non-spatially« (Pearson, 2002: 95), or in Bergson's own terms of *Creative Evolution*: to finally acknowledge that while it seems to us as if the world ›is‹ first of all in a spatial, and not a temporal sense, because it appears to our intellects that time is just one more dimension of space, »[t]he universe *endures*« (CE: 11), and »I change... without ceasing« (CE: 1).[20] Neither the world nor I myself can be adequately thought of by cutting up the movement of duration, and, thus, producing a kind of photographic all-round perspective. We have to learn again how to »access the real continuity that constitutes life in its concreteness« (Grosz 2004: 155); we have to learn to think movement itself, to place ourselves within movements, and to attune ourselves to these movements.[21] The task of philosophy is not to compete with scientists on their plane, nor is it to join common sense in perceiving all actions in regard of their use-value.[22] Rather, it is to focus attention

---

20 This negligence of time as an independent category of space has an extremely long history in philosophy—the human-all-too-human perspective that what ›is‹ has to be thought in terms of extension rather than duration. This—in Bergsonian terms—misconception even affects the most attuned sciences such as mathematics and the physical sciences. Thus, even the theory of Relativity of which Bergson otherwise thinks that it is the most advanced thinking of time, does not reach beyond a spatialization of time: space-time. In his book on Bergson Leszek Kolakowski writes in regard to the former's evaluation of the conceptualization of time: »Both in science and in our daily life we perceive time as if it were another kind of space: a set of homogeneous segments placed next to each other and together composing an indefinitely long line. This time is an artificial, abstract concoction that we need for practical purposes« (Kolakowski 1985: 3). For a useful and short recapitulation of Bergson's ambivalent but very intriguing criticisms of the theory of Relativity as he develops them in *Duration and Simultaneity*, cf. Pearson 2002: 55–58.

21 Cf. also Rosi Braidotti's concern with thinking movements rather than states of being in her *Metamorphoses. Towards a Materialist Theory of Becoming*, and her emphasis on what a difficult task this is: »Thus, it is by far simpler to think about the concept of A or B, or of B as non-A, rather than the process of what goes on in between A and B. Thinking through flows and interconnections remains a difficult challenge.« (Braidotti 2005: 1–2)

22 For Bergson, perception ›in general‹—if we can even use such language in relation to this philosopher—is not an objective and neutral vision in search

on what is inevitably left out in both science and daily life, and to produce a new philosophical plane. »Common sense, which is occupied with detached objects, and also science, which considers isolated systems, are concerned only with the end of the intervals and not with the intervals themselves.« (CE: 9) It is the engagement with the ›intervals themselves‹—the *invisible in-between*, the movement of duration itself—the ›how‹ rather than the ›what‹, that according to Bergson distinguishes philosophy from both *doxa* and the sciences. In such a move, in re-directing philosophical thought, he does not make philosophy the henchman of the sciences, passively accepting their practices and discourses, but rather he makes philosophy, as Grosz states,

> a productive concern that both functions *alongside* the sciences, operating with different aims and methods but able to make collateral use of the sciences as much as of the arts, and also functioning as it were *underneath* the sciences, making explicit their unacknowledged commitment to philosophical and ultimately ontological concepts (Grosz 2004: 157).

2. Differences in Kind vs. Differences of Degree

Giving the Bergsonian *method*—intuition—such a prominent place, Deleuze in *Bergsonism* distinguishes three different aspects or *acts* that define intuition as a philosophical method, and that provide us with a clearer picture of the manner in which he himself approaches the task of philosophy. At the beginning of his discussion, he says:

---

for the truth—unproblematically assuming that there is only one truth. It is always already a directed look, determined by our interests, by the actions we are about to take. Perception, instead of striving to find *the* truth, is the production of *a* truth: it might see only what it needs to see in order to act on it. Such fundamental reflection on viewpoint relates Bergson to Leibniz, the ›other‹ 17th century thinker to whom Bergson again and again refers—though he does so with a necessarily critical stand, as he sees the latter also as one of the strictest finalists (cf. esp. CE: 346–354, but also in the early section on ›radical finalism‹, CE: 39–44).

> Bergson distinguishes essentially three distinct sorts of acts that in turn determine the rules of the method: the first concerns the stating and creating of problems; the second, the discovery of genuine differences in kind; the third the apprehension of real time. (B: 14)

Instead of focusing purely on the outcome such as methods of knowledge usually do, that is, focusing on the solution of a problem or the object of knowledge, intuition in its specificity as a method of *thinking*, of approaching the world in its reality, starts with a concern for the problems themselves. This is the first *act* determining this method. The test of true and false, normally applied to solutions alone, already finds its application here on the level of problems.

The Leap into the Unknown

At first sight one might not recognize the great significance that such a move implies. A second look, however, makes clear that what is happening here radically changes what we assume thinking itself to be. Deleuze explains:

> We are wrong to believe that the true and the false can only be brought to bear on solutions, that they only begin with solutions. This prejudice is social... this prejudice goes back to childhood, to the classroom: It is the school teacher who ›poses‹ the problems; the pupil's task is to discover the solutions. In this way we are kept in a kind of slavery. *True freedom lies in a power to decide, to constitute problems themselves* (B: 15, my emphasis).

›Thinking‹, understood in this strong sense, requires first of all the positing of real problems and the avoiding of false ones, rather than purely focusing on the right solution to an already given problem. This step back in the manner in which we approach what it means to think is the reason why Bergson so often chooses to position his argument in the collision of two seemingly opposed systems of thoughts — his famous binaries of idealism vs. materialism or realism, mechanism vs. finalism, mind vs. matter, and others. Instead of producing such a clash to bring about a simple victory of one category over the other, i.e. the claim that the one is right while the other is wrong, Bergson strives for something else in this clash.[23] Kolakowski calls this »[Bergson's] favourite method... what he called *recoupage*« (Kolakowski 2001: 6), and he goes on to explicate what this Bergsonian method of a production of intersections means:

> [W]hen trying to answer a question [Bergson] confronted two existing solutions embedded in opposite conceptual systems and then asks at what point they overlapped, that is, what they had in common, whereupon he showed that they shared a false assumption concealed in the very way they phrased the question. (Ibid)

Without neglecting our interest that, of course, also lies with the solution in the confrontation of problems, all solutions — as Bergson and Deleuze dare to say — are always already that which is ›given‹ in a problem. For Bergson, solutions might have to be discovered or uncovered, but they cannot bring anything new into being, since — as also Deleuze explains — »the problem always has the solution it deserves, in terms of the way in which it is stated« (B: 16). In »Introduction II: The Stating of Problems« of *Creative Mind* Bergson tells us,

> [t]he truth is that in philosophy and even elsewhere it is a question of *finding* the problem and consequently of *positing* it, even more than of solving it. For a speculative problem is solved as soon as it is properly stated. By that I mean that its solution exists then, although it may remain hidden and, so to speak, covered up: The only thing left to do is to *un*cover it. But stating the problem is not simply uncovering, it is inventing (CM: 51).

Equating solving the problem with thinking it, speaks, according to Bergson and Deleuze, of a very limited concept of thought, a ›solution‹ both of them reject. In contrast to this they suggest that intuition as true philosophical method, must »invent« the problems so that »through it something is *presented*, is *given in person*, instead of being inferred from something else and concluded« (Deleuze 2004a: 23, my emphases). Only then does the *act* of thinking (intuition) give

---

23 We could formulate this again in the Deleuzian way as ›to move somewhere else‹; this is the task in every act of thinking.

expression to what is not yet there. Only then does it open itself to the ›new‹ and constitute ›true freedom‹.[24] While this emphasis on the new in relation to thought will be most relevant for our discussion of the ethical dimension in and potential of such a thought later on, right now it is important to realize that this intuitive thinking, rather than being conceptualized as mere causal or logical procedure, describes an *act*, a leaping into the unknown. Intuition as an *act* of thinking that poses the problems themselves is innovation and invention: it »gives being to what did not exist; it might never have happened« (B: 15).

Real Presences

The re-formulation of the test of true and false problems brings us straight to the second *act* by which intuition distinguishes itself as a method of thinking: intuition is the mode of thinking capable of approaching difference in itself, or—as Deleuze in *Bergsonism* calls it—of discovering genuine differences in kind. Once more, we are referred back to the problem of intellectualization which—because

---

24 In order not to misunderstand this claim, let me again refer to Bergson's lecture »Philosophical Intuition« in which he unfolds the difference between an intuitive thinking and a thought of categorization, the latter of which is always our first reaction when we encounter something that we wish to understand. For, as Bergson says, »the human mind is so constructed that it cannot begin to understand the new until it has done everything in its power to relate it to the old« (CM: 108). But how then does intuition proceed differently from categorization, which is always already a process of categorization into the old? In exposing this difficult process of penetrating a philosophical thought, Bergson gives the examples of Spinoza and Berkeley, two thinkers exemplifying the method of intuition. According to Bergson, in the case of these two philosophers we see that what intuition in the most serene sense means is the philosophical realization of the simple »single point... something simple, infinitely simple« (ibid), the one thing a philosopher worthy of the name has ever tried to say (and maybe he never actually comes to say it). Bergson, thus, writes about such a real philosopher: »[H]e has said only one thing because he has seen only one point: and at that it was not so much a vision as *contact*: This contact has furnished an *impulse*, this impulse a *movement*, and this movement, which is as it were a kind of swirling of dust taking a particular form, *becomes visible to our eyes only through what it has collected along its way*, it is no less true that other bits of dust might as well have been raised and that it would still have been the same whirlwind.« (112, my emphases) There is no better way to describe the *act* of thinking, thinking as an *act* or *practice*, which I am after in my pursuit of Deleuze's thought of becoming.

of its structuring everything in an ordered, hierarchized, and categorized world, a world according to our interests—propels us into positing problems the wrong way, and even into positing the wrong problems.

In his discussion of the two evolutionary tendencies intellect and instinct in *Creative Evolution*, Bergson shows that because of the way our intellect functions »its chief object [is] the unorganized solid« (CE: 153). And later on he writes that »*[t]he more consciousness is intellectualized, the more is matter spatialized*« (CE: 189). What is made explicit in these statements is that our intellect, rather than thinking the world, subsumes everything it encounters under its (innate) tendency to practically engage with the world. Our intellect, which for Bergson includes what is called consciousness, is not as is so often assumed an objective perception of the world. Rather, what Bergson explicates in this investigation into the theory of evolution is that the two ›attributes‹ (to speak in Spinoza's terms) that have developed over time, the »*two divergent solutions*« (to speak with Bergson again), are »*equally fitting, of one and the same problem*« (CE: 143). What he shows, thus, is that the intellect is but one response—a very complex response, yes, but in no sense ›better‹ than any other—to the problem of life. It is one particular way of approaching the world, and it is always already directed in a certain way. Our intellect is a »manufacturing« approach (CE: 92) that has the tendency to conceive of every difference in terms of hierarchies rather than to acknowledge *real* differences as differing in themselves (cf. CE: 139ff). This is particularly well exemplified in the human habit to see instinct and intelligence not as two equally suitable *response systems* to life (univocity of Being), but as vertical developments whose comparison is judged by the measure of the ›higher‹ development.

> The circumstances are not a mold into which life is inserted and whose form life adopts: this is indeed to be fooled by metaphor [of which only the intellect is capable of, KT]. There is no form yet, and the life must create a form for itself, suited to the circumstances which are made for it. It will have to make the best of these circumstances, neutralize their inconveniences and utilize their advantages—in short respond to outer actions by building up a machine which has no resemblance to them. Such adapting is not *repeating*, but *replying*,—an entirely different thing. (CE: 58)

Instead of seeing in both instinct and intellect impulses to find new and different responses to the various obstacles that life poses at every moment of its concrete form, we — as these conscious/intellectual beings — make ourselves believe that intelligence, because of its capacity to detach from the object, to represent, and to rationalize, is the ultimate, that is, the *truest* approach to the world. Such attitude only proves our tendency to spatialize — to hierarchize — what actually is a matter of diversity. By measuring everything in terms of a logic structured by more and less, intelligence ends up with isolated blocks that seem no longer to come from one and the same life as duration. While Bergson, to be sure, does not suggest that thinking in terms of such categorizations, blocks, and states, is wrong *per se*, he nonetheless claims that Life, in the way we experience it, comes at the level of impure composites — this is the condition we live in, matter *and* memory — and this means the operations of the intellect cannot be its truest representation. Every-thing living that *exists* in this world is a mixture of both extensity and duration — two directions of the same movement. All specific actualizations (including ourselves), therefore, cannot totally avoid re-presenting and being represented as such mixtures. While this condition is, therefore, simply a matter of fact, and for Bergson nothing to be rejected but rather to be enhanced, what is indeed problematic for him, and this is where his critical intervention digs deeper, »is that we no longer know«, as Deleuze says, »how to distinguish in that *representation* the two component elements which differ in kind, the two pure *presences* of duration and extensity« (B: 22). Bergson's obsession with the *pure* in all of his works (be it memory in the case of *Matter and Memory*, or duration in the case of *Creative Evolution*) strives for the adequate restoration of these differences in kind, reduced to mere differences of degree by our intellect and our daily life. This means — in the Bergsonian sense — moving beyond the badly posed questions and returning to the problems themselves. Any reduction of this complex situation — instead of re-connecting us to life — ultimately leads to the idea of a universe as mysteriously ›created‹, and obscures the reality of but *one* life which without losing its Oneness is capable of *manifold* responses (to itself): organized and unorganized bodies, matter and memory, instinct and intellect.

After announcing the Bergsonian method as »intuition«, therefore, Deleuze announces the »Bergsonian leitmotif«, according to which »[p]eople have seen only differences in degree where there are differences in kind« (B: 23). While one has to add that Deleuze's Bergsonism here takes its distinctly Deleuzian turn, nevertheless emphasizing Bergson's work as fundamentally concerned with *difference* and a logic of differentiation is to my mind still one of the most important contributions Deleuze made to the study of Bergson himself. It is this gesture that sets Bergson apart most rigorously both from attempts of phenomenological recuperation and from vitalist inscriptions to which his terminology so often seems to lend itself.[25] The way in which Deleuze *reads* Bergson, the way in which he *replies* to Bergson by taking him up as his subject of investigation, is to take »[i]ntuition as... a method of division« (B: 22).[26] This he develops out of no other issue but Bergson's perspective on life—that is, the whole as One-All—itself. In *Creative Evolution* again, Bergson says: »*Life does not proceed by the association and addition of elements, but by dissociation and division*« (CE: 89). Intuition, as thinking the movement itself, looks for the ›real presences‹ of the composite—the constitutive elements structuring our phenomenal world. In taking on the task of dissociating the always already composite nature of our experience, intuition brings us to the ›at least two‹ constitutive elements of

---

25 While I think that this claim for distinction between Bergson and the phenomenological tradition is of major importance for an adequate understanding of him, and was made here before, it in no way means disavowing the specific parallels existing between the two contemporaneous thoughts of Bergson and Husserl, and thus of what follows from them, from Sartre to Merleau-Ponty, Levinas, and up to Derrida and Deleuze. Since our aim in this discussion is, however, mainly to determine in which sense Deleuze's philosophical work is influenced precisely by a different philosophical lineage, it is important to emphasize the Deleuzian divergence from the phenomenological tradition—a difference that e.g. would be of major significance for any comparison between Derrida and Deleuze. In support of this divergence from phenomenology, cf. Murphy: »As the principles of Deleuze's ontology have come to light, it has become clear that it does not fit into the dominant phenomenological line of descent of Western philosophy« (Murphy 1998: 212).

26 Already in »Bergson, 1859–1941« Deleuze stresses this direction: »Intuition as a method is a method that seeks difference. It presents itself as seeking and finding differences in nature, the ›articulations of the real‹« (Deleuze 2004a: 26).

this experience, *beyond* its being consciously lived by us.[27] Departing from *our* experience, Bergson sees intuition as a movement of differentiation that »seek[s] experience at its source, or rather above that decisive *turn* where, taking a bias in the direction of our utility, it becomes properly *human* experience« (MM: 184). Intuition, as a method of thinking, aims at ›liberating‹ thought from the human condition in order to »restore to intuition its original purity and so recover contact with the real« (MM: 185). For Bergson (and Deleuze follows him in this conviction), such a thought—as was already said—is *possible*, and does not mean speculative immodesty. In his critical response to Kantian critical philosophy, which represents the turn »the ordinary course of philosophical thought« (MM: 184) has taken after the *Auseinandersetzung* between dogmatism and empiricism,[28] ›pushing‹ thought beyond *the turn of experience*, beyond the human condition, is what Bergson envisions in order to move from a thought of conditions in »general« (the Kantian *a priori* structures) to one that takes on the task to think *precisely*. The mistake—as we discussed earlier on—that continues in Kant is, according to Bergson, the following: since Kant approaches the real always already under the servitude of our intellect, he believes—and joins his philosophical predecessors in this assumption—that we have to »flee our beloved homeland« as Plotinus has articulated it, and that we have

---

27 Although the opposite of addition and association seems to be subtraction and dissociation, this task of dissociation must, in my opinion, not be misinterpreted as a movement of subtraction, such as it becomes more frequently read today by scholars influenced by Badiou's set theoretical and psychoanalytical thinking. Instead, it has to be understood as a movement of ›differentiation‹, such as the term division, a different mathematical operation, and the Deleuzian expression ›*at least* two‹, speak for. While this remark cannot be argued for properly in this book, it is important to state it here, and expose yet another disagreement between my argument and e.g. Peter Hallward's discussion of Deleuze, to which I have already referred on different occasions.

28 For Bergson the argument between dogmatism on the one hand and empiricism on the other hand remained ineffectual because both traditions substituted »the living unity, which was one with internal continuity, [with] the factitious unity of an empty diagram as lifeless as the parts which it holds together« (MM: 183). And he continues: »Empiricism and dogmatism are, at bottom, agreed in starting from phenomena so reconstructed; they differ only in that dogmatism attaches itself more particularly to the form and empiricism to the matter« (ibid).

»to turn towards something else« entirely (cf. CM: 139). For Bergson, however, this is not the case.

> The impotence of speculative reason, as Kant has demonstrated it, is perhaps at bottom only the impotence of an intellect enslaved to certain necessities of bodily life and concerned with a matter which man has had to disorganize for the satisfaction of his wants. (MM: 184)

Instead of following the internal lines, i.e. the structure of things, in the way the Bergsonian intuition suggests, speculative reason here bends reality to »its superficial and acquired habits, to the contingent form which it derives from our bodily functions and from our lower needs« (ibid). The task for philosophers, however, following Bergson is to

> open us up to the inhuman and the superhuman (*durations* which are inferior or superior to our own), to go beyond the human condition: This is the meaning of philosophy, in so far as our condition condemns us to live among badly analyzed composites and to be badly analyzed composites ourselves (B: 28).[29]

---

29 For Deleuze it is important to tear Bergson away from any consciousness-related or subjectivist philosophy in order to do full justice to the Bergsonian claim we cited from *Matter and Memory* that sees the task of the philosopher as moving beyond the human condition, beyond the decisive turn where experience becomes properly human, i.e. consciousness-related. Bergson himself on the other hand and in difference to Deleuze claims this to become—as we heard above—a force of consciousness itself. For Bergson, consciousness always remains the anchor in his philosophy, consciousness being capable of »[ultimately] opening to itself an unlimited field«. At this peculiar point in *Creative Evolution* Bergson goes on: »Once freed, moreover, [consciousness] can turn inwards on itself, and awaken the potentialities of intuition which still slumber within it. From this point of view, not only does consciousness appear as the motive principle of evolution, but also, among conscious beings themselves, man comes to occupy a privileged place.« (CE: 182) Bergson defines the living endowed with consciousness *by right*, thus truly opening the latter to so much more than what we usually think of it. Deleuze, however, would never want to call the *inhuman* movement that a radical philosophy of difference demands a task of consciousness. He thus departs from Bergson, but he does so out of important reasons that concern a true thought of immanence which cannot remain based on any notion of subjectivity related to the anthropocentric notion of »consciousness«.

»Philosophy« Bergson writes, »can only be an effort to dissolve again into the Whole« (CE: 191). The Whole in Bergson is nothing but life itself—life not as it is seen by our intellect, which already puts it to its own service, but a life superior and inferior to human life, too; life as One-All within which everything remains, however much detaching from and reflecting on it becomes possible throughout. Thus, while the »intellect has detached itself from a vastly wider reality... there has never been a clean cut between the two« (CE: 192–193), Bergson writes. And it is the task of philosophy—if there is one, according to Bergson, this *must* be it—to bring intelligence to re-live its own genesis. *»[T]o philosophize means to reverse the normal direction of the working of thought«* (CM: 190), Bergson concludes in »Introduction to Metaphysics«. This might all sound esoteric or mystical at first, but there is not a more constructive and non-naturalizing attitude to what true thinking implies: to reverse the normal direction, and to precisely undo what seems to us to be ›human nature‹. And intuition, the method that seeks difference—differences in kind—is the philosophical instrument with which we reach ›beyond‹ our (natural) intellectual representations of life in terms of states and differences of degree to become capable of grasping the articulations of the real—life as the impetus to differentiate—the *élan vital*.[30]

Pure Tendencies

The leap into the unknown we described as the first act of intuition; intuition as a method that reaches the level of constitutive elements—of *real* presences—and thus discovers differences of nature instead of categories of degree is the second act. Such differences of nature must, however, not be understood as oppositional differences.

---

30 The vital impetus is not, as many commentators of Bergson want to suggest, a special essence of life, and Bergson's relation to the vitalist tradition should be taken as a much more complicated (hi)story. Because we—as human intellects—will always encounter a limit of articulation (it is difficult to ›fool‹ on intellect for longer than a short moment), the *élan vital* can never be grasped ›directly‹, i.e. find articulation ›as something‹. It is also in this sense that claiming a ›beyond‹ of our habitual representations is no longer problematic *per se*. Instead of another realm or world above or below, here we speak of levels of intensity—a deepening gesture which nonetheless remains on but one plane—so that what is supposed to be vertical becomes a gesture of horizontal spreading: diversification and multiplication.

Difference as opposition or contradiction is one intellectual conceptualization of difference, representing just one particular form—a very limited one as it were—that difference can take.[31] Rather, what an understanding of differences in kind means to suggest is that at this ›deeper‹ level, if we want to go into this metaphor of depth for a moment, that which differs changes itself. It means that the way we understand difference alters. We usually assume that differences appear between things, between different life forms such that an animal is not a man, or that matter is opposed to life. Bergson shows that this is a thinking of degree, always working according to the logic of more and less, a logic that starts from a stable ground on which the measurement of degree can only ever be applied. In rediscovering differences in kind that can no longer be on a level of opposition but of intensity, we realize that real differences are

> [n]ever between two products or between two things, but *in one and the same thing* between the two tendencies that encounter one another in it. Indeed, what is pure is never a thing; the thing is always a composite that must be dissociated; only the tendency is pure, which is to say that the true thing or the substance is the tendency itself (Deleuze 2004a: 26).

With intuition we learn again to differentiate what has been mixed together in our lived experience. In this process of division we arrive at differences in kind that now are no longer composites (essences, things as we commonly see them) but *pure tendencies*.[32] Difference

---

31 This is, of course, the dialectical, and especially the Hegelian definition of true difference as determined negation, which pushed to its extreme, becomes opposition or contradiction. According to the logic we are presenting here, this conceptualization reveals already a complete submission to the requirements of a logic of representation, whose inherent premises pre-determine the matrix according to which difference will be understood from the very start: categorization as the function of thought. As Deleuze puts it in *Difference and Repetition*, such a dialectical fixation *mediates* difference »to the extent that it is subjected to the fourfold root of identity, opposition, analogy, and resemblance« (DR: 29).

32 Cf. Bergson in *Creative Evolution*: »A perfect definition applies only to a *completed* reality; now, vital properties are never entirely realized, though always on the way to become so; they are not so much *states* but *tendencies*.« (CE: 13)

thought ›in itself‹—the Deleuzian *credo*—is no longer a difference between two things but difference in one and the same thing, between two tendencies of one and the same substance, a substance, however, that itself is nothing but movement or tendency. Life ›is‹ tendency; it is what differs in itself from itself. Life is not a ›given‹ that by differentiation becomes other, rather, life is *becoming-other*.

Before we devote ourselves with sufficient energy to this *One* that only ›is‹ *in difference*, let us get back to our discussion of method and summarize the difficult claims that this second act of intuition produces.

Intuition, instead of looking merely at the phenomenal world, follows the internal lines of things ›up‹ to where they become tendencies, pure tendencies that encounter each other. This is what Bergson means when he speaks of intuition as a means to push the thought of difference *beyond the human condition*. It is to restore differences in kind and to encounter ›real presences‹ (nothing but tendencies, that is, movements). Thus, it is not a ›beyond‹ or some transcendental *a priori*. On the contrary, Bergson's endeavor was to return to the things themselves, but in the sense of following the internal rather than the external lines to the point where they become pure tendencies in order to then follow their intersections and restore a way (back) into experience (which will—as we will see later on—also become the potential to produce something new, a new way for experience).[33] In saying that, re-turn is as important as the turn ›beyond the human condition‹:

> Let us then go down into our inner selves: the deeper the point we touch, the stronger will be the thrust which sends us back to the surface. Philosophical intuition is this contact, philosophy is this impetus. Brought back to the surface by an impulsion from the depth, we shall regain contact with science as our thought opens out and disperses. (CM: 125)

---

33 »But intuition has a second characteristic: understood in this way, it presents itself as a return, because the philosophical relationship, which puts us in things instead of leaving us outside, is restored rather than established by philosophy, rediscovered rather than invented.« (Deleuze 2004a: 23)

And this is the reason why also Deleuze after placing so much stress on the *turn* beyond experience, highlights *return,* the rediscovery of

> the point at which [the lines of divergence] intersect again, where the directions cross and where the tendencies that differ in kind link together again to give rise to the thing as we know it... After we have followed the lines of divergence beyond the turn, these lines must intersect again (B: 28–29).[34]

After strict division—rigorous dualism—re-formation of monism; »after the broadening out, a final narrowing follows, just as integration follows differentiation« (ibid): these are the two—precision-demanding—movements, or better (in)directions of thought in Bergson's philosophy. Turn (beyond experience) *and* return (to the concrete or singular), however, must not be misunderstood to imply that the movement itself would not have been necessary since we arrive at the very same point from where everything began—the concrete thing.[35] This would again mean to fall for the naturalization of our intellect in the sense that, stating the problem in the wrong way, we imagine a distance spanned between a pre-given A and a pre-given B, which determines the movement all along and prescribes linearity. Succeeding in the difficult movement of ›indirection‹

---

34 To return one more time to Bergson's highly illuminating essay on »Philosophical Intuition«, the way in which he expresses the movement of intuition here is the following: »Let us take all that the philosopher has written, let us bring back these scattered ideas to the image from which they had descended; and let us raise them enclosed now in the image, up to the abstract formula enlarged by its absorption of the image and ideas, let us now attach ourselves to this formula and watch it, simple as it is, grow simpler still, all the more simple for our having pushed into it a greater number of things; finally let us rise with it, go up to the point where everything that was given extended in the doctrine contracts in tension: we shall picture to ourselves this time how from this center of force, which is moreover inaccessible, there springs the impulse which gives the impetus, that is to say the intuition itself.« (CM: 120)

35 Returning to *recoupage* as the Bergsonian method according to Kolakowski, Deleuze's complementary rule to the second act of intuition explicates that »[t]he real is not only that which is cut out *(se découpe)* according to natural articulations or differences in kind; it is also that which intersect again *(se récoupe)* along the paths of converging toward the same ideal or virtual point« (B: 29).

in which no-thing really travels — for we are, of course, not brought into another place — but rather every-thing is *thought differently*, the method of intuition is not merely descriptive but must be understood as an *act*ion that »breaks the circle« (CE: 192) in which our intellect naturally seems to be caught up — this vicious circle according to which, as Bergson writes in *Creative Evolution*, we could never »go beyond intelligence... except by intelligence« (ibid). In one of the most incisive passages of this work Bergson explains that while this objection (the impossibility of going beyond intelligence) »presents itself naturally to the mind« (ibid), this cannot be the hindrance to true thinking which has only this drive to go beyond or further, to multiply and differentiate.[36] How, he asks, would we otherwise ever learn of something new? If we take just the well-worn example of the way we learn to swim, mere »[r]easoning« as Bergson says »in fact, always nails us down to the solid ground« (ibid). With reasoning alone we would never learn to swim. »But if«, he goes on,

> quite simply, I throw myself into the water without fear, I may keep myself up well enough at first by merely struggling, and gradually adapt myself to the new environment: I shall thus have learnt to swim (ibid).[37]

---

36 As most commentators on the Bergsonian intuition agree, intuition is not the absolute opposite to intellect, although at points it is presented in this way. Rather, as Bergson himself in *Creative Evolution* writes, »intuition may bring the intellect to recognize that life does not quite go into the category of the many nor yet into that of the one... by the expansion of our consciousness which it brings about, it introduces us into life's own domain, which is reciprocal interpenetration, endlessly continued creation. But, though it thereby transcends intelligence, it is from intelligence that has come the push that has made it rise to the point it has reached« (CE: 177–178).

37 Deleuze follows up on this example of swimming in *Difference and Repetition* when it is up to him to explain what it means to learn, and how we learn to think differently: »Learning«, he says, »takes place not in the relation between a representation and an action (reproduction of the Same) but in the relation between a sign and a response (encounter with the Other)... The movement of the swimmer does not resemble that of the wave, in particular, the movements of the swimming instructor which we reproduce on the sand bear no relation to the movement of the wave, which we learn to deal with only by grasping the former in practice as signs. That is why it is so difficult to say how someone learns... We learn nothing from those who say: ›Do as I do‹. Our only teachers are those who tell us to ›do with me‹, and are able to emit signs to be develo-

This is what ›thinking‹ in its superior mode — philosophical thinking as intuitive thinking — is asking from us. Intuition is leaping into the unknown; it is performing an *act* by which one leaves one's own environment and throws oneself into the movement of duration itself. Intuition then arrives at the creative stream — the impetus as Bergson calls it — the *élan vital* that is nothing but the force of differentiation of that which differs in and from itself: difference in itself.

3. Time of the Virtual vs. Space of the Possible

We have now arrived at the final stage of the discussion of method that gives structure to Deleuze's *Bergsonism*, the stage at which it also becomes clear what kind of far reaching consequences such an approach ultimately brings about. Thinking about problems (rather than solutions) so that they themselves become re-formulated by pushing thought to a limit that is *beyond* ›our‹ (conscious) terrain; reaching, thus, the impersonal tendencies that differ in kind and constitute the phenomenal world — in this movement of thought, the way we think and think about thinking changes radically. Deleuze states the third rule of intuition:

> Third rule: *State problems and solve them in terms of time rather than of space*. This rule gives the ›fundamental meaning‹ of intuition: Intuition presupposes duration, it consists in thinking in terms of duration. (B: 31)

The rule of temporalization carries the fundamental meaning for Deleuze because with it we arrive at the condition of possibility of such a thought of duration and, thus, of difference in itself. We started our discussion of intuition because of Spinoza's heritage of a thought of univocity that Deleuze introduces to us in his reading of Spinoza. Instead of representing merely one side of the opposition between the One and the Many, this thought of One-ness moves beyond every dualism. The question, however, remaining to us was: *how* is such a

---

ped in heterogeneity rather than propose gestures for us to reproduce. In other words, there is no ideo-motivity, only sensory-motivity« (DR: 23).

thought possible? We were looking for a way of thinking movement instead of separate states in an already distributed space; a way of thinking change and endurance rather than the timeless eternity that represents the traditional horizon of philosophical thought.

Time as Duration

With intuition as the philosophical method that goes further than merely noting differences of degree, and instead pays particular attention to differences of intensity, we now encounter a thought of difference that is able to overcome the apparent contradiction of indivisible Oneness on the one hand and (the process of) differentiation as that which constitutes — i.e. ›is‹ — this very Oneness on the other. We arrive at a different texture of what ›there is‹, and at the same time at a different perspective on how we think ontologically: *substance* — an image of totality — becomes *tendencies*; but tendencies, though different in kind, are not separate in the strict sense, but are rather *two directions of the same movement*; and this movement — this ›new‹ image of the One — is *duration*. While it would be wrong to assume intuition to already be duration, intuition »is... the movement by which we emerge from our duration« (B: 33), Deleuze says. It is the movement that throws us onto our own duration, and that makes it possible »to affirm and immediately to recognize the existence of other durations, above or below us« (ibid).[38] With intuition we are no longer dealing with essences and categories postulated as given — always reliant on the separation of two different worlds or orders. Instead we think in terms of duration, »duration, which ›tends‹ for its part to take on or bear all the differences in kind« (ibid). This one movement — duration — tends towards extension *and* duration, matter *and* memory, relaxation *and* contraction. It is two direc-

---

38 It should be added that, while for Deleuze this plurality of durations is of no question, he himself notes in the chapter »One or Many Durations?« in *Bergsonism* that »Bergson's texts seem to vary considerably on this point« (B: 76). Although in *Matter and Memory* Bergson still affirms a radial plurality of durations, *Creative Evolution* assumes only a single time, that is one duration. Deleuze, in his way of productively *reading* antagonistic claims, takes issue with the Bergsonian inconsistencies in terming the latter's thought as one of multiplicity — where »[t]here is only one time (monism), although there is an infinity of actual fluxes (generalized pluralism) that necessarily participate in the same virtual whole (limited pluralism)« (82).

tions of one and the same movement, or in yet another of Deleuze's expressions: »What differs has itself become a thing, a *substance*« (Deleuze 2004b: 37). Reading Bergson's complicated conceptualization of the series: substance is duration as pure difference,[39] Deleuze here finds for himself a thought of multiplicity that overcomes the logic of the One vs. Many.

To avoid two separate worlds (immobile eternity on the one hand and mobile temporality on the other), and, thus, to avoid the methodological problem of choosing the ›right side‹ in the question where to begin, Bergsonian thinking shows that motion, One-ness differing in itself, comes before rest, a One that only repeats and distinguishes itself from something else. Duration is real time for Bergson, and it is this changing which is all that ›is‹. Duration is that which differs from itself—»the continuous progress of the past which gnaws into the future and which swells as it advances« (CE: 4).

Being as Alteration

Deleuze has already explicated the logic of differentiation in »Bergson, 1859–1941«. In its essential process of differentiation into *two directions ›at once‹* (past *and* future) duration as the concept of time, Bergson suggests, brings about both what interrupts this movement, i.e. matter, *and* what turns back and retraces its steps—movement itself (cf. Deleuze 2004a: 24). The distinction of differences in kind and differences of degree, or qualitative multiplicity and quantitative multiplicity, thus always leads us back to the side of the differences in kind, that is of duration itself, without, however, collapsing the difference between the two distinctions: »The Absolute is difference, but difference has two facets, differences in degree and differences in kind« (B: 35).[40]

---

39 How complex this thought of duration, difference, change, or movement is (they are all interchangeable for this reason in Bergson) is shown by the following passage from »The Perception of Change«: »*There are changes, but there are underneath the change no things which change: change has no need of a support. There are movements, but there is no inert or invariable object which moves: movement does not imply a mobile.*« (CM: 147) Bergson's difficult concept of the *élan vital* has to be understood as precisely such a movement with no inert object that ›is‹ the impetus the *élan* itself expresses.

40 In her discussion of Bergson's notions of difference and multiplicity, Grosz goes even so far as to push the distinction between difference of degree and

It is with the conceptualization of such (paradoxically) *affective multiplicity* that we gain a new and truly immanent ›solution‹ to the problem of ›beginning‹ and ›grounding‹ in philosophy, very similar to that which stood at the end of our discussion of Deleuze's Spinoza: a One that is nothing but *movement* and *alteration*, a One, thus, of multiplicity and pluralism, a One that is never ›given once and for all‹ since »the first time is already the second; such is the notion of foundation« (Deleuze 2004a: 24). In »Bergson's Conception of Difference« Deleuze then draws conclusions from this thought of alteration for philosophy itself: »Difference is the genuine beginning« (Deleuze 2004b: 50), he says, and Bergsonism for him »is a philosophy of difference, a philosophy of the actualization of difference; in it we meet difference in person, which actualizes itself as the new« (Deleuze 2004b: 51).[41] In such a philosophy we rediscover not only differences in nature, but we go from there to the very nature of difference that ›is‹ *nuance*.[42] Nuance is the infinitesimal movement that makes all the difference.

In saying that with intuition as the method of such a philosophy of difference we move beyond our actual experience of things towards the conditions of experience in the concreteness of ›at least‹ two series—differences in kind—which encounter each other, we claim that it is possible to move towards a new thought whose consistency has changed at last: instead of the usual spatio-temporal foundation or ground that is taken as given and that is supposed to

---

difference in kind—a distinction first of all of qualitative nature—in its most extreme case to a continual one, that is (terminologically) a difference of degree. She asks her reader to think quality and continuum together, and comes to the following conclusion: »The distinction between these two kinds of multiplicity or difference is itself qualitative and nonoppositional; the terms provide extremes of a continuum, a difference of tendency or impetus, an ›endosmosis‹, that is, a difference of degree.« (Grosz 2004: 163)

41 Cf. also Pearson in his *Germinal Life. The Difference and Repetition of Deleuze*: »To neglect the move being made from causes to tendencies is, in effect, to reduce differences of nature to differences of degree and to loose sight of the inventive character of duration which actualizes itself only as ›novelty‹.« (Pearson 1999: 37)

42 »In other words, being is difference and not the immovable or the undifferentiated, nor is it contradiction, which is merely false movement. Being is the difference itself of the thing, what Bergson often calls the nuance.« (Deleuze 2004a: 25)

give birth to ›what is‹ in an eminent, analogical, or dialectical way, Bergson and Deleuze are »committed to *saving* time and to saving it ›for us‹« (Pearson 2002: 168), so that we learn to think the movements themselves in their different intensities, which means to think their singular degrees of contraction and expansion (*complicare/explicare*) without moving outside duration. Difference in itself is *first and foremost* differing from itself. We are dealing here with a One that not only ›is‹ by *falling out of step with itself*,[43] that is in an infinite process of (dis)continuity, but in this way we also deal with an ever only *productive* One — ›the continuous progress of the past which gnaws into the future and which swells as it advances‹. This One is no simple unity, because it is time dividing itself in two directions, one as the past and the other on the way to a radically open future. In contrast therefore to the image of a One conceived in terms of parts and Whole that relies on a logic of possibility, i.e. *a priori* conditions of possibility, and is thus always already dependent on what is realized, here we are able to think the *One as virtual* that lives of its always differing actualizations.[44] With Bergson we move

---

43 This is an expression Gilbert Simondon uses for explaining the meaning of ontogenesis as a process of individuation: »The meaning of the expression ›ontogenesis‹ will be given its full weight here if, instead of being understood in the more limited and secondary sense of the genesis of the individual (…), it is made to designate the development of the being, or its becoming — in other words, that which makes the being develop or become, insofar as it is, as being. The opposition holding between the being and its becoming can only be valid when it is seen in the context of a certain doctrine according to which substance is the very model of being; but it is equally possible to maintain that becoming exists as one of the dimensions of the being, that it corresponds to a capacity beings possess of *falling out of step with themselves*.« (Simondon 1992: 300, my emphasis)

44 Because of the centrality of this thought of time as duration in Bergson's work, I would like to take the opportunity to refer the reader at this point to the significant textual references in Bergson's work. For the thought of the virtual linked to his thought of a coexistence of past and present, cf. *Matter and Memory*, esp. chapter III, in which he develops the famous picture of the time-cone, and also his essay »The Possible and the Real« (CM: 91–106). The distinction between a logic of the possible on the one hand and one of the virtual on the other is taken up by Deleuze in reference to Proust's formula that virtuality is »real without being actual, ideal without being abstract«, while »[t]he possible has no reality (although it may have an actuality)« (B: 96). For a detailed discussion of Bergson's thought of time, cf. Grosz 2004: 185ff, and for a thought of the One as virtual, cf. Pearson 2002: 97ff. I would also like to refer the reader

from substance, a One of mere matter or space, to a One that can never present itself in these traditional senses of the word, since it is a One of time, *being* only ever in the past and always *becoming* in its present into the future.

The One as Multiplicity

Before we end this discussion of Bergsonism and of the transformation that the plane of immanence undergoes in it, we should, without really being able to treat it in due detail here, nonetheless consider what actually happens when the issue of time is taken into consideration in this — enduring or virtual — way. Duration, Bergson explains, never ›is‹ in a conceptual framework in which being ›is‹ present or is nothing at all, while the past ›is no longer‹, and the future ›is not yet‹. Such is an understanding of time that cannot do justice to the thought of duration that we tried to unfold in this chapter. For Bergson, a linear image of time is nothing but our intellectual attempt to find spatially separated categories that not only center us as subjects but also chain us to a present as the only realm of the ›there is‹, limiting both the ›there‹ and the ›present‹ to each other by a representational thought based on presence as visibility. When Bergson begins *Creative Evolution*, he challenges such a thought, arguing — as he also had already done in *Matter and Memory* — that such a thought of time does not think time in itself but only according to the spatio-temporal terms of our intellectual habit. Thinking time in itself, to the contrary, means to think *endurance* (cf. CE: 4), that is, time in terms of intensity and continuity rather than in terms of before and after. Such duration as enduring cannot ever *be* in any present moment. Rather, Being — this state we take as the normal condition of our presence — can be attributed only to the past.

> In reality, the past is preserved by itself, automatically. In its entirety, probably it follows us at every instant... What are we, in fact, what is our *character*, if not the condensation of the history that we have lived from our birth — nay, even before our birth, since we bring with us prenatal dispositions? Doubtless we think with only a small part of our

---

to our last chapter in which the question of virtual and actual will reappear in more detail.

past, but it is with our entire past including the original bent of our soul, that we desire, will and act. (CE: 5)

»The past«, as Deleuze says in his interpretation of this peculiar Bergsonian claim, »has ceased to act or to be useful. But it has not ceased to be. Useless and inactive, impassive, it IS, in the full sense of the word: It is identical with being in itself« (B: 55). The ›identity‹ spoken of here is, of course, a virtual one. It speaks both of a coexistence of past and present, and yet absolutely separates the two.[45] Since we »cannot go through the same state twice« (CE: 5) when we truly think duration, the *present*—unceasing change—never ›is with itself‹. It is always only ever differing from itself, on the way to something new because duration—though not infinite in the strict sense—is nonetheless irreversible. Presence or existence never ›is‹ any-thing,[46] it is always only (in its) *becoming* (cf. B: 55). While a presence, thought of as *realization*, always already works according to the logic of resemblance and limitation because »the real is supposed to be in the image of the possible that it realizes« (B: 97), becoming in the sense of *actualization* never resembles the virtual. And this is not—in Plato's sense—a catastrophe but a virtue! It is only in this way that we arrive at a true thought of difference (one that does not reduce it to a secondary effect) but also at a satisfying response to the question of how to *dynamize* the whole without having to refer to something outside. Deleuze, in reference to Bergson, makes clear

---

45 This, however, must not be misunderstood as the virtual again being some sort of ideal or ›possible‹ level—introduced purely out of reasons of analogical reference. We have to think back to the Spinozist logic of expression that—as we said—›flattens‹ the thought of difference without, however, collapsing what differs in kind. Deleuze in *Difference and Repetition* also clearly points out that »[t]he virtual is opposed not to the real but to the actual. *The virtual is fully real in so far as it is virtual*... Indeed, the virtual must be defined as strictly a part of the real object—as though the object had one part of itself in the virtual into which it plunged as though into an objective dimension« (208–209). As was said above, Deleuze's differentiation of virtual/actual vs. possible/real as borrowed from Bergson and further developed in his own philosophy will be taken up once more in our last chapter.

46 It is not even ›outside itself‹ as the thought of existence as ek-stasis or Hegel's emergence of self-consciousness suggest. Such is already a too oppositional thought of difference, limiting and taming the latter to one form of representation.

that »the rules of actualization are not those of resemblance and limitation, but those of difference or divergence and of *creation*« (ibid, my emphasis).[47] Since the virtual possesses absolute reality in this thought and the processes of actualization do not work according to a logic of representation but differentiation, such ›creation‹ is no theistic *creatio ex nihilo* or creationist utopia, but the immanent production of something truly ›new‹: the continuity of change and alteration that ›is‹ discontinuity to the reproduction of the same.

We thus arrive at a new turning point in our investigation of the Deleuzian ›image of thought‹. We have developed an ontological plane that is a One as multiplicity, overcoming both the opposition between the One and the Multiple and the structure of its corresponding thought. We have arrived at a thought of a One-All that never merely ›is‹ but that continuously *endures* and, thus, gives itself the shape that it is ›capable of‹. A *productive* or—as we have called it before—*affective* ontology has now become possible in the sense that it was said that ›thought again is possible‹ with Deleuze.

And yet, one question remains. It is the question of how a thought of becoming that is creative in this sense actively affirms itself as the production of difference rather than sameness. How it is that this thought can pass the test that it is truly difference and differing, which characterizes the movement of becoming, and not the sedimentation of the ever-same. Thus we arrive at the question in what sense this thought already speaks of a practical attitude towards the world rather than merely describing what there is.

It is with this question that we again will have to move somewhere else, and it is the task of our next chapter to look closely at the production of the actual as *real* differentiation and creation. Bergson himself shows a concern for *practice* in all of his major works; this

---

47 In her article »Time, Life, Concepts: The Newness of Bergson«, Paola Marrati in a similar way argues: »The virtual and the actual do not resemble each other. The very process of actualization is here one of *differentiation*. From this perspective, existence *does* make a difference: it implies a creative process of differentiation« (Marrati 2005: 1109); and she concludes her article by repeating that »[t]he tendency of life, which is its very essence, is not the coming into existence of a possibility. It is an ongoing process of actualization that creates new and different forms of life along with new concepts, ideas, and affections« (ibid).

is his affinity to the philosophical tradition of pragmatism. However, except for his very last book *The Two Sources of Morality and Religion*, he treated this *ethical turn* in and of thought — the *demand* to produce difference and not sameness — in a rather negligible way. Here, in my opinion, lies the difference between the last metaphysician Bergson and the post-structuralist philosopher Deleuze, whose concern with the question of what it means to think, and what thinking is, always affirms its ethical and practical attitude. The task of liberating thought from the (traditional) image »is, thus, for Deleuze, unmistakably, an ethical undertaking«, Rodolphe Gasché writes in his essay »Thinking within Thought« (Gasché 2007: 255). It is to this aspect of Deleuze's plane of thought that we will have to devote ourselves next in order to complement further the practical re-construction of Deleuze's philosophy of becoming, so fundamental for our move towards the ethical dimension of this thought.

IV.

»To Affirm!« or the Thought of Repetition: *Nietzsche*

> And he alters both the theory and the practice of philosophy. He compares the thinker to an arrow shot by Nature... According to him, the philosopher is neither eternal nor historical but ›untimely‹, always untimely.
>
> (Deleuze, *Nietzsche and Philosophy*)

If we learn to think of the world in fundamentally temporal terms, the world as nothing but movement and becoming, duration and differentiation; if, thus, we no longer think of it as self-identical substance, given once and for all, in need of the determination of ›what it is‹, and forcing us as a consequence into the construction of two different realms, the ideal (how things ›must be‹ because they ›should be‹ that way) on the one side and the real (always incomplete, never good enough, and the point of view from which the ideal is only ever conceivable) on the other side; if, therefore, we change the registers of our thinking itself, we learn of a new approach to ontology, a new way of how to think about, and that is, of how to *express* the world.[1] It will be the task of this chapter to show that it is, thus, that thought becomes a question of ›how to live‹. Thought itself becomes practice.

The inherent links between questions of thought and life, theory and practice, ontology and ethics lie at the heart of my argument in favor of a thought of becoming as a poetics of life. In a first step we introduced Spinoza's serialization of God *or* Nature, set against classical dialectics and negative theology, in order to argue for but *this world*. A radically immanent, i.e. ›flat‹, ontology is able to ›liberate‹ thought from an infinity above or below, be it a transcendent God,

---

1 Ontology (the logic of ›what there is‹) in this sense is always already inherently related to epistemology (the logic of ›how we know the world‹) in the way Bergson spoke of a new metaphysics, that is, philosophy proper, in which a *theory of life* is inseparable from a *theory of knowledge*. For this Bergsonian claim, cf. chapter III.

Idea, or Being, which supposedly gives structure to ›what is‹. In a second step, and with the help of Bergson, we then developed a way of thinking such immanence without reducing it to either brute materialism or an even strengthened positivism. We saw the emergence of a ›superior empiricism‹—›metaphysics‹ in the Bergsonian sense or ›transcendental empiricism‹ in Deleuze's words. What remains to be done, however, in this re-construction is to show that such a departure from the all in all idealist canon of philosophy—from Plato to Kant and beyond—truly changes the way we normally think of thought itself. In a most general sense, thought is always taken as abstraction from and contemplative reflection of practice and experience in this world. In a philosophy of radical immanence, however, a philosophy of becoming that does affirm its ›immanating‹ and superior empirical heritage, ›a new *image* of thought‹—as Deleuze calls it—arises. We now speak of a thought that distributes the distinction between theory and practice in philosophy in new and different ways, because theory is not only a practice in but also a construction of this world. In order to fully understand what this peculiar claim really implies, we have to engage with the third and perhaps in this regard the most active influence in Deleuze's work—Friedrich Nietzsche.

Although my argument in no way pursues a ranking among the here presented philosophical influences for the thought of Gilles Deleuze, the following series might nonetheless contain some truth when reflecting on the kind of effects each of the different thinkers investigated here actually has on the latter. The series that I would like to propose at this particular moment, which is the beginning of the last chapter that concerns the *conceptual* investigation into Deleuze's plane of thought, is the following: while Deleuze *thinks* (conceptualizes) the world in a Spinozist way, while he *senses* (envisions) it in a Bergsonian way, it will be the task of this chapter to exemplify that Deleuze *acts* (intervenes) in it in a Nietzschean manner. All three dimensions—thinking, sensing, and acting—are, of course, equal in their relation to the question of philosophy itself. There is no hierarchy between them, and only in their interplay does the force of Deleuze's thought truly unfold. In the two preceding chapters, our presentation slowly moved towards a productive and affective thought of immanence. We have dealt sufficiently with the pressing problem of stasis as the greatest hindrance of such a productive thought of immanence, and by suggesting the dynamization of this thought we have developed an adequate understanding of Deleuze's thought-structure based on the notion of difference, which, understood as difference in itself, is movement. Yet, while on the conceptual level we have thus traversed quite a large terrain, it is only with the »incorporation« of the Nietzschean spirit (if an arrow — such as the epigraph describes — can ever become such a thing) we ultimately leave the merely de-scriptive level and arrive at the active plane of thought — thought aiming at affecting and constructing the world — that is indispensable for such a *productive* logic of thinking.[2] It is by investigating this affectivity as activity of thought itself that we are also brought back to the important but still unfamiliar equation of ›ontology = ethics‹ which I attempt to unravel in this work.

***

Thus, turning towards the history of philosophy one more time, it is in the extraordinary philosophical œuvre of Friedrich Nietzsche that we find a way of thinking which is affective and effective *both* as analysis and reflection (the way we normally perceive of thinking as the method moving us from mere perception to true knowledge) *and* as movement and action that makes its force a *real* force of and in the world (a thought that is, thus, also a practice, that only ›is‹ as

---

2 This momentary ranking of thought according to a degree of effectuation into the world does, of course, not want to suggest that either of the two other thinkers, Spinoza or Bergson, belong to a philosophical tradition that hopes for nothing but to remain neutral in its conception of the world — a neutrality that in the spirit of all four thinkers discussed here should be rather called pseudo-neutrality. Both Spinoza and Bergson understand thought as a true investment and construction, and, thus, treat it as a kind of physiology, a practice that affects the question of life, and as such as a way of philosophizing for which Nietzsche then became famous for. They both therefore belong without question to what Deleuze once called »the other family of philosophers« (Deleuze 2004e: 138). On the other side, however, nobody ultimately has developed a thought so extreme and has posed the question of thinking so radically as Friedrich Nietzsche did, who in his work experiments with the interrelatedness of thought and life to an extend that something entirely new emerges. I would go as far as to argue that his elevated position, not only in our discussion but also in the whole history of philosophy, stems from this extreme — and often misunderstood — rigor. In what follows, I hope to illuminate the uniquely Nietzschean turn that also gave Deleuze's thought its unmistakable direction.

practice). For Nietzsche, thought is a motor of creation and production. It is always already an *attitude* towards the world. Thought has to make a difference or it is nothing at all. The question of ›style‹ in Nietzsche's way of thinking has to be understood as precisely pointing to these often neglected dimensions of the philosophical work. Rather than interpreting his emphasis on stylistic and thus ›formal‹ criteria as mere longing for aristocratism, the concern was to save thought from both indifference and pathetic cliché.

In putting the stakes so high for the question of true thought, Nietzsche alters both the theory and the practice of philosophy. Staying with our picture that for Deleuze Spinoza is the first true *thinker* of the world, and that Bergson develops the most precise *vision* of it, it is with Nietzsche that such a thought finds its singular *actualization* for the very first time. For Deleuze, Nietzsche possesses such an outstanding position in the history of philosophy because the ›*Revaluation of All Values*‹—already in this articulation so much more than pure theory—is at the very heart of his philosophical thought. In his essay »Nomadic Thought« written for the conference *Nietzsche aujourd'hui?*, taking place in Paris in 1972, Deleuze says that Nietzsche is the dawn of a *counter-culture*. Referring the reader to the ›holy‹ trinity of modern culture, Freud, Marx, and Nietzsche, Deleuze here writes:

> The trinity of Nietzsche, Freud, and Marx is thought to be the dawn of our modern culture. Never mind that by doing so you defuse the explosiveness of each from the start. Perhaps Marx and Freud are the dawn of our culture, but Nietzsche is something else entirely, the dawn of a counter-culture. (Deleuze 2004d: 253)[3]

---

3 This comment by Deleuze in the context of this colloquium cannot but be understood as critique on both dogmatic Marxism and psychoanalysis, and also as marking a slight difference in regard to the Nietzschean arrow thrown into philosophy between himself and Foucault, who at an even more famous colloquium on Nietzsche, organized by Deleuze himself in 1964, gave his significant talk on »Nietzsche, Freud, Marx« in which he called the three together the founders of »the possibility of a hermeneutic« in the then new *post*-structuralist sense. Foucault's text was published for the first time as »Nietzsche« in *Cahiers de Royaumont. Philosophie No VI*: 183–192. The English version is published as »Nietzsche, Freud, Marx« in *Aesthetics, Method, and Epistemology. EssentialWorks of Foucault 1954–1984*, Vol. 2. For the publication of the conference

Deleuze's particular interest in Nietzsche lies in this ›something else entirely‹ that Nietzsche's thought provides us with. »[A]n aphorism by Nietzsche is a sense-producing machine, in that order specific to thought« (Deleuze 2004e: 137), he says. In this respect, Nietzsche overtakes even the provocations of Spinoza and Bergson who — their re-evaluation of thought notwithstanding — did not make the bridging of the gulf between thought and life their ultimate central concern. This is, however, what Nietzsche's project speaks for all the way through. It is Nietzsche's unique force — brought about by a matchless style — that we are forced to rethink what we believed quite naturally, be it in regard to the question of what thinking means, what a subject is, or how and in what sense the world is given to us. Nietzsche stages his thought — he *dramatizes* it, as Deleuze says[4] — so that it alters and *acts* on us. In a way similar to Spinoza but conceptually much more daring, *concept* and *affect* are intrinsically linked in Nietzsche.[5] And Deleuze, once asked about the privileged position that Nietzsche occupies in his work, confirms this impression by giving the following significant example, which demonstrates the specific quality of Nietzsche's thought.

Referring to the philosophical statement »God is dead«, which so often is taken as a short-hand for Nietzsche's whole œuvre, Deleuze points out that what is important about the catchy phrase is not that

---

Nietzsche aujourd'hui?, cf. Boudot 1973.

4 In a very short talk given in front of the French Society of Philosophy at the time of writing *Difference and Repetition* in 1967, Deleuze relates »The Method of Dramatization« to a thought of difference/differentiation as dynamic multiplicity instead of one of opposition and contradiction. »Through dramatization, the Idea is incarnated or actualized, *it differentiates itself*«, he announces his own argument at the beginning of his text (Deleuze 2004c: 94). In what follows he delimits such an approach from a way of thinking that privileges the question »*What is this?*« which »prematurely judges the Idea as simplicity of the essence; from then on, it is inevitable that the simple essence includes the inessential, and includes it *in essence*, and thus contradicts itself« (95–96). While such schematization of the history of philosophy is harsh, and simplifies what is more nuanced, the fact that this extreme statement wonderfully expresses the philosophical antagonism between Nietzsche's approach to thought on the one hand and that of his fierce enemy Hegel on the other hand seems to legitimize the »dramatization«.

5 »Like Spinoza, Nietzsche always maintained that there is the deepest relationship between concept and affect. Conceptual analyses are indispensable and Nietzsche takes them further than anyone else.« (NP: xii)

it was truly Nietzsche's invention, which it actually was not. Rather than speaking this sentence for the first time, what is so significant about Nietzsche, Deleuze says, is that in making this formula the structure of his thinking as such, he becomes

> the first to believe this phrase to have no importance whatsoever as long as the human occupies the place of God. Nietzsche was trying to uncover something that was neither God nor Human, trying to give voice to these impersonal individuations and these pre-individual singularities (Deleuze 2004e: 139).

By daring to think beyond the human, criticizing precisely the too easy substitution of God by the human via the logic of Subjectivity, Nietzsche pushes thought to the ›impersonal individuations‹ and ›pre-individual singularities‹. He does not just articulate a critique of transcendence from within the logic of the Subject, thereby merely secularizing the philosophical heavens, but, in further radicalizing the philosophical lineage we are following here, he criticizes even this critique and pushes us further than what ›we‹ can bear. Pierre Klossowski, a reader of Nietzsche contemporary to Deleuze, and one who is of major relevance for Deleuze's understanding of Nietzsche, follows in his *Nietzsche and the Vicious Circle* such an evaluation of Nietzsche's thought, and sees the claim of the *death of God* as concerning »Nietzsche's relationship with the guarantor of his *ego's* identity—namely, the abolition, not of the divine itself, which is inseparable from *Chaos*, but of an identical and once-and-for-all individuality« (Klossowski 2005: 140).[6]

It is in the *Gay Science* that Nietzsche himself gives the hint for such an understanding of this thought. There he writes:

---

6 It is important to note that in the French reception of Nietzsche's work this part of the latter's thought is not understood as determining merely Nietzsche's last period of writing, an interpretation earlier commentators of Nietzsche often wanted to suggest in order to save him from too dangerous (political) misunderstandings. It is from such a Nietzschean thread that Foucault's expression of the ›death of man‹ or the ›end of man‹ in *The Order of Things* (Foucault 1994b) develops. In an interview with Didier Eribon on Foucault, Deleuze says that the latter »develops [the Nietzschean theme] in a very originary way« (Deleuze 1995: 99). On a more extended discussion of this Foucaultian theme, cf. also the appendix in Deleuze's *Foucault* (F: 124–132).

> *New battles.*—After Buddha was dead, they still showed his shadow in a cave for centuries—a tremendous, gruesome shadow. God is dead; but given the way people are, there may still for millennia be caves in which they show his shadow.—And we—we must still defeat his shadow as well. (GS #108)

This makes Nietzsche a true successor of the heretical times of the 17th century that were encountered earlier in our discussion. Taking only Spinoza as his equal,[7] Nietzsche, the ultimate *untimely* companion, accomplishes, according to Deleuze, what back then still presented an irresolvable problem: the inversion of Platonism without falling into oppositional regress.[8] With Nietzsche *we* move somewhere else, or better, we are *forced* to move somewhere else—if we pretend otherwise, we do not understand Nietzsche at all. Understood as no longer hiding behind cliché and the melancholy caused by »God is dead«, serene philosophy demands from us a different attitude to thought and thinking itself: instead of merely theoretically criticizing abstraction, in thought we must move towards the *incorporeal* invention of a new body. It is by giving thought a new body, after stripping it of the limited human(ist) body that transcendental philosophy is based upon, that Nietzsche pushes the relation of thought and life, of theory and practice—in our understanding the relation of ontology and ethics—in a profoundly new direction.[9]

---

7 »Apart from the Pre-Socratics of long ago he [Nietzsche] recognized only one predecessor—Spinoza.« (NP: ix)

8 Though it is always theoretically ambivalent to point out a Heideggerian trait in Deleuze, there is no question that it is Heidegger's lecture-courses on Nietzsche that inspired all of the engagements with Nietzsche after WWII. What I want to call to mind at this moment before we will discuss it in more detail in the following subchapter, is the Heideggerian criticism of Nietzsche's inversion of Platonism on the one hand, and his interpretation of the late Nietzsche as »a twisting free of it« on the other hand (Heidegger 1991a, Vol. I: 202). Heidegger's interpretation of Nietzsche became the starting point of a renewed interest in the most radical Nietzschean concepts such as the *will to power* and the *eternal return* that also became the major focus of Deleuze's Nietzsche. For Heidegger's extended interpretation of the inversion of Platonism in Nietzsche, cf. Heidegger 1991: 200ff, and for his acknowledgement of the late Nietzsche, cf. Heidegger 1991b, Vol. III, esp. part I. For a very helpful discussion of the apparent »double-bind« in Nietzsche, and the different ways in which it is read by Heidegger and Deleuze, cf. Bell 1995.

9 »For Nietzsche, it is about getting something through in every past, pre-

1. Pluralism vs. Metaphysics

While we understand that, for Deleuze, Nietzsche is the first true *actualization* of a radical thought of immanence, we must not forget what happened in our last chapter when we spoke of the Bergsonian influence on Deleuze. In looking back we must note that however unknown the lineage remained to the two authors themselves, Nietzsche and Bergson share what could be called a similar universe of thought—they both develop the same stand in and towards *cosmology*, a concern so alien to the contemporary philosophical business of their own time. And the reason for positioning Bergson chronologically *before* Nietzsche in our discussion lies precisely in Deleuze's obvious choice to read Nietzsche's aphoristic philosophy again through the lenses of Bergsonian systematicity. Before we thus enter into the specifically Nietzschean turn of Deleuze's thought—the *(im)personal actualization* of a thought of immanence that thinks immanence only in itself and thus commits itself to a world of difference, nothing but differentiation—let us clarify Nietzsche's ontological or meta-physical plane in relation to what we have already learned from (Deleuze's) Bergson, who in his work put so much emphasis on developing a differential mode of thinking the world.

Nietzsche's Double-Bind

Forcefully rejecting all philosophical urgency towards metaphysics and ontology in what he explicitly says, Nietzsche nonetheless remains deeply committed to these high philosophical endeavors. However strong the denunciation of Platonism we already spoke of above, or his refutation of »Darwinism«, not to speak of the contempt he felt towards Christianity as the majoritarian value system, Nietzsche, in fact in a very ›timely‹ fashion, always contextualizes his thought philosophically, and he remains devoted to the big questions of philosophy. In his lectures on Nietzsche, Martin Heidegger states

---

sent, and future code, something which does not and will not let itself be recoded. Getting it through on a new body, inventing a body on which it can pass and flow: a body that would be ours, the body of Earth, the body of writing....« (Deleuze 2004d: 253)

this clearly, and he makes of this ambivalent relation that Nietzsche has towards the tradition of philosophy »the end of metaphysics, inasmuch as it reverts to the very commencement of Greek thought«, thus closing »the ring that is formed by the very course of inquiry into being as such and as a whole« (Heidegger 1991a, Vol. II: 199–200).

While it was precisely the take on Nietzsche that Heidegger developed in his lecture series of the 1940s that initiated a new interest in the philosopher, it is the insinuation of a ›new philosophical beginning‹ after Nietzsche in the Heideggerian turn, exemplified in the expression ›the end of metaphysics‹, that became the critical issue for the generation that followed after the Second World War. In contrast to the emphasis on metaphysics coming to an end or completion with Nietzsche, Deleuze as one of these ›followers‹ was concerned above all to bring to mind the infinite *productivity* in Nietzsche's thought, a productivity beyond beginning and end that manages to *endure* and to *affirm* the philosophical double bind, and thus alters how we think of ontology or metaphysics itself.[10] According to Deleuze, Nietzsche does not fulfill the logic of the One by completing the circle and returning to its origin, as is claimed by Heidegger, who thus justifies his criticism of Nietzsche as leaving us philosophically with no way out (cf. Heidegger 1991, Vol. II: 200ff). To the contrary, in his radicalization of the Kantian critical philosophy Nietzsche is not after any ultimate solution *beyond* metaphysics and by that fulfilling this very metaphysical — onto-theological — endeavor. Rather, in criticizing without any hope of redemption, Nietzsche pushes thought to such a degree that what is created by this pressure is a new productive logic able to overcome the classical philosophical double-bind notion of ›reversal‹ based on a logic of ›either/or‹. His thought moves, as we will see in the following, towards a serial logic — a logic of ›both/and‹.[11] Nietzsche (and according to Deleuze this is very similar

---

10 For Deleuze, Nietzsche, thus, joins the ›other‹ philosophical family that engages us throughout this project; and it is in this divergent interpretation or ›philosophical usage‹ of Nietzsche that we can see Deleuze originate his criticism of Heidegger, whose own relative silence about Spinoza also tells something, and whose criticisms of Bergson Deleuze would throw back at his own thought of *Being and Time*.

11 That the critique of metaphysics fails because such a critique presupposes already concepts and argumentative strategies that are at the heart of the metaphysical tradition is no new criticism fired at attempts such as Nietzsche's

in the case of Bergson) thinks philosophy no longer in the vertical terms of metaphysics but rather as a ›flat‹ or horizontal pluralism that lives through dynamisms rather than static systems. This is why in *Nietzsche and Philosophy* Deleuze points us to a hidden relationship between Bergson and Nietzsche:

> Nietzsche's philosophy cannot be understood without taking his essential pluralism into account. And, in fact, *pluralism* (otherwise known as *empiricism*) is almost indistinguishable from philosophy itself. Pluralism is the properly philosophical way of thinking, the one invented by philosophy; the only guarantor of freedom in the concrete spirit, the only principle of a violent atheism. (NP: 4, my emphasis)

Without forcing this relation too much, turning to the posthumously published fragments from 1881 that accompany Nietzsche's writing of *The Gay Science*, the resonance of a ›virtual Bergsonism‹ in Nietzsche (if such untimeliness is allowed for a moment) is irresistible.

> Unsere Sinne zeigen uns nie ein Nebeneinander sondern stets ein Nacheinander. Der Raum und die menschlichen Gesetze des Raums setzen die Realität von Bildern Formen Substanzen und deren Dauerhaftigkeit voraus, d.h. unser Raum gilt einer imaginären Welt. Vom Raum, der zum ewigen Fluß der Dinge gehört, wissen wir nichts. (KSA 9: 11 #155)[12]

---

or today's post-structuralism. However, as Bell in his article on the question of »philosophizing the double-bind« argues, »[a]lthough the critique of metaphysics, at least with Nietzsche, does claim to be reversing the tradition of metaphysics since Plato, what is being criticized or reversed is, we will show, the notion of reversal itself. What is therefore being criticized is the very premise upon which [the] critical strategy acquires its force — in particular, the faith in oppositions, or the logic of either/or, whereby either one opposes and reverses the tradition completely, or they remain stuck in this tradition« (Bell 1995: 371). For a more detailed discussion of the Kant-Nietzsche connection that Deleuze establishes via their equal concern for *critique* as philosophy proper, see *Nietzsche and Philosophy*, esp. chapter 3. The issue of thought as critique will also be taken up again in chapter V.

12 The complete Colli and Montinari edition of Nietzsche's work is not available in English. Only a very small part of the *Nachlaß* that has not been included into Kaufmann's *The Will To Power*, which offers a selection from Nietzsche's

Such *critical* diagnosis of ›our‹—that is, the intellectual—way of thinking (the world), which after our discussion of Spinoza and Bergson we feel already quite familiar with, also finds expression in *The Gay Science*. This time, however, it explicitly shows the peculiar Nietzschean twist—a form of *imperative* driving all of Nietzsche's thought and distinguishing this thinker from everybody else:

> *Let us beware.*—Let us beware of thinking that the world is a living being. Where would it stretch? What would it feed on? How could it grow and procreate?... Let us beware even in believing that the universe is a machine; it is certainly not constructed to an end, and the word ›machine‹ pays it far too high an honour.... Let us beware of attributing to [the universe] heartlessness or unreason or their opposites: it is neither perfect, nor beautiful, nor noble, nor does it want to become any of these things; in no way does it strive to imitate man!... Let us beware of saying that there are laws in nature. There are only necessities: there is no one who commands, no one who obeys, no one who transgresses. Once you know that there are no purposes, you also know that there is no accident; for only against a world of purposes does the word ›accident‹ have a meaning. Let us beware of saying that death is opposed to life. The living is only a form of what is dead, and a very rare form.... But when will we be done with our caution and care? When will all these shadows of god no longer darken us? When will we have completely de-deified nature? When may we begin to *naturalize* humanity with a pure, newly discovered, newly redeemed nature? (GS #109)

Comparable to Bergson's philosophy of the virtual that does not speak for or lead into a new essentialism of what the world truly ›is‹ but to the very contrary develops a most provocative way of thinking radical immanence—constructivism—for Nietzsche, according to Deleuze, »[t]he whole of philosophy is a symptomatology« (NP: 3). Instead of taking phenomena as mere appearances covering a deeper essence which itself remains unchangeable and unreachable (the idea(l) in the Platonic sense); instead, thus, of again dividing

---

notebooks of the years 1883–1888, has been published in a systematic English translation. Wherever this is the case, I cited from the original German edition of the *Kritische Studienausgabe* (KSA) followed by the volume, section, and number of aphorism.

the world into two realms, one of which is transcendental essence, the other its merely mundane *re*presentation, for Nietzsche everything—every thing—is always already *interpretation*:

> That things possess a constitution in themselves quite apart from interpretation and subjectivity, is a quite idle hypothesis: it presupposes that interpretation and subjectivity are not essential, that a thing freed from all relationships would still be a thing. (WTP #560)

The World as Interpretation

Rejecting all eternal guarantees—the notions of one given truth and a pre-given world included—everything exists or comes into existence only by appropriation; every thing is a question of force and possession. No longer the question ›what is it?‹, but its re-formulation into ›which one wants it‹ is Nietzsche's concern. His most general project, Deleuze writes, is »the introduction of the concepts of sense and value into philosophy« (NP: 1), which together make up what was just called interpretation. With the notion of sense, primal plurality is inscribed into every thing.[13] With the notion of value, however, and this is the crucial twist that distinguishes Nietzsche from the authors of our preceding chapters, this plurality itself becomes differentiated: although everything *is* interpretation, and this means that everything *must be* and will remain a contingent and always ›subjective‹ construction, there is still the question of *how* to interpret, of *how* to evaluate. To formulate it in even more Nietzschean terms, what remains to be dealt with is the question of *will* and what it means ›to will‹![14] Before we, however, elaborate on this crucial question of the Nietzschean will, which shall enable us to introduce a *critical* force into thinking itself, let me first come back to the Bergsonian universe

---

13 »There is no event, no phenomenon, word or thought which does not have a multiple sense. A thing is sometimes this, sometimes that, sometimes something more complicated—depending on the forces… which take possession of it.« (NP: 4)

14 »In fact, the notion of value implies a *critical* reversal… The problem of critique is that of the value of values, of the evaluation from which their values arises, thus the problem of their *creation*… Evaluations, in essence, are not values but ways of being, modes of existence…« (NP: 1)

one more time in order to provide the adequate framework for our argument.

We have to emphasize that in our discussion of Deleuze's Bergsonism we have inquired into a new mode of thinking. This path has led us into the thought of intuition as the Bergsonian method for a philosophy that avoids those »baggy clothes« of the One in general, as we have called it; it thus has led us into a mode of thinking which defines thought as an act or leap into the unknown rather than just the ever better definitional approaching of what is already known. According to Bergson, thought understood as act or leap is to be affirmed as the properly philosophical ›culture‹, as distinguished from the scientific model of thought, which always approaches the object by turning it into something *useful*, something always already useful ›to us‹. Intuition, a way of thinking that truly makes a difference (method of differentiation), de-centering the anthropomorphic image of the world (›beyond‹ the human turn), and, thus, opening up new possibilities for both thinking and acting, does not take its leave from the ready-made thing, taking it for granted as given. Rather, it approaches the supposed ›givenness‹ as a composite of which the true task for thinking is to find the constitutive internal lines that lead up to it. This methodological discussion provided us with the *real* possibility of a thought of substance as a One of multiplicity—the One as virtual—making understood, in a step after Spinoza himself, Deleuze's own very dynamic Spinozism.

Something comparable to the thought of substance is now happening in Nietzsche's approach to the question of thinking itself and, thus, to the way thought and what is to be thought relate to each other. For Nietzsche, thinking, adequately understood, is always and out of necessity an *act of creation*. As we have just heard above, nothing ever has but one meaning or sense. Instead of being a question of finding the (given) truth, thinking is a question of interpretation and evaluation. In as much as Bergson's superior empiricism, Nietzsche's pluralism is, however, no simple trick to avoid the serious issues at stake in philosophy. Rather, as Deleuze points out,

> [t]he pluralist idea that a thing has many senses, the idea that there are many things and one thing can be seen as ›this and then that‹ is philosophy's greatest achievement, the conquest of the true concept, its maturity and not its renunciation and infancy (NP: 4).

Instead of looking at a thing as it is ›for us‹, a serene philosophical thought has to ask from where and how it became what it is now, in as much as it has to ask how it can become something else.[15] For Nietzsche, essence is not something eternally given. Essence is that which amongst all the senses of a thing gives this thing »the force with which it has the most affinity« (ibid), as Deleuze says. According to such logic of forces, thinghood (*Dingheit*) is not something simple. It is always already a composition and production, and this means it is a temporarily settled struggle between ›at least two‹ forces. The question of what a body ›is‹ finds its answer in a relation, a relation of dominating and dominated forces. In this sense Nietzsche both revives Spinoza's question of ›what a body can do‹ and Bergson's understanding of substance as *nuance*, as *movement* itself. Being never ›is‹ simply One, but always more than this: it is ›at least two‹, and thus a relation substituting theoretical atomism with a thought of and as movement itself. In as much as this formula of thought as movement unites in particular Bergson with Nietzsche, for the latter — and this might be one of the greatest differences to Bergson's way of thinking — the question of force, of appropriation, and of taking possession of the world, does not just begin with *our* intellect. In his push ›beyond the human condition‹, Nietzsche instead describes all of life as *will to power*.[16]

> Here we must think things through thoroughly, and ward off any sentimental weakness: life itself is *essentially* a process of appropriation, injuring, overpowering the alien and the weaker, oppressing, being

---

15 Genealogy, Nietzsche's ›method‹ of thinking, is a question of both critique (referring all things back to values) and creation (giving birth; genealogy as ›new‹ origin). »The differential element is both a critique of the value of values and the positive element of a creation.« (NP: 2) It is this deconstruction of ›origin‹ as ›what a thing *is*‹ that makes genealogy the method of a pluralist philosophy.

16 »The will to power is, for Nietzsche, the only drive, the very drive governing not only all organic life, but all of matter as well.« (Grosz 2004: 125) While we will come back to the concept of will to power later on, that which *drives* life in Nietzsche is — to emphasize it again — the movement (of life) itself, understood in the way that our discussion tries to develop throughout as that which only *becomes* in the encounter of differential elements (Bergson) or forces (Nietzsche), a becoming that defies every logic of being, be it one of essences, presences, or visibilities.

harsh, imposing your own form, incorporating, and at least, the very least, exploiting—but what is the point of always using words that have been stamped with slanderous intentions from time immemorial? (BGE #259)

In contrast to the claim of mere self-preservation,[17] which he finds both in Schopenhauer's will-to-live, Spinoza's *conatus*, and the Darwinian survival of the fittest, life, according to Nietzsche, must in a double sense be something more pronounced.[18] If life or living would

---

17 »Physiologists should think twice before positioning the drive for self-preservation as the cardinal drive of an organic being. Above all, a living thing wants to *discharge* its strength—life itself is will to power —: self-preservation is only one of the indirect and most frequent *consequences* of this.—In short, here as elsewhere, watch out for *superfluous* teleological principles!—such as the drive for preservation (which we owe to Spinoza's inconsistency —).« (BGE I #13)

18 Cf. with regard to Schopenhauer: »Only where life is, is there also will; but not will to life, instead, thus I teach you—the will to power!« (Z ›On Self-Overcoming‹).

In our discussion of Spinoza, we have not touched on his concept of self-preservation or *conatus*. However, while Nietzsche's interpretation of the *conatus* is extremely critical, the fact that Deleuze sees in the Nietzschean *will to power* »a Spinozist inspiration« (NP: 62), and thus disagrees in this point with Nietzsche himself is not all too surprising to us. After our discussion of *Deleuze's Spinoza* we sense what this ›body‹ of work is capable of, having created an encounter in which the latter becomes the true predecessor of Nietzsche's thought, even if the *conatus* as the drive that governs life can only function as the starting point for Nietzsche's *will to power*.

Contemporary to Nietzsche and, thus, his most prominent socio-political and philosophical enemy during his lifetime is Darwinism. There are innumerable passages written against this ›English narrow mindedness‹. One of those passages shall be quoted here in its entirety as it shows in detail Nietzsche's razor sharp (mis)reading both of the Spinozist and the Darwinian tradition: »*Once again, the origin of the scholars*.—To wish to preserve oneself is a sign of distress, of a limitation of the truly basic life instinct, which aims at *the expansion of power* and in so doing often enough risks and sacrifices self-preservation. It is symptomatic that certain philosophers, such as the consumptive Spinoza, too and indeed had to take just the so-called self-preservation instinct to be decisive:—they were simply people in distress. That today's natural sciences have become so entangled with the Spinozistic dogma (most recently and crudely in Darwinism with its incredible one-sided doctrine of the ›struggle of existence‹—) is probably due to the descent of most natural scientists: in this regard they belong to ›the people‹, their ancestors were poor and lowly folks who knew all too intimately the difficulty of scraping by. English Darwinism

simply be a question of self-preservation, of merely staying alive no matter how, a thought of life that according to Nietzsche's perspective even Spinoza — his only equal — seems to share, the question that has to be posed is how and why differentiation — difference as the main force in life — could and should be possible at all. How life itself could ever become a question of difference — that is, a question of ›making a difference‹ — is, thus, the fundamental question of Nietzsche's way of thinking.

Life = Will to Power

The Nietzschean formula, life = will to power, that we will have to explore in more detail in what follows, not only stresses the essential dynamism that we already see with Spinoza and Bergson. It also — and this is extremely important for an understanding of Deleuze's work as a work concerned with *this* world — links this foundational dynamism in a most radical way to the question of *value* so that »to differ« (must) become(s) more than mere theoretical description or practical relativism.

> What are our evaluations and moral tables really worth? What is the outcome of their rule? For whom? in relation to what? — Answer: for life. But *what is life*? Here we need a new, more definite formulation of the concept ›life‹. My formula for it is: Life is will to power. (WTP #254)

---

exudes something like the stuffy air of English overpopulation, like the small people's smell of indigence and overcrowding. As a natural scientist, however, one should get out of one's human corner; and in nature, it is not distress which *rules*, but rather abundance, squandering — even to the point of absurdity. The struggle for survival is only an *exception*, a temporary restriction of the will to life; the great and small struggle revolves everywhere around preponderance, around growth and expansion, around power and in accordance with the will to power, which is simply the will to life.« (GS #349) It seems obvious that Nietzsche calls himself an ›Anti-Darwinian‹ because he wants to radically delimit himself from what became of Darwinism after Darwin, whom he may not even have read personally. Recent commentaries on both Nietzsche and Darwin suggest that Nietzsche might be read most productively as precisely a *philosophical* response to the *scientist* Darwin. For a helpful elaboration on the dispute and discussion of the complex relation between Nietzsche and Darwin/Darwinism, cf. Pearson 1997 and Grosz 2004: 95ff.

To believe that it is a universal or general will to live, the will to survival driving the living, mistakes even the most basic processes in and of life. Instead of such indistinguishable sameness, when it comes to the matter of life and living, the process of living is much more pronounced in its expression: »Wille zum Leben? Ich fand an seiner Stelle immer nur Wille zur Macht« (KSA 10: 5 #1), Nietzsche says. And while he acknowledges Schopenhauer's will-to-live as a »sehr glückliche[n] Fund... wir wollen diesen Ausdruck uns nicht wieder nehmen lassen und seinem Urheber dafür im Namen der deutschen Sprache dankbar sein«, he absolutely refutes that what life is about is »Dasein um jeden Preis« (KSA 8: 23 #12).

Neither Spinoza's *conatus*, Schopenhauer's will-to-live, nor Darwin's struggle for existence, thus, reach far enough in the most necessary reformulation of the concept of life. Life taken seriously, that is in Deleuze's reading *becoming a life...* as the expression of difference in itself and as that which makes a difference (how and why should we otherwise be aware of it?), cannot be just mere survival or static existence of a form of being. *A life...* only ever truly ›is‹ in differing. It is proliferation and excess; first of all out of necessity—all ›there is‹ is difference—but also in order to truly become what it is (in the sense of Nietzsche's *Ecce Homo. How One Becomes What One Is*). *A life...* in this sense always is (in) a process of becoming-more—a becoming-something-else.[19] In contrast to what so often is made of the concept of the will to power in misleading interpretations of Nietzsche, in a moment we will discuss the will to power as precisely this *differential element* in and of life. Before we do this, however, it is essential to realize that with this thought Nietzsche opens a perspective on life understood as a process that must always be and remain *a becoming....* Life as this process of becoming can never be defined *a priori*. Neither what nor why it is. The only thing that can be said of it *a priori* is that it cannot be determined in advance. There is no final ›what‹ to which becoming *should* become. The recurrent emphasis in Nietzsche's work on the interrelation of chaos and order in life is precisely this: the emphasis that »one must still have chaos

---

19 »Life is not about mere survival, but about profusion and proliferation, not existence but excess, not being but becoming-more, that is, becoming, but a becoming-what that cannot be determined in advance, that is always itself in the process of becoming-something-else.« (Grosz, 2004: 104)

in oneself to be able to give birth to a dancing star« (Z ›Zarathustra's Prologue‹). The process of life as will to power is thus this process in which we are »to impose upon chaos as much regularity and form as our practical needs require« (WTP #515). What for Nietzsche is at stake here is not a mere ›more‹ or a simple ›something else‹ in any additive sense (a movement that remains so dependent on a logic of parts and Whole — the latter being finite or infinite). Such would only underscore a thinking of life as mere survival. For Nietzsche, the only ›more‹ that really makes a difference is a ›more‹ of intensity and of variation, a ›more‹ as multiplication that comes about through the process of differentiation itself. It is a ›more‹ that is restricted by nothing but immanence itself — category of pure intensity. Instead of fixing life to ›what it is‹ and to ›what is‹, instead of anthropomorphizing life in the way expressed in his warning »*Let us beware.* —«, Nietzsche's imperative is: »To impose upon becoming the character of being — that is the supreme will to power« (WTP #617).

2. Force vs. Subject

But we have to be careful not to misunderstand the will to power in too simple a sense. In asking ›what the will to power is‹, we probably fall already into one of Nietzsche's various philosophical traps and are in danger of missing what is productive about this thought. As soon as we ask ›what something is‹, in our striving for the essence of what is under investigation, we smuggle in the subject/object divide that is based on an image of thought starting from some-thing given — an approach whose shortcomings we have discussed in detail in our previous chapters. And yet, after having re-constructed Spinoza's substance as self-expressive multiplicity, which becomes self-differentiating tendency in Bergson's philosophy of the virtual, we must still tackle the difficult question of how to adequately understand the ontological force of the formula ›life = will to power‹. In order not to fall prey to the conceptual impasse, we have to learn to think life no longer according to the mere *extensive* coordinates of time and space, such as Kant suggested, but think it also in an *intensive* way — the concept of the will to power as *intensive* category. This will then lead to a different understanding of what *a life…* means.

First of all, we thus have to strip the concept of will from any supposedly Subjective agency that the recurrent ›self-› even in the above mentioned serialization might still suggest. If we look to Nietzsche directly, we see that his response to the question »Aber wer will Macht?« is the assertion, »Absurde Frage: wenn das Wesen selbst Machtwille... ist« (KSA 13: 14 #80). Instead of asking the personified question of who wants power, we must learn to think on the level of force—impersonal force to be precise. We must dare a way of thinking that—if we succeed in our presentation—will not lead to the extinction of all agency, not even of the subject itself, but to their radical reformulation.

Heidegger's Nietzsche

It has long been recognized that Nietzsche's thought emphasizes the importance of force—»at least since Heidegger« as Jeffrey Bell points out in »Philosophizing the Double-Bind« (Bell 1995: 373). In his lectures on Nietzsche Heidegger re-writes »Life is will to power« as »[w]hat is the *pervasive character* of the world? The answer is: ›*force*‹« (Heidegger 1991a, Vol. II: 86). He, thus, develops an interpretation of Nietzsche that acknowledges the impersonality of the latter's thought, a thought that refuses to blindly believe in the necessity of a Subject *prior to* and *behind* the will, and instead asserts only a will ever producing subjectivity. At the very beginning of his discussion, Heidegger clarifies this point of view, which is fundamental to an adequate understanding of Nietzsche's thought of will to power:

> According to the usual view, will is taken to be a faculty of the soul. What will is may be determined from the essence of the psyche. The latter is dealt with in psychology....Now, if in Nietzsche's view will determines Being of every sort of being, then it does not pertain to the psyche; rather, the psyche somehow pertains to the will. But body and mind too are will, inasmuch as things ›are‹. (Heidegger 1991a, Vol. I: 37–38)

In the section ›What is the Will to Power?‹ of *Nietzsche and Philosophy*, Deleuze also emphasizes the will to power »as ascribed to force« (NP: 49).[20] Both Heidegger and Deleuze, therefore, agree that

---

20 In his interpretation of the concept of will to power, Deleuze still works

whenever we speak of the will to power, willing is not ascribed to a subject, even less so to a Subject, one that possesses a desire for (more) power. »Every time«, Deleuze says, »we interpret will to power as ›wanting or seeking power‹ we encounter platitudes which have nothing to do with Nietzsche's thought« (NP: xi). The will to power is, as Grosz also explicates,

> before, under, and beyond any self, sense of agency, or subjective intention. It is not the desire of a subject directed to an object, but a force directed only to its own expansion, for which objects take on the function of enabling or opposing forces (Grosz 2004: 126).

Nietzsche's will to power is not related to a Subject as a form of being, but always to forces that *become.*[21] Instead, of referring us to the world of persons and things, the will to power must be understood as the *impersonal* drive, that which first of all *structures* this — visible or present — world.[22] This is how we need to understand Nietzsche's

---

with a version of Nietzsche's writings known in the English translation as *Will To Power*. It is Walter Kaufmann's translation and edition of Nietzsche's unpublished notes from the 1880s. This edition is understood as a more authentic version than the infamous edition Nietzsche's sister Elisabeth Förster published in 1901/1906 under the very same title. However, while — as the new critical Nietzsche edition initiated by Colli and Montinari shows — the aphorism in question in the original German version reads: »Der siegreiche Begriff ›Kraft‹, mit dem unsere Physiker Gott und die Welt geschaffen haben, bedarf noch einer Ergänzung: es muß ihm eine *innere Welt* zugesprochen werden, welche ich bezeichne als ›Willen zur Macht‹« (KSA 11: 36 #31, my emphasis), Deleuze still speaks of the *inner will* that must be ascribed to force, instead of the inner world of which the original actually speaks. Without disregarding this mistranslation, the correction of which is one of the many merits of the new critical Nietzsche edition, Stefan Günzel's argument in »Wille zur Differenz. Gilles Deleuzes Nietzsche-Lektüre« in regard to this occurrence seems too strong to me. He seems to employ this fact in order to point to a weakness of the interpretation of Nietzsche's will to power that Deleuze provides in *Nietzsche and Philosophy* (Günzel 2002). Deleuze's understanding of the will to power as distinguishable and yet inseparable from the notion of force does, however, in no sense depend on these two words and precisely draw attention to the non-identity of force and will.

21 »Nietzsche's concept of force is therefore that of a force which is related to another force: in this form force is called will.« (NP: 7)

22 »Nietzsche's provocation to philosophy is his contention that the will to power is the underlying explanation of the world, of those who live in that

claim that »there is no ›being‹ behind doing, its effect and what becomes of it: ›the doer‹ is invented as an after-thought — the doing is everything« (GM: 1 #13). Not simply the negation of a willing Subject, the taking away of all conscious acts, but the staging of a different order of thought altogether: beginning from somewhere else, and moving beyond the human condition towards »*the inhuman* that makes the human possible and at the same time positions the human in a world where force works in spite of and around the human, within and as the human« (Grosz 2004: 130). Therefore, while with regard to the question of the inseparability of force and will to power Deleuze finds himself in the rare situation of agreeing with Heidegger, and in my opinion can be even said to rely on his earlier interpretation, there is a further differentiation that Deleuze introduces, which leads him to a different conclusion with regard to Nietzsche than the one chosen by his predecessor.

When Heidegger writes that the will to power as the universal character of the world is force, the notion of force is substituted for the will to power; both are taken as interchangeable. According to Deleuze, however, such equalization is misleading, and his indebtedness to Heidegger, thus, ends at this point. One must be more careful, Deleuze says, since »[i]nseparable does not mean identical« (NP: 50). Heidegger's paraphrasing jumps to conclusions too quickly and provides too easy a solution to the Nietzschean riddle of the relation between his logic of forces and the will to power. The distinction between force and will to power, a distinction that might better be called a *differentiation*, cannot be reduced to one of mere terminology — and this precisely in order not to misunderstand the concept of the will to power as yet another some-thing (logic of Being) or, even worse, as something else (analogy). Although Deleuze ascribes the will to power to force, this is so »in a very special way«, he says and continues: »[the will to power] is both a complement of force and something internal to it« (NP: 49). Agreeing that »[t]he will to power cannot be separated from force without falling into metaphysical abstraction«, Deleuze significantly adds that »to confuse force and will is even more risky« (NP: 50).

---

world, and of philosophy itself.« (Grosz 2004: 134)

Where lies the significance of this warning? In my opinion it consists in the following: Deleuze — again — demands that we should not confuse different levels. The difference in kind between forces — actualizations of active and reactive, dominating and dominated qualities — must not be misunderstood as being the same as their internal »principle«, that is, as the primordial will to power itself.

> It is therefore essential to insist on the terms used by Nietzsche; *active* and *reactive* designate the original qualities of force but *affirmative* and *negative* designate the primordial qualities of the will to power... This distinction between two kinds of quality is of the greatest importance and it is always found at the center of Nietzsche's philosophy. There is a deep affinity, a complicity, but never a confusion, between action and affirmation, between reaction and negation. (NP: 54)

In order not to *subjectify* (in the ambivalent sense of the term) the logic of forces itself — this is Heidegger's mistake — but to escape such limitation, it is important to listen carefully to Nietzsche and to recognize that although the will to power is inseparably related to the notion of force, the two are in no way the same. Deleuze, in his early engagement with Nietzsche in 1962, is probably the first of a generation of Nietzsche-readers who cautiously differentiate here, a differentiation of course that for Deleuze's own thought is most relevant, underscoring once more the difference between a thought still caught up in the split of Being/being and a rigorous thought of becoming. Appropriating the Nietzschean question of the will to power, which Deleuze phrases as ›which one?‹ (avoiding a ›who‹, i.e. the subjectification of this very question), he writes: »[W]e cannot say that force is *the one that* wills. The will to power alone is the one that wills; it does not let itself be delegated or alienated to another subject, even to force.« (NP: 49)[23] While forces certainly ›are‹ in the sense that they directly confront each other, or as Deleuze says,

---

23 That Deleuze is right in stressing absolute depersonalization is shown by the following reference to one of Nietzsche's notes regarding the will to power from 1885/86, which even provides us again with the link between the notions of interpretation, i.e. *valuation*, and this will: »One may not ask: ›who then interprets?‹ for the interpretation itself is a form of the will to power, exists (but not as a ›being‹ but as a process, a becoming) as an affect.« (WTP #556)

»[t]he concept of force is, by nature, *victorious* because the relation of force to force, understood conceptually, is one of domination« (NP: 51), the drive that governs all life, that ›is‹ life, is not another subject, another ›what‹ — a presence to be represented — but rather is *movement* itself, a movement that *inheres* and *subsists* within forces and that cannot even be ascribed to the struggling forces themselves, for this would already be the confusion of being and becoming. Referring to Heideggerian ontology as a philosophy of power, Deleuze states, »[f]orce is what *can*, will to power is what wills (*La force est ce qui peut, la volonté de puissance est ce qui veut*)« (NP: 50, my emphasis).[24]

The Practical Element of Difference

In his definition of the will to power, Deleuze stresses the non-confusion of essences and calls the will to power »*the element from which derive both the quantitative difference of related forces and the quality that devolves into each force in this relation*« (NP: 50). The will to power is no will or desire in any of the traditional senses. Rather it is the differential and thus invisibly moving element that drives or structures everything without ever being »present in the strict sense«, because it will only ever *become* in this process. In contrast to the counter-posing forces or series themselves, it is *complementary*, as Deleuze says, the complement that »this victorious concept of force needs,... and this complement is *internal*« (51). It is internal in the sense that it only ever ›is‹ — inheres or subsists rather than exists — in-between, in the very middle or inherent to the relation of forces that encounter each other. The will to power, understood in this way, is thus again (and similar to Deleuze's understanding of Bergson's *élan vital*) the non-identifiable — singular — element that, instead of moving beyond or outside the encounter (and always being directed towards a transcendental idea(l)), is »an essentially *plastic* principle that is no wider than what it conditions, that changes itself with the conditioned and determines itself in each case along

---

24 It seems as if Deleuze implicitly refers us to Levinas who so convincingly claims that (Heidegger's) »[o]ntology as first philosophy is a philosophy of power« that comes down to the »I can — to an appropriation of what is, to an exploitation of reality« (Levinas 2000: 46).

with what it determines« (50).[25] Deleuze here describes the same superior empiricism that »reconciles empiricism with principles« (ibid) which he already has found in Bergson: a new mode of thinking—of the *mapping* and *creation* of the world—that affects both the ontological and the practical dimensions of thought. When we here claim a privileged position for Nietzsche—although for Deleuze *the* thinker of a superior empiricism is Bergson—we do this out of no other reason than that only in Nietzsche is the emphasis so clearly put on »the practical element of *difference*«, as Deleuze says (NP: 9), which for our purpose is of course of major significance. Because Nietzsche pushes the practical, the actively transformative side of difference in an unsurpassed way, Deleuze calls him »in this sense« an empiricist (ibid). That such a first conclusion is in no way exaggerated exemplifies the following citation from Nietzsche's unpublished notes from 1885, coining a philosophical tone that no other thinker had expressed before him:

> And do you know what ›the world‹ is to me?... This world: a monster of energy, without beginning, without end; a firm, iron magnitude of force that does not grow bigger or smaller, that does not expend itself but only transforms itself; as a whole, of unalterable size, a household without expenses or losses, but likewise without increase or income;... not something endlessly extended, but set in a definite space as a definite force, and not a space that might be ›empty‹ here or there, but rather as force throughout, as a play of forces and waves of forces, at the same time one and many, increasing here and at the same time decreasing there; a sea of forces, flowing and rushing together, eternally changing, eternally flooding back, with tremendous years of recurrence, with an ebb and a flood of its forms... this, my *Dionysian* world of the eternally self-creating, the eternally self-destroying, this mystery world of the twofold voluptuous delight, my ›beyond good and evil‹, without goal, unless the joy of the circle is itself a goal; without will, unless a ring feels good will towards itself—do you want a *name* for this world? A *solution* for all the riddles? A *light* for you, too, you best-concealed, strongest most intrepid, most midnightly men?—*This world is the will*

25 Cf. also Jeffrey Bell in »Philosophizing the Double-bind« where he develops such an understanding of Deleuze's reading of Nietzsche's will to power (Bell 1995).

to power—and nothing besides! And you yourselves are also this will to power—and nothing besides. (WTP #1067)

Immanent Creation

The extraordinary mixture thus expressed of both a new mode of thinking ›the world‹ and of actualizing it in a new way as will to power completes the difficult collection of the *Will To Power*. It brings together the conceptualization of the world as force-relations and the plastic principle driving and only ever becoming in this process. We are able to *see* Nietzsche's ›world of will‹, of order *and* chaos, as *a becoming...*, a world that must remain ›false‹, because it is but an *act* of interpretation. An interpretation, however, which instead of merely representing ›what is‹ necessarily *produces*, *creates*, and *maps* this world in a new and different sense. It does so without concealing its necessary relatedness to what has already happened. There is no creation *ex nihilo* in Nietzsche's thought. Such could not be further from this thinker of radical immanence.[26] And it is because of this immanent thought of the new, without the need to claim such ›creation‹ as absolute, i.e. as stirred by *nothing*, that it comes of no surprise that in his *Untimely Meditations* Nietzsche demands precisely contact with and examination of or debate about history, if we do not want to succumb to ›what there is‹. In »On the Uses and Disadvantages of History for Life«, the second essay of the *Meditations*, Nietzsche develops his thought of untimeliness precisely as a *critical* analysis of and attitude towards a world capable of generating something new. And as Elizabeth Grosz in her discussion of Nietzsche elaborates, this is what ›unfashionable‹—the older translation of Nietzsche's *unzeit-*

---

26 A creation *ex nihilo* always implies the however shadowy existence of transcendence serving as the legitimate measure of such a creation. This stands in complete opposition to the Nietzschean, and also to the Deleuzian endeavor, which begins precisely with the active affirmation of the death of God—every God, as we have heard above, including the deification of the Human. With regard to what the emphasis on creation for Nietzsche means, the following quote from Deleuze is helpful: »The world is neither true nor real but living. And the living world is will to power, *will to falsehood*, which is actualized in many different powers... Being, truth and reality are themselves only valid as evaluations, that is to say as lies.« (NP: 184) The world understood provocatively as the production of lies claims ›artificiality‹, i.e. the active production of the world, as opposed to a thought of ›naturalness‹, against which Nietzsche forcefully argues throughout his work.

gemäß— means: »What history gives us is the possibility of being *untimely*, of placing ourselves outside the constraints, the limitation and blinkers of the present... There is a place for the ahistorical, the pure present« (Grosz 2004: 117). Nietzsche's thought asks from us to push the past—that which we cannot escape—in a new and different way »hopefully for the benefit of a future time«.[27] The practical disposition Nietzsche himself assumes towards thinking, towards the questions of what thinking is for and how true thought might be possible at all, is by now more than apparent. It is thought itself that changes the world: either thought makes a difference or it is nothing at all.

3. Repetition vs. Sameness

Since with Nietzsche it is always a question of value, of what thinking happens for at all, the question of how he himself becomes the thinker of the *active affirmation* of difference, rather than of its *reactive annihilation*—and it is for this reason that we can speak of Deleuze as a true Nietzschean—still needs to be investigated. And we cannot understand it by focusing our discussion purely on the one concept of the will to power. In order to truly grasp the particular emphasis Nietzsche gives to a thought of difference, an emphasis decisive for the relation of philosophy and ethics in which we are interested, we have to turn to the other of Nietzsche's two ›unbearable‹ philosophical concepts. This is the eternal return, which as the second axis of his thought (as the *doctrine* of the will to power as Deleuze calls it), differentiates this thought of becoming one more time. Taking seri-

---

27 Cited in Grosz 2004: 117. The notion of »*aternal*«, introduced by Deleuze and Guattari in *What is Philosophy?*, has to be read in a very similar way to that of *untimeliness*. Taking this notion from the nineteenth-century French writer Charles Péguy who created this concept for *adequately* thinking the event, the *aternal* »consists in reassembling the event installing oneself in it as in a becoming, becoming young again and aging in it, both at the same time... It may be that nothing changes or seems to change in history, but everything changes, and we change in the event« (WPH: 111). In their explanation, Deleuze and Guattari even refer to Nietzsche's *Untimeliness*: »Is this not something similar to that which a thinker far from Péguy designated the *Untimely* or *Inactual*—the unhistorical vapor that has nothing to do with the eternal, the becoming without which nothing would come about in history but that does not merge with history?« (WPH: 111–112).

ously what a radical thought of difference entails, we have to differentiate difference itself so that the conceptualization of the world as will to power and eternal recurrence does not succumb to the return of the self-same that would simplify Nietzsche's complex logic of repetition, but instead creates something new. Thus, instead of speaking of any (shortsighted) sameness, the teaching of the eternal return, in particular Nietzsche's *Zarathustra*, has to be understood as a *selective thought* of the return of (only) that which differs. Far from remaining stuck in the philosophical double-bind, the eternal return as the doctrine of the will to power provides ›a way out‹ by transforming the constraint of sameness through active affirmation (this is a question of willing in the most impersonal sense) into a question of difference. This leads us to a new expression of thought and life itself: the imperative ›to will—always and ever—becoming!‹

> Becoming active... presupposes the affinity of action and affirmation; in order to become active it is not sufficient for a force to go to the limit of what it can do, it must make what it can do an object of affirmation. Becoming-active is affirming and affirmative, just as becoming-reactive is negating and nihilistic. (NP: 68)

Eternal Return as the ›Being‹ of Becoming

Let me begin the discussion of the eternal return with the recapitulation of the relation of the will to power as the principle *creating* ›this‹ world, and the latter's image as eternal recurrence in the way Nietzsche himself has expressed it in the long quote from *The Will To Power* cited above. Deleuze, in his reading of this thought, calls it the »*First Aspect of the Eternal Return: as cosmological and physical doctrine*« (NP: 47).

Both the old Platonic horizon of an ideal world above the one we are living in and his contemporaries' pseudo-secularized physical belief (be it mechanist or finalist—ultimately, as we know from Bergson, the same orientation anyway) that the universe moves towards a final state of equilibrium, cannot but remain unconvincing for Nietzsche and his thought of force-relations. For Nietzsche, if such should be the case, why had the world not already reached this status in its long course of becoming?

> If the world had a goal, it must have been reached. If there were for it some unintended final state, this also must have been reached. If it were in any way capable of a pausing and becoming fixed, of ›being,‹ if in the whole course of its becoming it possessed even for a moment this capability of ›being,‹ then all becoming would long since have come to an end, along with all thinking, all ›spirit.‹ The fact of ›spirit‹ as a form of becoming proves that the world has no goal, no final state, and is incapable of being (WTP #1062).

Although a strange reminiscence of Hegel might irritate in this statement at first, it is Nietzsche's emphasis on the world's ›incapability of being‹ that is most significant, and from the start it defies all similarity to a Hegelian ›systematicity‹. There is no final state, no goal for this world but only ever *a becoming...* — eternal becoming.[28] Contrary to a world that ›is‹, and thus is eternally fixed, or a world developing towards an ultimate but always already pre-determined (eternal) Being, the world ›is‹ nothing but changing — eternally changing.

> ›Timelessness‹ must be rejected... ›Change‹ belongs to the essence, therefore also temporality: with this, however, the necessity of change has only been posited once more conceptually. (WTP #1064)

Life, according to Nietzsche, and we have seen this already in Bergson, is nothing but this ›essential change‹; it is ›enduring difference gnawing on matter‹ as Bergson has said. And Nietzsche's interest in

---

28 Without attempting to simplify the most complicated issues in philosophy, what will become clear in the following and should be stated right at the beginning of the discussion of the eternal return, is that Nietzsche's logic of the eternal return as eternal becoming does, according to Deleuze, in an active sense ›overcome‹ the metaphysical logic of Being and, thus, also Heidegger's so called post-metaphysical ›ontological difference‹, which — for Deleuze — falls short precisely when it comes to the question of immanence as thinking difference in itself. Heidegger, by keeping two separate ways of being — Being/being — eventually gathers Being, contrary to what in Deleuze is called ›becoming‹ as a thought of being belonging only to difference: »[D]oes [Heidegger] effectuate the conversion after which univocal Being belongs only to difference and, in this sense, revolves around being? Does he conceive of *being* in such a manner that it will be truly disengaged from any subordination in relation to the identity of representation? It would seem not, given his critique of the Nietzschean eternal return.« (DR: 66)

›us‹ as one figuration that life takes, as *a life…*, is none besides such a differential perspective. Either *a life…* is affirmation of difference, as we have already said, or it is nothing at all. Instead of being, we only have to think in terms of movement. There is no other ›being‹ of becoming but becoming itself; becoming ›is‹ eternal — impersonal, inhuman becoming working in spite of, within, and as the human, as Grosz expressed it in the passage we have cited before. Or as Deleuze says: »All we need to do to think this thought is to stop believing in being as distinct from and opposed to becoming or to believe in the being of becoming itself« (NP: 48). Again what is needed, is to ›flatten‹ the relation between eternal form and changing content, a flattening, as we by now know, that in no way eliminates the essential difference, i.e. differentiation as ›all there is‹. We ›are‹ nothing but *a becoming…*, as much as the world ›is‹ only ever as *becoming* — becoming as that which always differs from and in itself; a becoming, therefore, that is always already *un*becoming.[29]

And yet we are pressed to think the ›being‹ of this becoming — our language cannot but press for this question. It is the question of how to think difference as continual self-differentiation. And we have to find a different solution than the one both traditional ontology (Heidegger included) and all other philosophical attempts denying the ontological any value have found for it. Instead of searching for a thought that starts by avoiding the (im)possibility (or *aporia*) that is fundamental to the question of beginning and, thus, tries to eliminate it once and for all, Nietzsche's refusal to produce a final solution to it while criticizing and rejecting everything that has been said about it so far is not, as Heidegger would seem to have it, a proof of his belonging to the old metaphysical tradition — bringing it to its end. Rather, if we make use of Jacques Derrida's critique on Heidegger's reading of Nietzsche in *Of Grammatology*, in

---

29 In order to think becoming in a non-teleological and, thus, radically immanent way as that which emerges and remains *in-between* or ›in the middle‹ of an encounter of forces — relations which could always also be different — every becoming is unbecoming. Becoming and unbecoming must be thought as a figure of (un)becoming; only in this way the dynamism that is the most important character of this concept has a chance to survive within conceptual language. For a very helpful discussion of this notion of ›unbecoming‹ when everybody focuses mainly on ›becoming‹, cf. the special issue of *parallax* 2005.

> [r]adicalizing the concepts of *interpretation, perspective, evaluation, difference,* and all the ›empiricist‹ or nonphilosophical motifs that have constantly tormented philosophy throughout the history of the West,... Nietzsche, far from remaining *simply* (with Hegel and as Heidegger wished) *within* metaphysics, contributed a great deal to the liberation of the signifier from its dependence or derivation with respect to the logos and related concept of truth or the primary signified, in whatever sense that is understood (Derrida 1997: 19).

Instead of looking for a ›less naïve‹ ontology — Heidegger's project *after* Nietzsche — for Derrida as much as for Deleuze the problem must be transformed into a question of »*accentuating*« (ibid), or as Deleuze has said we simply have to »*stop believing* in being as distinct from and opposed to becoming« (NP: 48, my emphasis).[30]

What this means is not to mistake the logic of the eternal return as a ›solution‹ intended to resolve the problem of origin once and for all, but rather to take it as an enduring challenge of thought — the eternal as eternal becoming, that is, as eternal differing — with no beginning and end because becoming ›is‹ always only ›in the middle‹ and *in-between*, so that what returns can no longer be the self-same — becoming turned into being — but only that which differs — being of becoming. The already cited Fragment 617 of *The Will To Power*, often entitled *Recapitulation*, expresses precisely this:

---

30 This reference to the most important of Derrida's early works seems appropriate here, since it gives me the possibility to mention that Derrida and Deleuze in their early career seem to have a lot more in common — theoretically — than it feels to us today, after the immense attention deconstruction has achieved over the last decades, and after the direction Deleuze, too, has taken in his collaborations with Guattari. And yet, latently, the difference between Derrida's thought of differ*a*nce and Deleuze's differen*c/t*ial thought is already apparent in the above quoted passages — a choice of words, if you want, but one that is significant to each of them. To come back to the example that we find in the matter at stake: Derrida calls Nietzsche's ›naiveté‹ a breakthrough to be »accentuated«, that is, letting it become a deconstruction of the philosophical corpus from within, while Deleuze ›simply‹ claims ›to stop believing‹ in this corpus, a thinking of thought that for him ›is possible‹. For further discussions of the ›nearly total affinity‹ — Derrida's claim in the only text addressing the other directly (cf. Derrida 2001) — and points of diffraction between the two thinkers, see Kuiken 2005; and Lawlor 2000 and 2003b.

> To impose upon becoming the character of being—that is the supreme will to power.
> That *everything recurs* is the closest *approximation of a world of becoming to a world of being:* — high point of the meditation....
> Becoming as invention, willing, self-denial, overcoming of oneself: no subject but an action, a positing, creative, no ›causes and effects.‹...
> Presupposition: bravery, patience, no ›turning back,‹ no haste to go forward. (N.B. Zarathustra adopts a parodistic attitude toward all former values as a consequence of his abundance.)

The ›being‹ of becoming is ongoing, never-ending return. Becoming, that which is differing first of all from itself, is all that ›stays the same‹ in this eternal return. Deleuze says: »What is the being inseparable from that which is becoming? *Return is the being of that which becomes*. Return is the being of becoming itself, the being which is affirmed in becoming.« (NP: 24) It is with the logic of the eternal return which transforms being into movement, i.e. difference, that the will to power as the non-identifiable differential element is differentiated once more so that what returns is difference and nothing else.

Rather than being secularized, i.e. substituted by a limited notion of finitude which is all that is left for the human within the logic of transcendence, in Nietzsche the ›eternal‹ is in Giorgio Agamben's sense *profanized*,[31] so that it no longer stands in opposition to temporality (as the dualism eternity/ideal vs. temporality/real usually is understood) but is rather the expression of a thought of immanence that has nothing left besides itself—immanence immanent only to itself, or, as Rosi Braidotti calls it, an »eternity within time« (Braidotti 2006: 236). Instead of a vertical ›eternal‹ that again divides the world in two, Nietzsche re-inscribes the eternal in a purely immanent way, and in that provides us with an immanence from which something new can be created. Rather than the static nature of an eternity high up in heaven—essence or presence in the strict sense—determining what is possible in the world, we find a *productive* logic (willing = creating) of that which will always differ, come again, and repeat itself. Only in this way does becoming not loose its character

---

31 Cf. Giorgio Agamben *Profanations*, esp. its central essay ›In Praise of Profanity‹ (Agamben 2007).

of radical openness, an openness limited by immanence alone.

> That the present moment is not a moment of being or of present ›in the strict sense‹, that it is the passing moment, *forces* us to think of becoming, but to think of it precisely as what could not have started, and cannot finish, becoming. (NP: 48)

Again we might want to think back to our last chapter and to draw yet another line to Bergson. Comparable to what was shown as a parallelism between Nietzsche's will to power and the Bergsonian *élan vital*, the latter's philosophy of time, substance as duration, also matches Nietzsche's conceptualization of the world as eternal return.[32] To say this in such a way is, however, to underscore also the major differences that separate these two thinkers who are so significant for Deleuze. Without denying any of Bergson's practical significance, and once more acknowledging the fact that it is his Bergsonism that most of all enables Deleuze to develop such a powerful interpretation of Nietzsche, it is only in the work of the latter thinker that philosophy reaches beyond, i.e. wills more than the purely descriptive level that we usually expect from (philosophical) thought.

---

32 To recapitulate the Bergsonian argument again: in his thought of duration, Bergson responds to the same question of how to think ›becoming‹. His ›solution‹ is an essence or substance that always tends, i.e. that is becoming-other and as such alteration, with, as Deleuze showed us, a concept of duration that is both one and many — a multiplicity — a one that is always based on difference. In the case of matter, it allows but for minimal difference (which nonetheless is difference); and in the case of the living, it is capable of imagining an infinitely high degree of variation. Setting difference thus at the beginning, starting with nothing but differing, the question wherefrom and whereto change is taking place acquires a new meaning. Instead of asking for an origin and an end at which difference again turns into identity, everything always starts and happens in the very middle, i.e. in that which already differs. While it seems that in such a thought the aspect of direction has been lost altogether, it actually regains a new dimension. In the preceeding chapter we have distinguished thinking in terms of degrees from thinking in terms of intensities — intensity as that which is always already a repetition; a repetition, however, that in its singularity is unrepeatable. Only this way does identity not smuggle itself again before difference (a one that ›originally‹ was one and only differs in a second step, even if from itself). The question of immanence would again be handed over to something beyond it, and the attempt to think difference as such, that is, true immanence, would again be canceled out.

Nietzsche, and here Deleuze's Nietzscheanism is the strongest, leads us towards a thought that thinks and affirms its own *act*ivity and pushes both thinking and acting in new directions. As much as everything else, thinking at its best is (=) the expression of the will to power. And such willing is (=) creating in a most *practical* sense. Rather than remaining within the dualism of thought and practice, Nietzsche links the two, and leads us towards a thought that reflects on its own precariousness in and for the world it *both* describes *and* creates.

Speculating on what a true actualization of Nietzsche's *critique* would be, Deleuze reformulates not only the ontological question but encounters also an inherent *ethical* quality — the question of *attitude to life* in thought and thinking itself.

> But does not critique, understood as critique of knowledge itself, express new forces capable of giving thought another sense? A thought that would go to the limit of what life can do, a thought that would lead life to the limit of what it can do? A thought that would *affirm* life instead of a knowledge that is opposed to life. Life would be the active force of thought, but thought would be the affirmative power of life. Both would go in the same direction, carrying each other along, smashing restrictions, matching each other step for step, in a burst of unparalleled creativity. Thinking would then mean *discovering, inventing, new possibilities of life*. (NP: 101)[33]

---

33 We might also want to think of what Michel Foucault in his essay »What is Enlightenment?« called ›attitude‹ when he re-inscribes Kant's *Was ist Aufklärung?*. Let me briefly point to two moments in Foucault's text, which seem to be most relevant for the approach we develop here. »Thinking back on Kant's text, I wonder whether we may not envisage modernity as an attitude rather than a period of history. And by ›attitude,‹ I mean a mode of relating to contemporary reality;... a way of thinking and feeling; a way, too, of acting and behaving that at one and the same time marks a relation of belonging and presents itself as a task. No doubt, a bit like what the Greeks called an *ethos*.« (Foucault 1997: 309) At the very end of his argument, summarizing and coming back to Kant, Foucault states: »The critical ontology of ourselves must be considered not, certainly, as a theory, a doctrine, nor even as a permanent body of knowledge that is accumulating; it must be conceived as an attitude, an ethos, a philosophical life in which critique of what we are is at one and the same time the historical analysis of the limits imposed on us and an experiment with the possibility of going beyond them.« (319)

And yet, we again have to slow down. In order to adequately understand this link between thought and life, or between thinking and acting if you will, we have to come back one more time to the logic of repetition that Nietzsche suggests with his concept of the eternal return. The eternal return still seems truly problematic for our thought of becoming. For while we might have found a way to make compatible the eternal with true immanence by flattening verticality, the notion of ›return‹ that is posed as a ›way out‹ of the paradox of thinking the being of becoming on the plane of immanence itself, seems to throw us at the foot of an insurmountable wall again — contradicting what was just emphasized in the equation of willing = creating. For, how can willing as fundamentally linked to return bring about any creation at all? How can becoming overcome what cannot be surpassed because it is all there is, because there is nothing besides or beyond it? In Nietzsche's long note from 1885 that we already cited above, he made clear that ›this‹ world for him is

> a monster of energy, without beginning, without end; a firm, iron magnitude of force that does not grow bigger or smaller, that does not expend itself but only transforms itself; as a whole, of unalterable size, a household without expenses or losses, but likewise without increase or income;... not something endlessly extended, but set in a definite space as a definite force (WTP #1067).

How does Nietzsche, and together with him Deleuze as maybe his most faithful successor in this regard, manage to tear away the understanding of the world as eternal return from the reproduction of the ever-same — repetition without a reasonable chance to produce something truly new; how do these thinkers envision a transformation of the law of the eternal return into a most relevant — untimely timely, *aternal* — ethical task?

Here, we come up against Nietzsche's ultimate question; the heaviest of all knowledge he himself calls it, demanding the impossible from us: to actively transform into affirmation what must necessarily be our downfall.

> *The heaviest weight.* — What if some day or night a demon were to steal into your loneliest loneliness and say to you: ›This life as you now live

it and have lived it you will have to live once again and innumerable times again; and there will be nothing new in it, but every pain and every joy and every thought and sigh and everything unspeakably small and great in your life must return to you, all in the same succession and sequence — even this spider and this moonlight between trees, and even this moment and I myself. The eternal hourglass of existence is turned over again and again, and you with it, speck of dust!‹ Would you throw yourself down and gnash your teeth and curse the demon who spoke thus? Or have you once experienced a tremendous moment when you would have answered him: ›You are a god, and never have I heard anything more divine.‹ If this thought gained power over you, as you are it would transform and possibly crush you; the question in each and every thing, ›Do you want this again and innumerable time again?‹ would lie on your actions as the heaviest weight! Or how well disposed would you have to become to yourself and to life *to long for nothing more fervently* than this ultimate eternal confirmation and seal? (GS #341)

In his interpretation of Nietzsche's eternal return according to its »*Second Aspect…: as ethical and selective thought*« (NP: 68), Deleuze tackles the problem by drawing first of all a comparison to Kant's practical and critical philosophy, and here not only to the latter's categorical imperative that has become so influential for the canonical philosophical tradition, but also to the potential of ›disinterestedness‹ that latently lies in Kant's *ethical* thought. While this is a far-fetched comparison, it is one that provides us with the adequate direction of where to look for a productive understanding.[34] Without question

---

34 While Nietzsche's ethical thought of »nobility« seems to be constructed precisely against Kant's great emphasis on »disinterestedness« as the ›measure‹ for true morality, the more recent psychoanalytical tradition in its approach towards the ethical reads Kant in a more extreme and thus perhaps more Nietzschean way, so that a ›radicalized disinterestedness‹ comes very close to what Nietzsche himself is after in his difficult thought of (in)difference. For the most interesting and challenging ›new‹ thoughts on the question of the ethical in the psychoanalytical tradition, we first and foremost think of Lacan's *Ethics of Psychoanalysis* which he develops in Seminar VII (Lacan 1997), and the contemporary discussion in the field, represented by authors such as Alain Badiou, Joan Copjec, Slavoj Žižek, and Alenka Zupancic. For Nietzsche's contempt when it comes to (moral) ›Disinterestedness‹, see BGE #260: »The noble and brave types of people who think this way are the furthest removed from a morality

Nietzsche takes up Kant's ›attitude‹ in his formulation of the law of the eternal return. »The eternal return gives the will a rule as rigorous as the Kantian one«, Deleuze writes, and a little later, he goes on: »As an ethical thought the eternal return is the new formulation of the practical synthesis: *whatever you will, will it in such a way that you also will its eternal return.*« (Ibid) Before we speak directly of such an ethical thought, we must stress again that the Nietzschean counterattack on nihilism and *ressentiment* lies in this (im)possible imperative that necessarily must overthrow all subjective agency. For is not what is asked from us total *indifference* towards what happens (to us)? Or are we misreading something here?

To begin with: yes, for Nietzsche there is nothing less but also nothing more than just *this world*—this is not only the speculative but also the practical synthesis, as Deleuze calls it, which the eternal return provides us with. In radically flattening the seemingly natural vertical direction of thought—what we normally call progress, and the striving for Truth, the Good, or the Ideal—we can no longer wait for eternal becoming to be triggered from outside, from some other—higher—place. Differing—difference in itself—is the process of becoming itself, and it must be produced from within. What we are left with in Nietzsche is, thus, nothing but radical *self-creation* without any self, the dice throw that in its absolute *indifference* must become actively affirmed—*in difference*, however, and this becomes the all-important addition. To think the eternal return cannot be done without the structure of *willing* as active affirmation of this very logic.[35] That we are not merely playing with words here will be

---

that sees precisely pity, actions for others, and *désintéressement* as emblematic of morality.« That this is no fair representation of Kant's moral philosophy is not hard to detect. However, when we think of what became of Kant's ethical thought in the field of moral and political philosophy, in the Neo-Kantian analytical philosophical tradition, Nietzsche's harsh criticism gains new significance and points us to the reduction of the problem of ethics that can still be found in these approaches.

35 In his *Introduction: Repetition and Difference* to *Difference and Repetition* Deleuze already warns us against the »Stoic error«, the Stoics expecting a »repetition from the law of nature« (DR: 3). In their cosmology, »[t]he wise must be converted into the virtuous; the dream of finding a law which would make repetition possible passes over to the moral sphere« (ibid). But »[t]here is always a *task to recommence*, a fidelity to be revived with a daily life« (ibid, my emphasis), as Deleuze concludes before citing Büchner's Danton on the weariness

demonstrated in what follows.

The recognition that there is nothing besides *this world* does of course mark an absolute limit, that is, irrevocable finitude. However, all our discussions so far have shown that such immanence in no way contradicts or excludes an infinity of expressions (Spinoza) or a virtual as real as the actual world (Bergson) and necessarily belonging to it. In Nietzschean terms, then, we have to think of the radical pluralism that is the only truth of everything that ›is‹. Any other assumption — as we heard at the very beginning of our discussion — is but a ›quite idle hypothesis‹.

If we now try to express this strange paradoxality of infinite immanence in terms of will, to will and re-will always and only ever the same, everything that happens to us, even the littlest things — this for Nietzsche on the one hand truly means radical *indifference*. We should not try to tame this thought just because ›we‹ simply cannot bear it. However, on the other hand, to despair of life because of this harsh evaluation is to forget that instead of the logic of being the eternal return means that we are always already within a logic of becoming. The eternal return cannot deliver itself in any form of ›being‹, so that what returns only in its lowest form results in the identical and the selfsame. The eternal return conceptualized adequately in a logic of becoming, and this is what Nietzsche hopes for in his thought, is not the return of the identical but only ever of that which differs — difference pushed to its highest degree: difference is that which returns. Deleuze sees this right away, and at the very beginning of *Difference and Repetition* he writes that

> [t]o repeat is to *behave* in a certain manner, but in relation to something unique or singular which has no equal and equivalent... This is the apparent paradox of festivals: they repeat an ›unrepeatable‹. They do not add a second and a third time to the first, but *carry* the first time to the ›nth‹ power (DR: 1, my emphases).

---

of life: »everything's done twice. It's all boring and very, very sad.« (quoted in ibid). Agreeing with everything that is said here *conceptually*, it is the different ›attitude‹ — active affirmation and joy, instead of boredom and sadness — that I find in Nietzsche's thought, and thus in Deleuze's poet(h)ics of life.

In an adequate understanding of the eternal return it is difference itself which returns. The eternal return calls for a repetition of that which is impossible to repeat in any traditional—*additive*—sense. It calls for the repetition of the singular, which although a paradoxical construction in itself nonetheless has to remain the task for the thought of the eternal return. And because of its inherent paradox, this movement of thought requires something more than just what it says: it is in need of a certain ›attitude‹ or ›behavior‹ of thought, that is, an activity of thought, which transforms thought into something else. Active affirmation—an impersonal force, emphasizing the *act* in ›active‹ because no willful subject could ever bear it—means ›to carry the first time to the ›nth‹ power‹, and thus to substitute intensification and multiplication for addition. That every other interpretation would return the thought of becoming to a logic of Being, is initially difficult to grasp. However, if we would not follow the interpretation presented here, return would again no longer approximate in the closest way the being of becoming but establish the reference to something else which returns—something that is first of all identical with itself and not always already differing from itself. The absence of something stable makes it so difficult to think of repetition in its truest sense as the eternal return, the repetition of that which differs. This is also one reason why Deleuze calls such repetition a miracle rather than something we can rely on naturally—a natural law to which the world regularly submits.

> If repetition is possible, it is due to miracle rather than to law. It is against the law: against the similar form and the equivalent content of law. If repetition can be found, even in nature, it is in the name of a *power which affirms itself against the law*, which works underneath laws, perhaps superior to laws. (2, my emphasis)

If we want to achieve a thought of becoming coherence on a purely conceptual level is not enough. Since the ›process‹ of becoming as repetition of difference is precisely that which contradicts the law because it speaks of the singular instead of the general, such a thought must also take on its inherently active dimension—it initiates and is initiated by an *act* itself. A thought of becoming cannot find expression in neutral disinterestedness but must lead into a new form of expression: infinite imperative! Before we learn to understand what this demand implies, what we have to take into account is that for Nietzsche the serenity of a moment of absolute stand-still characteristic to all substantial experience of thinking, as of all (human) existence, is crucial. But for him, we must not cover it up but rather affirm and live through it—to endure!—so that at a totally unexpected moment, if we only know how to be *(in)different*, we *will* ›move somewhere else‹. This is Nietzsche's logic of chance as ›necessity‹: starting with difference, that is, putting difference first, is active affirmation of the eternal return, which ultimately—if we stay with this difference—transforms the simple cyclical movement into a ›centrifugal wheel‹ by which only that which differs will be able to return. Here the joy, the dance, affirmation of the Earth of which Nietzsche speaks is reached; the transformation of the heaviest of all knowledge into the Dionysian world ›beyond Good and Evil‹.

In anticipation of what in a moment will conclude the Nietzschean turn of my argument, consider the following quote from Deleuze:

> Zarathustra recognizes that while he was sick, he had understood nothing of the eternal: that it is not a cycle, that it is not the return of the same, nor a return to the same; that it is not a simple, natural assumption for the use of men. Zarathustra understands [when he is convalescent, KT] the equation ›eternal return = selective Being‹. How can reaction and nihilism, how can negation come back, since the eternal return is the Being that is only said of affirmation, and becoming in action? A centrifugal wheel, ›supreme constellation of Being, that no wish can attain, that no negation can soil.‹ The eternal return is repetition; but it is the repetition that selects, the repetition that saves. (PI: 90–91)

The Nietzschean ethical/practical question that becomes Deleuze's own in all his thinking is thus a question of *how* to *repeat*, which means *how* to *affirm* (›carry to the ›nth‹ power‹) what happens to us in such a way that it is not nihilism which returns but true becoming of thought and life. This ambiguous—because somehow non-localizable—attitude that disturbs the usual distribution of thought and practice so fundamentally cannot be articulated otherwise than as an imperative that rather than merely prescribing truly *affects*: the infinit(iv)e *impersonal* imperative »To become!«.

Zarathustra's Laughter

Letting Nietzsche speak himself at this difficult and pivotal closure of our discussion via his fictive ›alter ego‹ *Zarathustra,* we see that even (t)he(y) needed a long time — an eternity — in the face of this unbearable thought to transform mere reaction into action and to become-active in the Deleuzian sense. This is *Zarathustra's* journey: After so many downfalls and withdrawals, in the work's third part[36] Zarathustra seems to be ready to take on his task:

> I am a wanderer and a mountain climber... I do not like the plains and it seems I cannot sit still for long.
> And whatever may come to me now as destiny and experience — it will involve wandering and mountain climbing: ultimately one experiences only oneself. (Z ›The Wanderer)

By then he knows only one thing. He now has to *face* his hardest and longest, his last peak, the (im)possibility of which he expresses in the following way:

> Indeed, I must start my hardest path! Indeed, I have begun my loneliest hike!
> But whoever is of my kind does not escape such an hour, the hour that speaks to him: ›Only now do you go your way of greatness! Peak and abyss — they are now merged as one!...
> And if all ladders should fail, then you must know how to climb on your own head — how else would you climb upward?
> On your own head and over and beyond your own heart! Now what is mildest in you must become hardest. (Ibid)

When at this moment he begins to tell his darkest vision to his audience of »searchers, researchers (*Versucher*)«, Zarathustra is able — for the first time — to remember a courage and strength to speak out against the dwarf who never stopped undermining the difficult path(os) of Zarathustra with his scornful

---

36 This third part was often even taken as the final part of this work. For the difficult history of the writing and publishing of *Thus Spoke Zarathustra. A Book for All and None*, cf. Robert B. Pippin's *Introduction* (2006: viii-x).

›Oh Zarathustra,‹...›You stone of wisdom! You hurled yourself high, but every hurled stone must—fall!

Oh Zarathustra, you stone of wisdom, you sling stone, you star crusher!

Your hurled yourself so high—but every hurled stone—must fall!

Sentenced to yourself and to your own stoning; oh Zarathustra, far indeed you hurled the stone—but it will fall back down upon *you*! (Z ›On the Vision and the Riddle‹)

But when the dwarf finally falls silent—bathing himself in shameless self-righteousness—it is courage, an *act* of courage that brings Zarathustra this time to act against his own deadly lethargy. Interrupting his heaviness, ›something in him‹—and this is essential, this moment does not seem to be voluntary in the traditional sense—makes him speak:

But there is something in me that I call courage: this so far has slain my every discourage. This courage at last commanded me to stand still and to say: ›Dwarf—you or I!‹ (Ibid)

While this first becoming-active challenges the dwarf, and with the help of quizzing him Zarathustra even manages to assign him to his appropriate place, this time Zarathustra's triumph over the »spirit of gravity«, which instead of exposing itself to the heaviest of all knowledge finds a solution far too easily, nonetheless must remain a temporary one.[37] Reflecting on the obscure Nietzschean text as a whole, it seems that at this moment Zarathustra is still too *personally* engaged with his other, the dwarf: »Dwarf—you or I!«, this other tearing Zarathustra down again and again.

---

37 The dwarf's sloppy answer to Zarathustra's quiz of the gateway ›Moment‹ at which two contradicting eternal paths come together is: »›All that is straight lies,‹ murmured the dwarf contemptuously. ›All truth is crooked, time itself is a circle«. Zarathustra's angry response to this sloppiness has its reason in the mindless superficiality that is expressed by the dwarf who thinks to have won the game by simply speaking the right vocabulary—without taking into account the effects that such a thought implies, that is, its transformative (productive *and* destructive) quality.

Therefore he has to be overcome once more by yet another nauseating vision, one making Zarathustra not only speak up against his personal adversary — a task difficult enough — but against the impersonal pettiness of life as such.

And this time the vision is even more horrific and unbearable. It contains a young shepherd who, »writhing, choking, twitching, his face distorted, with a thick black snake hanging from his mouth« (ibid), appears from the seeming nowhere. In his interpretation of the scene, Deleuze points out that »the snake is an animal of the eternal return« (NP: 65). Pictured as heavy and black, however, it is the animal of the eternal return for as long as it is still that of *reactive* instead of *active* forces. The scene with the snake, thus, both symbolizes the black nihilism that befell man — in his sleep, as Zarathustra himself says, »where it bit down firmly« (Z ›On the Vision and the Riddle) — and it shows Zarathustra's disgust overwhelming him, his physical strength so pointless — »in vain« — with nothing to be done! There is no help, »[a]ll too small the greatest one! That was my surfeit of humans! And eternal recurrences of even the smallest! — That was my surfeit of all existence!« (Z ›The Convalescent‹).[38]

While it seems as if this scenario can never have a productive outcome, we must keep on reading. For if we keep on reading carefully and do not jump ahead, the vision of the shepherd with the snake has not found an end yet. Despite the essential paralysis, where nothing is to be done because there is no *beyond* the unbearable recognition of this eternal returning of even the pettiest of all things, again, and all of a sudden, *it* — it is again not Zarathustra »in the strict sense« — shouts:

> Bite off the head! Bite down! — Thus *it* cried out of me, my dread, my hatred, my nausea, my pity, all my good and bad cried out of me with one shout. — (Z ›On the Vision and the Riddle‹, my emphasis)

---

38 In his notes from spring 1887, Nietzsche writes on the ›in vain‹: »That this ›in vain‹ constitutes the character of present-day nihilism needs to be shown. The mistrust of our previous valuations grows until it becomes the question: ›Are not all ›values‹ lures that draw out the comedy without bringing it closer to a solution?‹ Duration ›in vain‹, without end and aim, is the most paralyzing idea, particularly when one understands that one is being fooled and yet lacks the power not to be fooled.« (WTP #55)

And while Zarathustra seems a bit off *his* head with regard to the task awaiting him (he still wonders and reflects too much about whose face/vision it truly is: »*Who* is the human being into whose throat everything that is heaviest, blackest will crawl?« (ibid)), the shepherd on the other side, in an act *impossible* to him, does as he is told and »bit down as my shout advised him; he bit with a good bite! Far away he spat the head of the snake—and he *leaped* to his feet« (ibid, my emphasis).

It is only a few chapters later that Zarathustra finds full understanding of the vision that unfolded before him.[39] However, in experiencing it he already became the witness of a moment where only an (im)possible *act* transforms everything—overthrowing all rational willfulness, because how do you make yourself bite into that which actually you want to get rid of, how do you find a way out of this bleak scenario without ending up swallowing the whole thing? The outcome leaves us with no doubt:

> No longer shepherd, no longer human—a transformed, illuminated, *laughing* being!
> Never yet on earth had I heard a human being laugh as *he* laughed!
> Oh my brothers, I heard a laughter that was no human laughter—and now a thirst gnaws at me, a longing that will never be still.
> My longing for this laughter gnaws at me; oh how can I bear to go on living! And how could I bear to die now! (ibid).

---

39 Again only in the second attempt, after yet another deep sleep of seven days: »Scarcely had he spoken these words, however, when Zarathustra collapsed like a dead man and long remained as if dead… Finally, after seven days, Zarathustra, sat up on his bed, picked up one of the red apples, smelled it, and found its aroma lovely. Then his animals believed the time had come to speak with him.« (Z III ›The Convalescent‹) Zarathustra seems to have to sleep through, oversleep, the eternal time of God's world-creation as biblical Scripture tells it. Only after having moved beyond it, is transformation possible. And yet even in ›The Convalescent‹, Zarathustra is not »directly« the ›one‹ of the eternal return, as much as Nietzsche never gave a direct exposition of the eternal return, for reasons, as Deleuze in *Difference and Repetition* says, »which pertain both to the simplest ›objective criticism‹ of the texts and to their most modest dramatic or poetic comprehension« (DR: 297). *Zarathustra* remains »unfinished« (ibid).

A transmutation characterized most of all by laughter (no Being but action), a laughter so inhuman, it can no longer belong to the shepherd's form of being—›no longer shepherd, no longer human‹ but »[a]nother sensibility, another becoming«, as Deleuze sees it (NP: 65). Having ›pushed‹ and this means having endured the vision of *ressentiment*, bad conscience, and black nihilism long enough so that something else *must* happen, the *reactive* forces—the »foundation of the humanity of man« (NP: 64)—are transformed or turned into *active* ones through this (im)possible *act* of affirmation, an *act* which—as we know—cannot be ascribed to a Subject, but only ever *wills through* the shepherd so that he himself becomes transformed and turned.

> What happens when the will to nothingness is related to the eternal return? This is the only place where it breaks its alliance with reactive forces. Only the eternal return can complete nihilism *because it makes negation a negation of reactive forces themselves*. By and in the eternal return nihilism no longer expresses itself as the conservation and victory of the weak but as their destruction, their *self-destruction*. (NP: 70)[40]

Thus spoke Zarathustra. The becoming-active of reactive forces, the destruction of nihilism by biting off and spitting out the snake's head. Only a repetition that wills itself eternally can ever achieve this, and only by way of such affirmation, an affirmation that wills nothing but itself, does becoming gain a power which throws it beyond its

---

40 Nietzsche on the *Sich-zu-Grunde-richten*: »[T]his perishing takes the form of self-destruction—the instinctive selection of that which must destroy...the will to destruction as the will of a still deeper instinct, the instinct of self-destruction, the will to nothingness.« (WTP #55) This martial description, however, is concluded by Nietzsche with the following paragraph that again makes clear the immense *precision* which he demands when speaking thus: »Who will prove to be the strongest in the course of this? The *most moderate*; those who do not require extreme articles of faith, those who not only concede but love a fair amount of accidents and nonsense; those who can think of man with considerable reduction of his value without becoming small and weak on that account: those richest in health who are equal to most misfortunes and therefore not so afraid of misfortunes—human beings who are sure of their power and represent the attained strength of humanity with conscious pride.« (Ibid, my emphasis) No super-man task, therefore, but a most (in)human one!

mere descriptive qualities towards the creation of something new in this world. It is thus that becoming ›becomes‹ *ethos*, and thought as active thought encounters its transformative practice. It is time that we devote ourselves to this thoughtful practice itself.

V.

»To Become!« or Deleuze's *Poetics of Life*

> The philosopher of the future is the explorer of ancient worlds, of peaks and caves, who creates only inasmuch as he recalls something that has been essentially forgotten. That something... is the unity of life and thought. It is a complex unity: one step for life, one step for thought. Modes of life inspire ways of thinking; modes of thinking create ways of living. Life *activates* thought, and thought in turn *affirms* life.
>
> (Deleuze, *Pure Immanence*)

Let us recapitulate what we have learned about ›what it means to think‹ in the three chapters discussing Deleuze's plane of thought, with its emphases on immanence, difference, and repetition. Although the argument presented here does not claim that its chosen *dramatization* is the only possible way of arriving at Deleuze's thought of becoming as inherently expressing an ›attitude‹, i.e. an *ethos*, the series we developed has its significance. In this series we moved from an understanding of pure ontology to a thought ›beyond good and evil‹ via the all-important recognition that the two sides inherently belong to each other: ontology = ethics. While in this sequence we thus learned about the different thought-dimensions of Deleuze's philosophical plane, seen from a more general perspective all three philosophical inspirations — Spinoza, Bergson, and Nietzsche — must be read as expressing in a singular way the equation hypothesized since the beginning, and thus all of them produce a true line of flight for ethical thinking as *a concern for this world*. In analogous ways all three thought-universes create a thought of immanence that brings forth the dimensions characterizing the equation: thinking ›what is‹ in terms of a single yet always differing world, in which every approach to the world is always already the composition (creation) of a world. While the equals sign between ontology and ethics, of course, in no way speaks of an identity, if such an approach is understood with all the consequences I have drawn out in the last chapters, it follows that whenever one approaches the equation from one side one necessarily has to face or arrive at the other side. The question of ›attitude‹—›behaving‹ as Deleuze called it in his definition of repetition—the question of *how* to produce and *how* to create no longer remains at a distance. It is always already enfolded or implicated in the plane of ›what is‹, instead of representing a potential addition on a separate plane. Thinking back to the three very different yet equal ways to approach the question of such a creation, be it Spinoza's logic of expression, Bergson's intuitive precision, or Nietzsche's rigor in what was called a selective thought of the logic of the eternal return, to create and to construct already implicates the question of value and sense. »To become!« as both a theoretical and practical demand is, thus, always already an *ethical* question or it *is* nothing at all. It is linking an adequate understanding of what it means to create, i.e. what a creation truly is, with the question of how to become ›capable‹ of thinking and acting in this sense, which together is to *live* this world.

* * *

After our long discussion leading to this relation of thought and life, and culminating in Nietzsche's anti-moral (and in this sense radically ethical) approach to the question of ontology, the desire of *directly* moving into the field of ethics, an ›Ethics of becoming‹ so to speak, is more than comprehensible. If, however, we take seriously what was said about the ›consistency‹ of the thought of becoming, we must slow down and hesitate. Despite the fact that the side of the equation in question now seems to be crystal clear in what it says, much clearer than the side of ontology we spoke of at length up to now, we have to remember what we must deal with in thinking the equation ›ontology = ethics‹. In this relation, neither side can remain what it seemed to be at first. We are speaking of a *transductive relation*—to use a term Gilbert Simondon has coined in his essay on »The Genesis of the Individual«—that describes »a process—be it physical, biological, mental or social—in which an activity gradually sets itself in motion, propagating within a given area, through a structuration of the different zones of the area over which it operates« (Simondon 1992: 313). The processes of crystallization and morphogenesis have served this thinker as ways to find new expressions for the philosophical endeavor to conceptualize ›what is‹ as a relative *and* productive process. According to such differential logic to simply jump to the question of ethics and imagine it in overly simple terms — e. g. in an attempt to *define* the Ethics of becoming — is no possibility for this conclusive chapter. We again must proceed differently. We must continue the structure of doubling, which determines this project throughout: one step for ontology and one step for ethics — to reformulate what has been said by Deleuze about thought and life. The ontological inquiry into ›this world‹ is not only always already a practical *task* and a question of *construction* (Deleuze's *creation*), but simultaneously such an inquiry on the side of ethics no longer imposes a second — an other — world that saves us from this one, providing us with an ethical discourse with normative measures according to which we only have to model ourselves. In as much as ontology *is* ethics, ethics *is* also ontology. Instead of putting either ontology or ethics first, it is important to allow for the difficult — the (im)possible — thought of the indispensable concurrence of ontology *and*, and *as*, ethics. Daniel W. Smith points out that ethics in the Deleuzian equation then cannot »*precede*« ontology as for example in the structurally similar meta-ethical discourse of Emmanuel Levinas. While it is not difficult for any careful reader to find affinities in the way both thinkers approach the question of ethics,[1] in contrast to the Levinasian gesture of ultimately putting the ethical Subject first — the ›I‹ unconditionally and absolutely responsible for the other as absolute Other — what is asked from us by Deleuze is to *de-subjectify* the question of ethics and to radically *impersonalize* ethics so that it always already ›is‹ ontology (cf. Smith 2001: 179). Because the fol-

---

1 Levinas, too, approaches the question of the ethical from an ontological perspective, with the significant difference, however, that — remaining within a phenomenological perspective, and thus focused on a strong notion of the ethical subject (›I‹) — he wants to think the ethical as the »Otherwise than Being« (Levinas 1998), ethics as before or beyond ontology. Derrida in his discussion of Levinasian ethics pointed out that every ontology for Levinas always already implies violence in which the absoluteness of the Other is reduced to the Same (cf. Derrida 1978). It is thus that Levinas must of course be categorized as a thinker of transcendence when we approach him puristically from the position of radical immanence. However, an encounter between Levinas and Deleuze precisely in regard to the question of what philosophy is ›at its best‹ — which for both thinkers is implied in the question of the relation between transcendence and immanence — would nonetheless be most interesting, precisely because of the affinity between Levinas' notion of transcendental infinity and Deleuze's approach to an immanent one.

lowing discussion is in this sense incapable of satisfying the apparent need of all ethical discussions to precisely stop the infinite movement of the equation ›ontology = ethics‹ in order to arrive at a universally applicable and attributable ›what ought to be?‹, we instead must attempt yet another round of repetition. Only then do we avoid falling back into the transcendentalism that limits ethics to becoming nothing more than a morality (understood in the Nietzschean sense).

Revisiting the themes of immanence, difference, and repetition — this time however through the ethical imperatives of »*A life…, everywhere!*«, *Amor Fati*, and »*To Become!*« — we hope to show that the ethicality proposed here is not a merely catchy formulation in a time when ›nothing seems to be done‹ but a most difficult because most intens(iv)e task ›to become capable of‹, both in the practice of thought as an *ethos* to life and in what follows from there for the creation of *a life*….

1. »A life…: everywhere!«

How ›practical‹, then — this must be the question — is Deleuze's plane of immanence, that is, his ›attitude‹ to immanence? What implications arise from the acknowledgment that thought and life are so closely interrelated in this philosopher's work that ultimately, as Philip Goodchild summarizes it, »[e]thics becomes imperceptible, immanent within the entire plane of Deleuze's thought« (Goodchild 2002: 158)? To understand adequately, we have to return once more to the questions which engaged us throughout this book, questions which Deleuze himself addresses directly only in his last works: with Félix Guattari in *What is Philosophy?*, and in his very last text ›Immanence: a life…‹, so often taken — justifiably or not — as his ›testament‹. Since the former text has engaged us in more detail in our ›ontological‹ chapters on the question of immanence, it will be with the latter text that our discussion of the dimension of the ethical must take issue now.

Transcendental Empiricism

Right at the beginning of ›Immanence: a life…‹, Deleuze asks: »What is a transcendental field?« (PI: 25). The transcendental, not to be confused with the transcendent as Deleuze explicitly specifies (cf.

PI: 26), *must* and *can* be thought immanently; this is immanence immanent only to itself as we know; neither referring immanence back to transcendence nor reducing it to a base empiricism (cf. WPH: 47). The transcendental is not the transcendent because true immanence »doesn't refer to an object or belong to a subject (empirical representation)«, Deleuze explains (PI: 25). There is a ›superior‹ empiricist conversion of which he then speaks, and according to which the transcendental field is to be defined as a pure plane of immanence »because it eludes all transcendence of the subject and of the object« (PI: 26). Concurrent to his definition of immanence in *What is Philosophy?*, in ›Immanence: a fife...‹ Deleuze states:

> Absolute immanence is in itself: it is not in something, *to* something; it does not depend on an object or belong to a subject. In Spinoza, immanence is not immanence *to* substance; rather, substance and modes are in immanence... No more than the transcendental field is defined by consciousness can the plane of immanence be defined by a subject or an object that is able to contain it. (PI: 26–27)

This plane of thought claims not only to leave behind onto-theological transcendence but also the fundaments of modern philosophy in both the Cartesian and Kantian personal form of an ›I‹ as well as all forms of phenomenological consciousness (be it Hegelian or Husserlian). But what does it propose instead? In our attempt to respond to this question, we have emphasized from the very start that everything begins with the crucial issue of immanence and the way it articulates the difference between two logics that inscribe not only what it means ›to think‹ but also what it means ›to think *this* world‹. In the logic pursued here of becoming, which must be clearly delimited from the traditional logic of Being, »the plane of immanence is always single, being itself pure variation« (WPH: 39). Immanence, to repeat it one more time, does not have to be thought as ›immanence *to* substance‹, but as Spinoza showed us, substance and modes are in immanence so that the One becomes multiplicity or pure variation; a *One-All* in which one side cannot do without the other. In our presentation we have continuously emphasized that instead of being merely a unifying category, the One as multiplicity must be understood in a serial or different/ciating sense, be it Spinoza's thought of univocity (*deus sive natura*), Bergson's thought of duration (contraction *and* relaxation), or Nietzsche's thought of return (selection *and* affirmation).[2]

It is helpful at this point, to come back to the ontological dispute between Deleuze and Badiou, which latently has accompanied us throughout this study. Badiou's greatest mistake in his interpretation of Deleuze's thought, which ultimately makes him miss totally (though probably deliberately) what is so significant about Deleuze's *ontology of becoming*, lies precisely in this (im)possible thought of a One (a single plane of immanence) as multiplicity (pure variation). His whole critique circles around this »play of the One, composition, intensity of the plenum, the crystal (or logic) of sense« (Badiou 2007: 37) that he finds so disturbing, and from which he precisely delimits his own thought of the multiple and the event: »the event as disjoined from the One, [as] separation, assumption of the void, pure non-sense« (ibid). However, by reducing Deleuze's notion of the whole or the One as multiplicity to »a degraded, and even expendable, expression of an eminent power«, as Keith Ansell Pearson explains in *Philosophy and the Adventure of the Virtual* (Pearson 2002: 103), Badiou misconstrues Deleuze's logic of the virtual completely. Instead of being dogmatic in showing an empiricist rootedness (cf. Badiou 2007: 41), it is Deleuze's superior empiricism — transcendental empiricism — that alone makes it possible to think a whole that is *never given* as or in a totality, and yet is *absolutely real*. Thus, we can only agree with Pearson who states that Badiou »argues unconvincingly that because the real of the virtual is not given in its totality this means that the real ›consists precisely in the perpetual actualizing of new virtualities‹... This is a very odd construction of Deleuze's thinking of the virtual« (Pearson 2002: 104).

In Badiou's argument for a true thought of immanence, which he claims for himself rather than attributing it to Deleuze, he *pre-limits*

---

2 We have, however, not yet explicitly referred to the particular Deleuzian expression of the double directionality that characterizes Deleuze's thought of difference itself: differen*t*/*c*iation. In *Difference and Repetition*, Deleuze introduces the »complex notion of differen*t*/*c*iation«, in which the »*t* and the *c* here are the distinctive feature or the phonological relation of difference in person« (DR: 209). He specifies that »[w]hereas differentiation determines the virtual content of the Idea as problem, differenciation expresses the actualisation of this virtual and the constitution of solutions (by local integrations)« (ibid).

and *blocks* immanence conceptually by reducing all processes of actualization to the level of the Multiple, and doing so in opposition to and total rejection of the One. He thus thinks an immanence still delimiting itself from the transcendent One, which from a Deleuzian point of view, falls again in the very trap of transcendentalism, the logic of either/or, which it is meant to avoid. Instead of a One as pure variation—›flat‹ ontology—Badiou reifies the virtual, and thus conceptualizes it again in an eminent sense, by not reversing the terms of Being, i.e. the One as opposed to the Multiple, into a whole different register: the logic of becoming.[3] Thinking in terms of becoming, however, and thus emphasizing the differentiation between the actual and the virtual, without leaving the plane of immanence itself, Deleuze's notion of the virtual manages also to re-link both sides. It is such a thought—turn and re-turn on but one level that ›is‹ the movement itself—that is able to think the One as multiplicity (beyond the opposition of the One and the Multiple). This multiplicity is a radically open plane that although never given in a totality (because it is nothing but movement) is absolutely *real as virtual*. In following Bergson, Deleuze did spell out the important difference between the two logics that determine the ways we conceive of the ontological endeavor as an *approach to this world* from the very beginning of his philosophical life, and it is this dimension of Deleuze's thought that seems to me to be essential for an adequate understanding of his philosophy.

The Virtual as Task

Deleuze distinguishes a logic of the virtual (that is, of becoming) and a logic which is only ever concerned with the (in)finite possibilities of Being. He again and again warns of the confusion of the virtual with the possible. While, according to Deleuze, »[*t*]*he virtual is fully real in so far as it is virtual*« (DR: 208), »the possible is opposed to the real«

---

3 The entire Badiou-Deleuze-misunderstanding emerges once more from a particular image of thought: subtraction rather than differen*t*/*c*iation. While it leads too far to elaborate this issue in detail here, it should be clear that to understand the virtual as an eminent power above and beyond its actualizations represents a *mis*construction according to the interpretation of Deleuze we have developed in our discussion. It precisely misses everything about Deleuze's *different* consistency of thought.

(DR: 211). In contrast to the possible, which, as Deleuze also spells out in his book on Bergson, »has no reality (although it may have an actuality)« (B: 96), and only achieves reality in a process of realization functioning according to the rules of resemblance and limitation, the virtual—which at a later stage Deleuze starts calling the plane of immanence—»is not actual but *as such possesses a reality*« (ibid). The virtual and the actual cannot do without each other, and they are also not distinguished from each other by any measure of ›realness‹. The virtual is as real as the actual. At the same time, however, we also have to understand that the two are in no way related in terms of representation as resemblance, such as the distinction of the possible and the real functions. »As virtual«, Pearson explicates, »this open whole *cannot assemble* its actual parts that are external to each other« (Pearson 2002: 104, my emphases). But equally, »the actual *does not come to resemble* the virtual because actualization does not proceed by rules of resemblance or limitation« (ibid, my emphases). Rather, the actual ›embodies‹ and ›incarnates‹ the virtual, as Deleuze calls it. The process of actualization is a process of differen*t*/*c*iation. It takes place by creating difference and divergence between the actual and the virtual, and is precisely no longer a question of what comes first.

> Actualisation [sic] breaks with resemblance as a process no less than it does with identity as a principle. Actual terms never resemble the singularities they incarnate. In this sense, actualisation [sic] or differenciation is always a genuine creation. (DR: 212)

The virtual as plane of immanence—this is very important to understand—has to be seen as always already possessing two facets. As infinite movement it is double, it is Thought (virtual) *and* Nature (actual), as Deleuze and Guattari explain in *What is Philosophy?*, with only a fold (*pli*) ›from one to the other‹ (cf. WPH: 38):

> Infinite movement is double... It is in this sense that thinking and being are said to be one and the same. Or rather, movement is not the image of thought without being also the substance of being. (Ibid)

›Thinking and being are said to be one and the same.‹ This doubleness makes of being a becoming and of thought a practice of creation which enables Deleuze's thought of immanence to move on but one plane while leaving this very plane itself radically open, so that a breach, something radically unpredictable and new, can be expected from it.

There is, thus, always only one virtual. We do not, as Badiou would have it according to his interpretation of Deleuze, perpetually actualize new virtualities. This would only eliminate the potential of which true immanence as virtual ›is capable of‹. The virtual, however, is always already a multi*pli*city, and in this sense it ›is‹ only ever in the plural. To emphasize this exemplifies again that the virtual ›is‹ not according to or within a logic of Being. Rather it both announces and is already inscribed within a pure logic of becoming. As a logic of difference it no longer demands as its only legitimate ›use‹ the reproduction of true copies (presupposing an original that serves as the model or norm), seeing itself in the position to possess an inherent measure for it, but it is interested in the production, that is the creation, of something new. Such is becoming as infinite movement. By challenging this thought with the dimension of the new, however, we also have to keep in mind that the new is not new in the sense of a *creatio ex nihilo*: this would be a contradiction in terms for the logic of becoming. The new as actualization of the virtual cannot ever be an *ex nihilo* new beginning because the infinite movement of becoming does not have either beginning or end but always only and ever an ›in the middle‹. Therefore, instead of being able to (mis)use the process of actualization ›at its best‹ as a horizon saving us from error or evil (depending on which glasses we wear: the scientific ones or the moral ones), the creation of the new rather speaks of the *task* to infinit(iv)ely endure the never conclusively answerable question of ›*how to create (new) divergent lines*‹.

> For a potential or virtual object, to be actualised [sic] is to create divergent lines which correspond to—without resembling—a virtual multiplicity. The virtual possesses the reality of *a task to be performed or a problem to be solved:* it is the problem which orientates, conditions, and engenders solutions, but these do not resemble the conditions of the problem... Difference and repetition in the virtual ground the movement of actualisation [sic], of differenciation as creation. (DR: 212, my emphases)

By approaching even the virtual as a *task* and as a *problem to be solved*, the ethical dimension is truly immanent to the entire plane of Deleuze's thought. It is inherent to what it means to think for Deleuze: either thinking expresses *ethos* or it is nothing at all. Because of the breadth of the issue, however, ethics really becomes so imperceptible on this plane of thought that one could also think that it is missing altogether. That this is the most common impression Deleuze still gives is exemplified in particular by the rather quiet reception that Deleuze's rare explicit ethical statements, such as texts like ›Immanence: a life...‹, have met with. In his text-long engagement with precisely this last published article by Deleuze, Giorgio Agamben shows great insight, therefore, when he begins his discussion by pointing to the philosophical significance »of a striking coincidence« between Deleuze and Foucault, who both authorized as their very last published texts essays which »have at their center the concept of life« (Agamben 1999: 220).[4] This implies, Agamben says,

> the statement of a legacy that clearly concerns the coming philosophy, which, to make this inheritance its own, will have to take its point of departure in the concept of life toward which the last works of both philosophers gesture (ibid).

While I do not go along with what ultimately becomes of Deleuze's thought of immanence in Agamben's reading of it,[5] he is in my opin-

---

4 Years after Agamben wrote his text, Jacques Derrida in his very last interview for *Le Monde* on August 31, 2004 »Je suis en guerre contre moi-même«, also devoted all his energy to the question of life and what it could mean ›(not) to know how to live‹. For an English version of this interview under the title »I am at War with Myself«, cf. Derrida 2007.

5 Agamben turns Deleuze's virtual too much into his own—very Aristotelian—thought of potentiality, the concept under which the whole volume stands in which he has published »Absolute Immanence« in the English translation: *Potentialities. Collected Essays in Philosophy*. For such an ambiguous Aristotelian turn see especially Agamben's interpretation of Deleuze in regard to the Aristotelian distinctions of life-forms in *De Anima*, so that it appears as if Deleuze—like Agamben himself—remains within an Aristotelian understanding of life (cf. Agamben 1999: 236f). In our discussion of Spinoza's turn towards the Ancients, we already explained that Deleuze's immanence is no return to Aristotelian naturalism, which even in Agamben's re-evaluation of it cannot get rid of its biologistic bias.

ion nonetheless right in pointing us to the thought-strategic dimension, which Deleuze and Foucault initiate by re-introducing ›life‹ as one of the most important matters of philosophy. And he is also right in bringing the two thinkers in contact with each other here. Not only for the philosophical legacy that Foucault shares with Deleuze, but also precisely when it comes to the specific way of approaching this difficult ›point of departure‹ that a future philosophy will have to take on, these two intellectuals can be read as (virtually) complementing each other.

Impersonal Life

If we look at Foucault's work, his theoretical engagement with the issue of life is clearly marked by a caution so deep-seated that even today many of his readers are at a loss considering the question of how this thinker of omnipresent power relations and Bio-politics still could work on an ethics of the care of the self as an *aesthetics of existence*. These two opposing standpoints of the incorporation of life into thought appear to be unbridgeable.[6] In contrast to this rather suspicious treatment of the issue, Deleuze's philosophical attitude towards life is much bolder. He seems to act with much less care and caution. This can be exemplified in his very book on Foucault in which he remarks (and again — like with all discussions Deleuze has with other thinkers — we cannot really decide to whom to truly attribute this thought: is it Foucault pushed to his limits, or was it always already ›pure‹ Deleuze?):

> Contrary to a fully established discourse, there is no need to uphold man in order to resist. What resistance extracts from this revered old man, as Nietzsche put it, is the forces of a life that is larger, more active, more affirmative and richer in possibilities. The superman has never meant anything but that: it is in man himself that we must liberate life,

---

6 The irritation produced by the apparently different philosophical phases that run through Foucault's work determines the reception of him until today. While again I cannot elaborate further here, I do not agree with arguments that suggest conceptual inconsistency in his work. I rather would like to see a whole work devoted to the evaluation of the different levels on which the thinker has approached ›this world‹, in order to adequately understand the vectors running from epistemology to politics and ethics in his work.

> since man himself is a form of imprisonment for man. Life becomes resistance to power when power takes life as its object. (F: 92)

To turn the Foucaultian insight of an all-encompassing power structure into a creative possibility for life itself, as the creation of *a life...* as resistance to power—Foucault himself could not go that far, at least not explicitly. And whereas Deleuze of course also knows that, as Agamben articulates it, »he enters a dangerous territory in displacing immanence into the domain of life« (Agamben 1999: 232), the liberation of life in this creation of *a life...* is undoubted by Deleuze. Only when we reach an indefinite, unattributable, impersonal life can we speak of »pure power and even bliss« (PI: 30). The discourse of ›Man‹ must be overcome so that the potential of life as *becoming*—as resistance to the striated space-time—takes shape. In ›Immanence: a life...‹ Deleuze claims that only when we dare to think and go this far, will

> [t]he indefinite aspects in a life lose all indetermination to the degree that they fill out a plane of immanence or, what amounts to the same thing, to the degree that they constitute the elements of a transcendental field... The indefinite article is the indetermination of the person only because it is determination of the singular. The One is not the transcendent that might contain immanence but the immanent contained within a transcendental field. One is always the index of a multiplicity: an event, a singularity, a life... (ibid).

Such is Deleuze's claim in regard to life in which he again knots together in his unique fashion the One as plane of immanence *and* as indeterminate one—as *a* singularity.

It is important not to misunderstand the difference between Deleuze and Foucault as a disagreement with no way left to go. While at first such an evaluation seems to be only appropriate, particularly in order not to harm Foucault's philosophical legacy, it is shortsighted to represent the Deleuzian position as a misinterpretation of Foucault's stand on life, as simply turning again into productive forces that which had finally gotten rid of any such ›utopian‹ alternatives.[7]

---

7 Simply reversing the ›silent‹ disappearance of ›Man‹ in Foucault's *The*

What is at stake here is again more complicated. For Deleuze absolutely shares his friend's (un)timely political realism in the face of the dangers that any ›actualized‹, that is spelled-out, vitalism harbors, according to which we could and should find a life beyond—outside, above, or below—power. A rigorous Nietzscheanism in the way we presented it in our discussion earlier makes it impossible for both of these thinker to even desire any such beyond. However, rather than taking this limitation as a disillusionment, with the production of a politically relevant and ethically inspiring thought as the task of a philosophy worthy its name, Deleuze—explicitly—turns it into a virtue. For in his thought-map in which both the virtual and the actual are *equally* relevant and *real* dimensions of thought—and here he gives something back to the Foucaultian universe—his gesture of pushing thought's *potential* in order to find out ›what a body is capable of‹, however incapable ›we‹ *actually* will be of it, does not fall prey to mere vitalist utopias. Foucault has realized this, and he appreciates it in his claim that with Deleuze, »new thought is possible; thought is again possible« (Foucault 1998b: 367). It is a thought that pushes itself to the point where it becomes indistinguishable to practice (creation or action), without, however, ever closing the gap between the two such as a thought based not on difference but identity would have to have it. Only by presupposing this *complicated* interrelation of thought and life, theory and practice, or the virtual and the actual—each on its specific terrain—does Deleuze speak of the *possibility* of another form of life or another sensibility, such as he states it in ›Immanence: a life…‹:

> The life of the individual gives way to an impersonal and yet singular life that releases a pure event freed from the accidents of internal and external life, that is, from the subjectivity of what happens: a ›Homo tantum‹ with whom everyone empathizes and who attains a sort of beatitude. (PI: 28)

However, the passage cannot be taken in any ›direct‹ way. It must be understood literally, but literally only in its highest, and that is

---

Order of Things (Foucault 1994b) into the supposedly ›dancing‹ Nietzschean ›Superman‹ in Deleuze's own interpretation (cf. F: 124–132).

in a most complicated sense. While we also might want to add that it is as such nearly impossible to understand what Deleuze is really speaking of here—for how are we to imagine such a life?—the reasons for our command must be explained further. This passage must not be taken literally in any base sense, however tempting it may be for our wish to finally close the chapter on the thought of becoming as both *a thought…* and *a life…*, as a ›know-how of living‹. I claim this out of no other reason than out of the danger that by assuming too quickly what this ›alternative‹ life is all about, we loose its most fruitful potential. Looking closer at the concrete context in which Deleuze employs his thought of ›Immanence: a life…‹ we have to learn that (in this case as much as in many others), however ›practical‹ the Deleuzian imperatives often might sound, they are not suggested on the level of prescription, at which normative statements normally reside. On the contrary, if we only dare to expose ourselves to the Deleuzian style, his formulations do everything to precisely avoid any such directiveness.

The point that I wish to make here is so essential for an adequate understanding for Deleuze's work as a whole that it should be investigated on more than one occasion. But we must stay focused here and look closely at the complex situation in which for Deleuze it is possible to suggest ›a singular life that releases a pure event freed from the accidents of internal and external life‹. To be precise, it is first of all neither a very lively nor a very livable life that is referred to by Deleuze here. As we all know, it is the Dickens' scene of the living-dying Riderhood from his novel *Our Mutual Friend*, of which Deleuze writes that »[n]o one has described what *a life* is better than Charles Dickens, if we take the indefinite article as an index of the transcendental« (PI: 28). It is the ›spark of life‹ spoken of when »[b]etween… life and… death, there is a moment that is only that of *a* life playing with death« (ibid). Taking this literary situation as literal as it gets, one would be absolutely mistaken to approach the claim of the impersonal and singular life—*homo tantum*—as simply a new coat for the same old subjectivity, in which we would and could be told what we have to do in order to attain such singular life. No, we cannot tame this thought and bend it again to ›our‹ understanding. Deleuze is clear about what he is saying:

> It is a haecceity no longer of individuation but of singularization: a life of pure immanence, neutral, beyond good and evil... The life of such individuality fades away in favor of the singular life immanent to a man who no longer has a name, though he can be mistaken for no other. A singular essence, a life.... (PI: 29)

To choose, however, the opposite direction is also not right. We would misunderstand the thought of immanence just as much if we now assumed, because of such total decapitation of the Subject, that Deleuze simply neglects or has even totally done away with the structural *third* dimension, for which ›God‹, the ›I‹, or ›consciousness‹ stood for so long. No. While Deleuze does not hesitate to give the concept of *a* life an inhuman look, he is also very clear not to »enclose life in the single moment when individual life confronts universal death« (ibid). To the contrary, he says, »*A* life is everywhere, in all the moments that a given living subject goes through and that are measured by given lived objects« (ibid). Again and again we thus encounter the interweaving of the virtual (a life of pure immanence) and the actual (all the moments that a given living subject goes through) dimensions without ever losing sight of their fundamental distinctness; and it is these two directions together which produce something else — a more or a difference — that cannot be reduced to either side. It is only in what becomes in-between the two dimensions, that which cannot find direct expression, wherein lies the whole significance to this radical thought of immanence.

Figural Ontology

This is what our discussion wanted to make clear: by *flattening* the seemingly natural vertical orientation of thought into an equational and serial logic of encountering, we are not left with nothing. However difficult it is to grasp, a new direction is discovered that is characterized by indirection alone: *a* life as *becoming* that instead of alluding to transcendence deepens immanence.[8] It opens the imma-

---

8 Cf. Daniel W. Smith in »The Doctrine of Univocity«, where he determines Deleuze's thought of immanence not as »an appeal to transcendence, but rather a deepening of immanence«. He concludes: »What the drama of univocity exemplifies is the dynamic nature of Deleuze's thought, which must be defined and comprehended in terms of its *movement*.« (Smith 2001: 180)

nent so that the structural dimension of *the third* becomes an ingredient dispersed throughout immanence — everywhere.

> A life contains only virtuals. It is made up of virtualities, events, singularities. What we call virtual is not something that lacks reality but something that is engaged in a process of actualization following the plane that gives it its particular reality. (PI: 31)

This different logic of thought, rather than re-introducing a new vertical direction such as the ›I‹, and thus making immanence again immanent to something else, in being immanent only to itself, ›is‹ in this sense always already *figural*. It is a *figural ontology*, if we borrow from Deleuze's book on *Francis Bacon. The Logic of Sensation.*[9] The plane of immanence is never to be imagined as a ›given‹ space into which forces are introduced and distributed. There is no ›given‹ but always only a ›giving‹. If we have to think of an ›image‹ of this plane, we must envision it in a dynamic — a moving or fleeing — diagrammatic way, constantly in the making, »sketched out on and constituted by a living body, filled with forces that affect what happens

---

9 Cf. again Daniel W. Smith in his »Translator's Introduction« to Deleuze's *Francis Bacon*: »The fundamental concept in all these analyses, however, is that of the *Figure*. Modern art and modern philosophy can be said to have converged on a similar problem: both renounced the domain of representation and instead took the *condition* of representation as their object... Whereas ›figuration‹ refers to a form that is related to an object it is supposed to represent, the ›Figure‹ is the form that is connected to a sensation, and that conveys the violence of the sensation directly to the nervous system.« (Smith 2003: xiii) In their absolute (in)distinction from color and contour the ›Figures‹ in Bacon's painting must not be understood in a *figurative*, i.e. representational sense — »a screaming man, a smiling man, a seated man« (FB: 79) — but in their correlation to contour and color *»on a single Plane, equally close«* (FB: 9). »The contour, as a ›place‹, is in fact the place of an exchange in two directions: between the material structure and the Figure, and between the Figure and the field. The contour is like a membrane through which this double exchange flows. *Something happens in both directions.*« (FB: 13, my emphasis) It is in this sense that Deleuze speaks of *athleticism* — »the figure already demonstrates a singular athleticism« (FB: 14) — a double movement or deformation of which only the figure is ›capable‹. The first movement »that goes from the material structure, from the field, to the Figure« (ibid), coexists with another movement in which »the Figure... wants to pass through a vanishing point in the contour in order to dissipate into the material structure« (FB: 16).

there« (Goodchild 2002: 159). Instead of a measurement based on determinable distance and as such based on the category of essence, *affectivity*, *endurance*, and *intensity* express the proximity, the zone of indistinction or indiscernibility with which the difference between the two facets (thought and being) is overcome. If beings — if we for a moment still use this traditional ontological vocabulary — are »no longer distinguished by a [thought of] qualitative essence« which, as Daniel W. Smith is right to point out, refers us back to the ana*logy* of Being (Smith 2001: 178); if they instead rather express quantifiable degrees of power (in terms of speed/affectivity, duration/endurance, or return/affirmation), we move into »an important practical conversion in philosophy« (ibid) at which a radical shift takes place. It is a turn of philosophy *towards* ethical practice — ethical coming from *ethos* — and a turn *away* from it being the condition of any possible morality — the prescription of what ought to be. The significant difference between these two ways of relating thought and life is not to be underplayed, especially not today when we believe to have long done with this relation. While morality — as we know from Nietzsche's contempt for it — always only looks for the realization of one's essence, only looking at ›what is‹ as modeled on the demand of how things — ideally, always far away and in a different world — ›ought to be‹, the thought of radical immanence implies an ethicality that is always already *everywhere* — an infinit(iv)e imperative: ›*A* life is everywhere, in all the moments that a given living subject goes through and that are measured by given lived objects‹, we heard Deleuze state above.[10] Of a different ›texture‹ and ›consistency‹

10 It is really important to clarify here that the *everywhere*, though often related to the notion of the *everyday*, is precisely not to be understood in this way. To do so would mean to neglect again the very specific a/effect that a logic motivated by the distinction virtual/actual produces. There is probably no stricter adversary to the thought of the everyday, doxa, or common sense than Deleuze's everywhere-thought, which he also calls a *nowhere*-thought — nowhere as both ›no place‹ and ›here and now‹ (taking this from Samuel Butler's novel *Erewhon*). The *everywhere* surpasses every reference to an already determined notion of everydayness, and points instead to an indefinite and infinite singularity. We, therefore, totally agree with Claire Colebrook's critique of theories of the everyday that are still based on life as a norm or a telos of maximization, and precisely not — as we hope to have explicated here — as an open and indeterminable *intensity*. It seems fruitful to quote her argument as a helpful way to articulate the difficult thought-practice of *a life*..., which

from both the eternal or the ideal on the one side, and the factual or merely historical on the other side, such a thought and practice of life imagines *a becoming...* which as singularity remains open to, that is, remains ›capable of‹, the *reality of the virtual.*

2. »To think!« as *Amor Fati*

What makes Deleuze a true successor of the philosophers under consideration in this book is that he continues the legacy that is most characteristic of all of these philosophies. This is the ›attitude‹ to and of thought that they call forth: true thought, that is, philosophy at its best, is not merely knowing better what is already known—intellectual modesty—but producing something new and ›moving somewhere else‹—absolute immodesty. Rather than beginning with what ›everybody knows, and no one can deny‹ and striving for ›the Truth‹, a more creative approach to thought, a thought that affects and is affected by life, is asked for—and it is possible.

While all three inspirations, »Spinoza, Nietzsche, Bergson«, together with »Deleuze have pioneered the immanent critique of reasoning in ethics« (Goodchild 2002: 156), it is nonetheless Nietzsche who becomes Deleuze's ›real master‹ when we turn to the question of such a practical thought as what it means ›to do philosophy‹.[11] It is with

---

we also try to express here. Relating her own argument both to Deleuze and Irigaray's thought of the »feminine, thought beyond philosophies of life and the normativity of everydayness« (Colebrook 2002a: 688), Colebrook writes: »If one could imagine the everyday as nonactualized potential, as the thought of that which amounts to nothing, and is not only unproductive but also possibly counterproductive, then one might imagine a politics and ethics liberated from the knowledge of life. Such an ethics would be everyday, not because it released the potential of an already given ground, ultimately contributing to the emancipation and maximization of life, but because it began from the idea of thinking beyond life« (Colebrook 2002a: 689).

11 To state this again, Nietzsche is always one of the most obvious references for placing Deleuze within the philosophical tradition; in comparison to Bergson for instance, who for a long time did not even make it into these discussions. However, Nietzsche still did not receive the special attention in regard to Deleuze's *practical* philosophy that I believe him to deserve. For most Deleuze scholars, it is either Spinoza or Bergson who are called his »real masters«, to apply here to both a term Alain Badiou uses to describe Bergson's position for Deleuze (2000: 39). For extremely helpful investigations into the

Nietzsche that life and thought become interwoven so closely that, philosophically speaking, it no longer sounds bewildering when ›life *activates* thought and thought *affirms* life‹, as the quotation at the beginning of this chapter suggests. While active affirmation, as the most crucial aspect of what it means to think, is *implied* in Spinoza's univocal Being and, of course, most concretely *envisioned* by Bergson's method of thinking as ›leaping‹, it becomes truly *enacted* with Nietzsche's *style*. Since Nietzsche at the latest are we (post-)moderns thus forced to depart from picturing philosophy as neutrally reflecting on this world and to acknowledge the ethico-political explosiveness that pulsates through every creation.

Belief in this World

That the question of thinking, of philosophy, and of life as such, is a question of style, i.e. a question of *how* to create, Deleuze repeats and emphasizes throughout all of his works.[12] And in a conversation

---

Spinozian and the Bergsonian influences on Deleuze, cf. either the references made thoughout this book, or—on the Spinozian side—in particular Hardt's early study of the threefold Deleuzian plane of thought (1995), but also Alliez 2004, Goodchild 1997 and 2002: 156–163, and Hayden 1998. On the Bergsonian side, see esp. Grosz 1999, 2004 and 2005, and Pearson 1999, 2001, and 2002. I would argue that the slight negligence in regard to Nietzsche arises from the fact that Deleuze's thought is rarely understood as regarding what, after Foucault, we here call (ethical) ›attitude‹ to be a crucial aspect of thinking and philosophy itself. The argument we are pursuing thus positions itself within this ›Foucaultian‹ interpretation of Deleuze. With the publication of Deleuze and Guattari's *Anti-Oedipus* in 1976, Foucault publicly announced, that »*Anti-Oedipus* (may its authors forgive me) is a book of ethics, the first book of ethics to be written in France in quite a long time« (Foucault, 2004: xv). For an analogous interpretation of Deleuze's ›image of thought‹ to the one we are unfolding here, cf. Colebrook 2002b and Patton 2000. For a Deleuze-inspired interpretation of Nietzsche, see also Pearson 1997.

12 The examples are too numerous to give a detailed list of references. For two very prominent passages let us refer to Deleuze's »Preface« to *Difference and Repetition*, where he writes on the relation of philosophy, style, and Nietzsche: »The time is coming when it will hardly be possible to write a book of philosophy as it has been done for so long: ›Ah! the old style...‹. The search for new means of philosophical expression was begun by Nietzsche and must be pursued today in relation to the renewal of certain other arts, such as the theatre or the cinema.« (DR: xxi) In an interview »On Philosophy« twenty years later, Deleuze, one more time asked about style, again says that all »[g]reat philosophers are great stylists too. Style in philosophy is the movement of con-

with Antoine Dulaure and Claire Parnet in 1985, published under the title »Mediators«, Deleuze attests to this specific relating of thought and life in a very precise diagnosis of contemporary thought and of what he believes is needed for this world today:

> If things aren't going well in contemporary thought, it's because there's a return under the name of ›modernism‹ to abstractions, back to the problem of origins, all the sort of thing... Any analysis in terms of movement, vectors, is blocked. We're in a very weak phase, a period of reaction. Yet philosophy thought it had done with the problem of origins. It was no longer a question of starting or finishing. The question was rather, what happens ›in between‹? And the same applies to physical movements... [N]owadays we see movement defined less and less in relation to a point of leverage. All the new sports—surfing, windsurfing, hang-gliding—take the form of entering into an existing wave. There's no longer an origin as starting point, but a sort of putting-into-orbit. The key thing is how to get taken up in the motion of a big wave, a column of rising air, to ›get into something‹ instead of being the origin of an effort... if we're oppressed, it's because our movement's being restricted, not because our eternal values being violated. In barren times philosophy retreats to reflecting ›on‹ things. If it's not itself creating anything, what can it do but reflect on something? So it reflects on eternal or historical things, but can itself no longer make any move. (Deleuze 1995: 121)

What is needed, thus, is precisely a thought that is ›capable‹ of moving ›in-between‹, a thought of a different ›consistency‹ than both eternal ideality and mere factual historicity. What is needed are philosophers who create, in the *untimely* or *aternal* sense that we have followed here. A thought capable of ›getting into something‹, of making a move without at the same time establishing an origin, i.e. referring thinking back to transcendence.

»The philosopher creates«, Deleuze rigorously states, »he doesn't reflect« (Deleuze 1995: 122); and a little later in the conversation,

---

cepts. This movement's only present, of course, in the sentences, but the sole point of the sentences is to give it life, a life of its own. Style is a set of variations in language, a modulation and straining of one's whole language towards something outside it« (Deleuze 1995: 140).

he claims in the same vein that what ›this world‹ is really in need of are »people to think« (Deleuze 1995: 128). Such emphasis on the practice of ›thinking‹, and on the business of such thinking as one of creation—a creation that demands a lot: ›to move somewhere else‹—leads to a new logic of the ethical itself; it evokes a different understanding of where to place this dimension in philosophy as such. It is thus that Deleuze names the project ahead of us as ethology, or onto-ethology (and precisely not onto-theology) in Eric Alliez' reformulation.[13] Instead of demanding this world become everything that it is not, such ethically charged thought is based on the risks of experimentation. Rather than function through prescription it demands more than everything else a belief in this world—a task that Deleuze, together with Guattari, regards as most difficult for us today:

> It may be that believing in this world, in this life, becomes our most difficult task, or the task of a mode of existence still to be discovered on our plane of immanence today. This is the empiricist conversion (we have so many reasons not to believe in the human world; we have lost the world, worse than a fiancée or a god). (WPH: 75)

The problem has indeed changed; this is how Deleuze and Guattari see it. Worse than in Nietzsche's godless times of which we already spoke, and worse even than in the case of Kierkegaard's ›knight of faith‹, to whom we will come back in a little while, »[t]he modern fact is«, as Deleuze already said in *Cinema 2* a few years earlier, »that we do no longer believe in this world. We do not even believe in the

---

13 Cf. »Ethology: Spinoza and Us« in which Deleuze specifies: »The approach [of ethology] is no less valid for us, for human beings, than for animals, because no one knows ahead of time the affects one is capable of; it is a long affair of experimentation, requiring a lasting prudence, a Spinozian wisdom that implies the construction of a plane of immanence or consistency« (Deleuze 1992: 627). In a chapter of *The Signature of the World. What is Deleuze and Guattari's Philosophy?*, titled »Onto-Ethologies« Eric Alliez distinguishes a thought of analogy (that is onto-theology) from a thought of immanence. »I propose to call onto-ethology the establishment of a plane of immanence such that, *becoming and multiplicity being one and the same, becoming no longer has a subject distinct from itself* and carries thinking along with it as the heterogenesis of nature: a plane of nature. It is the plane of nature that provides the ›there‹ wherein to ›go in order to search would be to create‹.« (Alliez 2004: 76–77)

events which happen to us, love, death, as if they only half concerned us... it is the world which looks to us like a bad film« (C2: 171).

When it thus seems as if nothing can be done, what is needed — and according to Deleuze true thought (of whatever kind, be it artistic, scientific, or philosophical) by definition exposes itself to this task rather than avoiding it by looking for easier roles to take on — is the production of a creative and affective rather than a dogmatically coherent and normative response. The broken link between »man and the world« is so absolute that no better *ratio* could ever re-link it, so this constitutive (non)relation *must* become »an object of belief: it is *the impossible* which can only be restored in faith« (172, my emphasis). Instead of being merely the question of a more accurate knowledge that is to be gained in order to achieve mastery, thought here receives a radically different quality. As actualization of the virtual, and as such as *real* as any other practice, thought becomes the incorporeal force of a new mode of existence that is to be discovered on our plane of immanence today.

But it is essential to read carefully these rather un-Deleuzian expressions of ›belief‹ and ›faith‹ and to put them in adequate proportion so that we avoid falling back into both theological and idealist solutions. John Rajchman rightly points out that Deleuze's *empirical conversion* consists in claiming that »[t]o *think* is not to be certain, but, on the contrary, to *believe* where we cannot know for sure« (Rajchman 2002: 17, my emphasis). This belief, however, is not directed at a different world and thus has nothing in common with religious faith, but it is as we said a ›belief in *this* world‹. And as if this is not already a rather strange ethical demand for any action to take, Deleuze most significantly adds, »it becomes belief in this world, *as it is*« (C2: 172, my emphasis). Any lurking messianism or utopianism, which the formula ›belief in this world‹ may seem to imply, is radically transformed through the specification of the world such ›as it is‹. Instead of a belief in another sphere, providing ›this world‹ with the horizon of a ›better world‹, which ultimately, however, is never to be reached in the here and now, the belief suggested here is transformed into an infinite task of deepening immanence rather than fleeing it. It expresses what the paradoxical, two-directional moving equation ›ontology = ethics‹ speaks for. It does not mean any simple belief in the world, making of us Hegel's ›beautiful souls‹ who

»see... differences everywhere and appeal... to them only as respectable, reconcilable or federative differences, while history continues to be made through bloody contradictions« (DR: 52). ›The belief in this world, as it is‹ rather speaks a logic in which everything that ›is‹ only ever is as *becoming*. It speaks of belief as active affirmation of a world that in *every* practice must be affirmed in order to-become-itself as becoming-something-else. We again have to remind ourselves that the infinite movement that ›is‹ all there is, is always double. Thinking and being in this sense are said to be one and the same, Deleuze told us. What such a statement, therefore, exemplifies is that ethical imperatives do not have to depart from this world in order to produce the openness necessary for an ethics worthy of its name. Rather than moving into a realm of ideal values, which unambiguously, yet purely abstractly, could serve as criteria of ethical conduct, Deleuze with his paradoxical construction (›belief in this world, as it is‹) produces a movement of thought — a movement in the same place, a leaping, a becoming — which in being *the impossible* according to the measure of normative criteria is capable of affecting every-body.

We might gain illumination of this difficult way of thinking by remembering Nietzsche's theory of gambling, the throw of the dice about which he makes *Zarathustra* speak, and which for Deleuze in his interpretation of Nietzsche precisely demonstrates the at least two-directional movement of the infinitive as event that is both the release of the virtual and the affirmation of a most singular action.[14] Again, what is important about Nietzsche's dicethrow is not so much that it explicates chance as such — the dicethrow as an example of total arbitrariness in which each realization is as likely as any other. Rather, what an *adequate* understanding of the logic of the dicethrow must imply is the active affirmation of chance. Instead of »two worlds«, Deleuze says (NP: 25) of (1) the dice that is thrown and (2) the dice that falls back, throwing the dice is always the matter of a *singular* event in which both movements »are the two hours of a single world, the two moments of a single world, midnight and midday« (ibid). The affirmation of chance does not lie *either* in the throw of the dice *or* in their falling back. To the contrary, Nietzsche

---

14 »To think is to send a dicethrow«, Deleuze says (NP: 32). Cf. for the significant passages regarding ›sky *and* earth‹ in Nietzsche's *Zarathustra*, ›Before Sunrise‹ and ›The Seven Seals‹.

says, it is about affirming *both* earth *and* sky. The dicethrow affirms becoming *and* it affirms the being of becoming. No either/or but both at the same time; a logic of ... and ... or both/and to be precise, because both occurrences happen ›at once‹, without however collapsing into each other. Only in this way — as one double movement — is the necessity of chance not merely stated but actively affirmed as »the unique number which cannot be another« (NP: 32). And only thus does a thought of the necessity of chance become a thought of absolute *singularity* — a dancing thought. When Deleuze says that »*Nietzsche turns chance into affirmation*« (NP: 26) — and such an affirmation always means turning it into a demand — he exemplifies for us how thought has turned itself into an *a/effective imperative*.

New Image of Thought

We, thus, have reached an answer to the question of what philosophy is for Deleuze, of what his project of *transcendental empiricism* truly implies. With Colebrook we can speak of Deleuze's thought as ›a grammar of becoming‹ that in transforming the question of thinking is »an attempt to write a grammar of life« (Colebrook 1999: 129). We have thus also arrived at the Deleuzian ›image of thought‹, a concern that is at the center of so many of Deleuze's works.[15] If we take the equation of ›ontology = ethics‹ seriously, thinking this world ›is‹ (=) always already creating this world, this world that in itself ›is‹ (=) nothing but the movement of becoming(-other). Instead of being mere reflection on practice, thought has to be understood as a prac-

---

15 At this point I hope the idea that the quality of what an image is supposed to be changes in this transformation or ›destruction‹ of the dogmatic image of thought needs no further explanation. It is no contradiction that Deleuze speaks of a »New Image of Thought« in *Nietzsche and Philosophy* (NP: 103ff), while he seems to search for the liberation of thought from image altogether, looking for a *thought without image* in *Difference and Repetition* (cf. DR: 147ff). While, on the one hand, Deleuze aims at liberating thought from its traditional — dogmatic — image, he is, on the other hand, also attempting to tear away the image from a limited representational logic, something that, next to its (complicated) Bergsonian legacy (cf. Pearson 2001: 142), and also Kantian and Heideggerian influences (cf. Gasché 2007), I would also like to link to Walter Benjamin's important contribution to the thought of *reproducibility* (*Reproduzierbarkeit*), with all the ambivalent potential that this precise thinker developed in his essay on »The Work of Art in the Age of Mechanical Reproduction« (cf. Benjamin 1968).

tice whose exercise is already a question of *style* in the most substantial sense. It is always already a question of *how* to practice thought, the style of philosophy becoming much more than a simple mode of representation understood as merely the vehicle of communication. For Deleuze ›to think‹ or ›to do philosophy‹ is always already charged with this demand. ›To think‹ means to liberate thought from all presuppositions that dominate it and most of all from its subjectivist heritage which, by covertly re-introducing transcendence, produced an even stricter normative and moral image of thought than any thought before it. Deleuze's Nietzschean critique of *clichés* and *doxa*, but also of the modern image of thought as mere information and communication, is the call for a new way of thinking that confronts the task ahead. Instead of thinking thought as immanent to something, be it an objective truth or the expression of a subject, thought as the practice of thinking in a philosophy of radical immanence is itself expressing and unfolding *a*, and that means *this*, world. Only this way will we keep thought alive.

> If we think of thought as the owner of statements, as the producer of sense, as the condition of existence, we can do so only by virtue of a way of speaking, by asking certain questions that will always enable us to *recognize* what we understand thinking to be. But this is a denial of the life of *thinking*; for thinking is not a *being* (a subject), but the event ›to think‹. (Colebrook 1999: 130–131)

While thinking and being can be said to be one and the same in Deleuze's ontology of becoming, thinking is not located within a being but freed from any such imprisonment. It is nothing but the event ›to think‹, as Colebrook rightly points out. Deleuze's antisubjectivism or *nomadology*, as he himself often has called it, consists most of all in the reversal of the traditional subject-predicate-structure of philosophy. Instead of starting with the subject, which as a substance receives attributes according to which it then acts in the world (the world as the other, the *Gegen-stand* of the subject), it is thinking as practice which effectuates *a* something, which was once called subjectivity. ›At its best‹ we also might want to add, since to release an event, i.e. ›to become virtual‹, is as we know anything but likely in our daily practice of thinking, such as we usually conceive of it. However, this claim is nonetheless what Deleuze demands from true thought as what it is ›to do philosophy‹. Rather than simply moving beyond the subject by letting it die once and for all, Deleuze demands a *complicated* movement: an *inhumanizing* movement of undergoing the *infinit(iv)e* imperative: »to think!« — »to become!« — »to live!«, with no prior ›who‹, nor objective ›why‹, nor teleological ›what for‹. This infinitive — grammar of the impersonal imperative — no longer distinguishes between the doer and the deed, or between what something is and what it does (cf. Colebrook 1999: 130). It no longer distinguishes between a primary essence and a secondary movement, which this substance acts out. Rather, it *is* the event itself, that is, absolutely disinterested necessity of radical contingency. The infinitive (like the indefinite article) is always already an imperative, an affective imperative that cannot but produce movement — singular movement. In its infinit(iv)e indetermination, or (in)difference if you want. It demands on the level of the event itself. It demands the active affirmation of the event.

This philosophy is always already acting. It is philosophy as *amor fati*, a thinking that is a question of loving, of the love of one's fate, which in fact is nothing but one's life, which is — if we only know how to be truly Nietzschean — nothing but the creation of *a life*....[16] Deleuze as a true Nietzschean thinks against the moral images of thought for a thought that lives up to its inherent ethicality in and as its full potential.[17] It is Nietzsche's philosophical style that, un-

---

16 Many references could be given for the notion of *amor fati* in Nietzsche's œuvre. The following ›formula‹ from *Ecce Homo* suits our purposes best: »Meine Formel für die Grösse am Menschen ist amor fati: dass man Nichts anders haben will, vorwärts nicht, rückwärts nicht, in alle Ewigkeit nicht. Das Nothwendige nicht bloss ertragen, noch weniger verhehlen – aller Idealismus ist Verlogenheit vor dem Nothwendigen –, sondern es lieben...« (KSA 6: 297 #10).

17 Cf. Deleuze's three theses of the dogmatic (that is, moral) image of thought with which he begins his subchapter ›New Image of Thought‹ in *Nietzsche and Philosophy*: »1) We are told that the thinker *as* thinker wants and loves *truth* (truthfulness of the thinker); that thought as thought possesses or formally contains truth (innateness of the idea, *a priori* nature of concepts); that thinking is the natural exercise of a faculty... 2) We are also told that we are ›diverted‹ from the truth but by forces which are foreign to it... *Error*... 3) We are told, finally, that all we need to think well, to think truthfully, is a *method*... Through method we ward off error« (NP: 103).

derstood as *critique*, is so radical that nothing escapes it, not even this world's most pertinent nihilism. Critique, understood in such radical way as critique without redemption, can be said to be the only true mode of thinking (cf. Bell 1995).[18] Emphasizing this means precisely not, as many (and among them Heidegger) have suggested, that Nietzsche does not really provide us with a true line of flight for thought and life, and as such leaves us with no way to go for ethical thinking. To the contrary, what Deleuze shows in his interpretation of Nietzsche is that in pushing »destruction« as far as the self-destruction of nihilism (nihilism being nothing but the other side of idealism), Nietzsche truly produces a ›new image of thought‹, a thought ›beyond Good and Evil‹—a thought taking seriously its ethological dimensions in practicing it as a way of life, as an active affirmation of

---

18 We can no longer avoid it: at this point we have to speak of Kant. *Kant*, who cannot be missing when we think of a new, a different *practical philosophy*; but also *Kant*, who did not yet receive adequate attention in our specific discussion of Deleuze's Nietzscheanism, in which he latently provided us with a background against which we were able to explore the Deleuzian expression of ›a new image of thought‹. In *Nietzsche and Philosophy*, one of Deleuze's most interesting theses, which we mentioned only in passing, is that Nietzsche is a true Kantian, more Kantian even than Kant himself. Deleuze sees Nietzsche's philosophy as a deepening rather than an absolute rejection of Kant's Critical Philosophy, and he points out that it is precisely the principle Kantian motif—*Critique*—that stands at the beginning of Nietzsche's philosophizing. In tracing back this line of thought from Deleuze and Nietzsche to Kant, Kant's genius was, as Daniel W. Smith writes in »The Place of Ethics in Deleuze's Philosophy«, that he has conceived of »a purely *immanent* critique of reason« (Smith 1998: 253). It is this potential of critique that leads to an ethical thought which »presents this immanent conception of ethics not, as one might perhaps expect, as a rejection of Kantianism but, on the contrary, as its *fulfillment*« (ibid). According to Nietzsche, Kant's critique of reason does not go far enough and still awaits its true fulfillment. On the very first page of his Nietzsche-book Deleuze indicates this limited appreciation of Kant when he writes: »Kant had not carried out a true critique because he was not able to pose the problem of critique in terms of values.« (NP: 1) An emphasis on evaluation and interpretation instead of *a priori* principles and judgment is the Nietzschean revolution in philosophy for Deleuze, which ultimately gives *critique* a new significance. While Kant was the first to discover that critique is philosophy proper, for Deleuze it is only with Nietzsche that the highest quality of thinking is truly inscribed in critique. The critique of reason, as Kant perceives of it, still makes halt before reason itself as the natural image of thought. It does not carry through its project of ›a total and positive critique that escapes nothing‹ (cf. NP: 89).

this world, such as it is.[19] The point of critique is thus not, as Deleuze says, »justification but a different way of feeling: another sensibility« (NP: 94). Such new sensibility, *active* and *affective* thought, is a thought ›beyond Good and Evil‹, because it refers back »all things and any kind of origin to values, but also [refers] back... these values to something which is, as it were, their origin and determines their value« (NP: 2). Thinking then is freed from the base presupposition that it is the natural exercise of a faculty (and one totally separated from sense(s)), and it becomes instead »an extraordinary event *in* thought itself, *for* thought itself«. Thinking becomes »the n-th power of thought« (ibid). It becomes the event, which, as Deleuze already said in his *Logic of Sense*, »is not what occurs (as an accident)« but »is rather inside what occurs, the purely expressed« (LS: 149).

3. »To become!« as *ethos*[20]

We have reached a level of speaking of thought—thought as becoming-event—that can no longer be made comprehensible in a purely descriptive language. Only by undergoing the movement of becoming itself will it be possible to speak adequately of the implications that such an affective thought effectuates. This is the last task ahead of us: we must follow the movement of becoming as the ethical movement itself.

While we have already concluded that Deleuze never explicitly elaborated an ethics, we can nonetheless dare the statement that his whole work speaks an ethical concern—*everywhere*. We have shown that the ethical gesture is always already *inhering* and *subsisting* on the most conceptual level of what he demands of thought. Thought, both in its philosophical practice of creating concepts and in all other aspects of life, is not about being ›good‹ by being coherent in the normative logical sense. It is worthy of its name only when it is creative, a thought to *affect*, to *produce* differences, and most of all *to-think-and-live-otherwise*. Thus, and here he finds himself in

---

19 »Affirmation is the highest power of the will. But what is affirmed? The earth, life....« (PI: 83)

20 An earlier, much briefer version of this subchapter was published in Diekmann/Khurana 2007.

agreement most of all with his philosophical opponents Kant and Heidegger, Deleuze's task was never to reach argumentative closure to ›what thinking is‹. Rather, his thought speaks of the continual effort to produce thought, to understand thinking as an event—in-between essences. ›To think‹, thus, is already one expression of becoming. It is, and this is precisely shown in Deleuze's own practice of creating concepts, not about the measuring and the appropriation of a clearly demarcated territory. Instead, it is a non-appropriative response to something, which comes from the outside and affects us. We only have to remember again how Deleuze introduces the notion of what it means to think in *Difference and Repetition*:

> It cannot be regarded as a *fact* that thinking is the natural exercise of a faculty, and that this faculty is possessed of a good nature and a good will. ›Everybody‹ knows very well that in fact men think rarely, and more often under the impulse of a shock than in the excitement of a taste of thinking. (DR: 132)

In this practice, ›we‹ are no prior ground on which secondarily such a becoming takes place. On the contrary, ›we‹ are nothing but the very effect of this responding. Only in the active affirmation of this reversal of prioritization can it be ensured that the infinite movement of becoming, of thought in particular and of life in more general terms, is not blocked by something other than immanence itself. This is Deleuze's most *explicit* ethical impetus: The movement of becoming as *the infinit(iv)e imperative: »to become!«* must always remain *implicit*. But it must never be forgotten in the discussion of Deleuze's plane of thought, because it is the movement produced by this insisting imperative that alone enables us to link the question of thought to life. In a last turn I would like to give life to such a notion of becoming in its practical and living dimensions such as it always already figures in Deleuze's work.

The Movement of Becoming

It is common today to present the Deleuzian becoming as a politically empowering, liberating, and transgressive potential for the thinking and practicing of a new, and this means a *different,* world that we want to inhabit.[21] Without disagreeing in content with such a motivated interpretation of Deleuze's philosophy, my argument throughout this book has pushed Deleuze's thought of becoming in a slightly different direction. Rather than merely assuming that all that is asked from us is to use becoming instead of Being, and the rest, i.e. a different ontological perspective on the world, one that is about expressing and transforming, will fall into place all by itself, I deliberately moved one step backwards. I attempted to slowly develop Deleuze's philosophical take on ›this world‹ in order to show that the notion of becoming as *both* ontological principle *and* ethical potential can only be adequately understood when, because of this interrelation of ontology and ethics, it is taken as a highly demanding and infinite task, and this again *both* in its theoretical conceptualization *and* in its potential practical actualizations. Such particular emphasis seems to be necessary because of the very fact that many discussions use the notion of becoming in its rich ethico-political potential, as if it directly explicates a different practice for our reality, and thus they necessarily overlook the specific ›virtuality‹ that characterize Deleuze's figures of becoming, a virtuality that does not lack reality but that will ultimately also always escape its concrete actualization. Out of a concern for an understanding of becoming in which the ontological implications are not again compromised by practical applications, I have stressed the structural incommensurability of, and that means the differentiation between, the virtual and the actual. And this precisely out of concern for practice, since this differen*t*/*c*ial relation, which is more than either side by itself, is constitutive of it. Thus, rather than looking at becoming as a ready-made category which provides us with a new model both of a way of thinking and a way of living, something that ›we‹ easily can take on, I aimed at stressing that not only in its theoretical but also in its practical dimensions becoming must be read as a more complicated figuration — an impossible movement. Rather namely than something which we *can* perform, we instead infinit(iv)ely must learn *how to become capable of*

---

21 To name just one famous Deleuzian inspired political discourse, which precisely takes up his thought of becoming as proposing a different mode of inhabiting this world, we should think of Antonio Negri's and Michael Hardt's *Empire* (2000), with its sequel *Multitude* (2004).

it. And it is precisely in this *indirect* sense that the figure of becoming expresses the ethical concern.

If we therefore are to get a better grasp of Deleuze's imperative »to become!« as »*a life...: everywhere*!«, we must above all avoid the mistake of re-introducing a willing subject that always already *can*—be it thinking or being—and devote ourselves to the movement of becoming itself. The figure of becoming is not to be misinterpreted: Becoming always remains in the state of a *problem to be solved*. »To become!« speaks of an infinit(iv)e task, one that we will never fully accomplish, one that, therefore, we *are* utterly *in*capable of. This, however, does not have to necessarily imply that because we as Subjects are not capable of it, the movement itself cannot be produced. To the contrary, Deleuze precisely asks for the impossible. What is asked in order to face up to radical immanence is to *become* capable of the movement in the liberating sense that Spinoza said that ›we do not yet know what a body is capable of‹. It means, in the Bergsonian sense, to *precisely* endure the infinite movement of continual change, and, in the Nietzschean sense, to will *a* becoming worthy its name: active affirmation of becoming effect rather than being cause of the movement.

To stress such heaviness—›the heaviest of all weight‹—should not be misunderstood as moralistic taming of Deleuze's thought of becoming. What such a pointed interpretation rather hopes to illuminate is the *implicated* reversal of the yardsticks of philosophy and ethics—based on the clear separation of theory/knowledge from practice/morals—which I see at the heart of the notion of becoming. For becoming works both as the category of Deleuze's ontology and as its practical imperative »to become!« With the notion of becoming, not only is every supposedly universal scope of ethics transformed into the absolute singular task »to become!«, but also the addressee, the subject, must undergo a metamorphosis so (in)human that in place of the individual ›I‹ that knows what it does, only the pre-individual indefinite ›*a*‹ survives, one which is not at all certain what it knows and who it is, but is rather damned to affirm the *belief in what is not certain*!

How »to become!«, therefore? If at the end of this project we again ask our reader to return to its beginning, to Spinoza as the prince of philosophy, whose *Ethics* is (=) ontology, and whose concepts are (=) affective rather than explicative; and then via our imagination to move again through Bergson's thought of duration, duration as that which can be approached only by a very precise intuition, a leaping into the unknown as we said; in order to arrive at the Nietzschean imperative of thinking as actively affirming one's fate as its very creation, we could spell out Deleuze's task of becoming in the following way: *»To become!« is (=) to bring to the highest degree the (in)capacity to be affected while at the same time to intensify the force to affect.* To put it in slightly different—less competitive—terms, it means *to become capable of precisely following the fold of affectivity (to affect and be affected), which is the fold of becoming as infinite movement.* Only by *indirection*, and this means in an *affective* way, will this become *effective.*

In Deleuze's thought of becoming nothing remains what it ›is‹, everything (must) *become(s)-other.* Closure remains inhibited by the radical exposition to always yet another series. The figure of becoming is, thus, both conceptually and practically *produced* in the very *in-betweeness* that is its only mode of existence—as movement itself.[22] That this is not the total elimination of ›agency‹ but rather a new thought of action as we have called it here is important. Out of necessity—this is the least that can be said—there is always something moving in this (in)capable becoming. However, »to become!« the only one ›capable of‹ undergoing the movement of becoming, this is the *singular task—everywhere.* The movement is, thus, to become a *patient of dynamisms.* It is to undergo the *athleticism* Deleuze's philosophy presents to us even on the level of thought. No Subject can ever be its ›ground‹; the *figure,* while substantial, is (=) always only the effect of the infinite movement that is working upon it.[23]

---

22 This in-betweeness is very well exemplified by Gilbert Simondon's paradigm of becoming as that which ›always falls out of step with itself‹ [*se déphaser par rapport à lui-même*], cf. Simondon 1992: 300.

23 For Deleuze's notion of athleticism, cf. FB: 13–19. It is important to again point out that this athleticism is not any kind of ›gymnastics‹, i.e. one exercise among others. Looking at the paintings of Francis Bacon, Deleuze stresses the pain and disturbance they express and how much loss and violence is implied. Bacon's figures, he says, are about a *deformation* that could not be more substantial. What is at stake here is the reversed but nonetheless structurally the same paradoxical process that Levinas describes as the necessary paradox of the experience of shame, which is being ›chained to oneself‹ and yet having ›the radical impulse to flee‹ oneself (cf. Levinas 2003).

While any spelled-out ethics *of* becoming would always already, and more or less explicitly, presuppose subjectivity, or at least take providing a new model for subjectivity as its stated endeavor, becoming as the infinite movement »to become!« ›merely‹ expresses an *ethos*.[24] It speaks an ›attitude‹ that must remain nearly imperceptible, because as soon as the ivory tower of the Truth as inherently ›Go(o)d‹ is built upon it, it loses what is most important about it: the (im)possibility that only a ›belief in this world, as it is‹ can restore, and the (in)capability that only a (pre-individual) singularity—a different sensibility—can endure. The loss of the ability and willful subjectivity that was so fundamental to Ethics must be pushed ›beyond the human turn‹, as Bergson said, so that the passivity resulting from it is not mere ›receptivity‹, as Deleuze says in *Difference and Repetition* (cf. DR: 78). The movement of becoming must express a passivity so passive that it is not only passive to anything outside itself but also, and maybe most importantly, *to itself*. This is what is meant when Deleuze speaks of ›passive syntheses‹, and the passive ›self‹ as ›larval subjects‹:

> These thousands of habits of which we are composed—these contractions, contemplations, pretensions, presumptions, satisfactions, fatigues; these variable present — thus form the basic domain of passive syntheses... This self, therefore, is by no means simple: it is not enough to relativise or pluralise the self, all the while retaining for it a simple attenuated form. Selves are larval subjects, the world of passive syntheses constitutes the system of the self, under conditions yet to be determined, but it is the system of a dissolved self. (Ibid)

---

24 This distinction is brought out clearly by Ewa Płonowska Ziarek who in her elaboration of *An Ethics of Dissensus* says that »[b]y the ›ethos of becoming‹ I mean first of all the task of resistance to power and, second, the transformation of the negative thought of resistance into a creation of the new modes of being« (Ziarek 2001: 15). In reading the notion of ethos in the context of Foucault's »What is Enlightenment«, which we also have made use of in order to express the ethos of becoming as ›attitude‹, I could not agree more with her conclusion in regard to this ethos: »Whether it is seen as resistance or experimental praxis, this ethos shifts the ethical problematic from the obedience to universal law or moral codes to the disruptive temporality of becoming manifesting itself in the creation of the yet ›improbable‹ modes of being« (45).

The movement becomes *incapable* of stopping itself, or, to put it the other way around: it becomes *capable* of being immanent to nothing but itself.[25] Everything such a movement encounters ›does something‹ to it. Everything has an effect on it. Yet this effect cannot be absorbed into any realm of Being. It will necessarily move on, escape, and thus lead to further affection. Deleuze and Guattari already explained in their *Anti-Oedipus*, that such an escape is precisely not mere withdrawal from life but an extremely skillful movement: »There is a whole world of difference«, they say, »between the schizo and the revolutionary: the difference between the one who escapes, and the one *who knows how to make what he is escaping escape*« (Deleuze/Guattari 2004: 374, my emphasis).

To give an example of this impossible move, let us think of the *figure* of Abraham in the story called ›The sacrifice of Isaac‹, which Kierkegaard so a/effectively tells in his great book on the question of the ethical *Fear and Trembling*.[26] There, a barely ›capable‹ Abraham responds to a call so inhuman and murderous that only a fool or a monster would take it up. And think of the way in which Abraham responds — HERE I AM!, he always utters — even at the most abstruse end when, after all he endured, he all of a sudden is prevented from killing his son though he first was precisely asked to do so and apparently asked by the same voice. And think of the way Kierkegaard praises this absolute anti-hero who alone is able to produce a movement, which the ›I‹ can never make.[27] He is precisely none of the ›knight[s] of infinite resignation‹ who »are easily recognizable — their walk is light and bold« (FT: 38). Pushing further, Abraham — the stupid one, the murderous one, ›knight of faith‹ — was not only ›capable of‹ the movement that was demanded of him (in such a way namely that ultimately nothing happened!), but also as Kierkegaard says, »he

---

25 In her article »Passive Synthesis and Life«, Colebrook discusses such a radical passivity. »Radical passivity« she states »allows us to think radical activity: a force of pure positivity not subordinated to any of the transcendent terms which are formed as its effects« (Colebrook 2001: 14).

26 Cf. Kierkegaard 1983. It will be quoted in the following as FT.

27 »But this movement I cannot make.« (Kierkegaard 1983: 51) This is only one occasion among many others in which the ›I‹ expresses the impossibility that is demanded of it. It is Kierkegaard's genius to present his ›deconstruction‹ of Ethics even on the level of textual reference.

neither arrived too early nor too late« (FT: 35). Both his (in)capacity in regard to the movements to be made and the untimely timeliness produced thereby—*precision brought to its highest power*—present to us a movement of becoming.[28] Did anything happen at all…? Yet, *everything* has happened![29]

Return to the Surface

But we have to come back to the movement itself. ›To be affective‹ — one possible short version of our (ethical) formula—does not have anything to do with simple, uncritical affirmation. Nietzsche's affirmation is a critique so radical that nothing escapes it. To be affective, that is »to become!«, demands more than pushing in just one direction. While traditional philosophy starting with Platonism always only looks to the heavens and establishes philosophy, in as much as life itself, as an ›ascent‹ (cf. LS: 127) or a way out of the cave, by contrast a philosophy of becoming (must) look(s) for a movement ›down-

---

28 This ›Abrahamic movement‹ could, of course, also be read as an ultra-transcendent movement, precisely ignoring everything that is of significance in ›this world‹ and giving up all worldliness in order to follow the call. However, while the issue of transcendence and immanence again would have to be investigated and elaborated in detail, in my opinion Kierkegaard's ›wit‹ lies precisely in re-inscribing the obvious reference of transcendence in this story into a radical thought of immanence. Such a reading of Kierkegaard's *Abraham* is based on the existing (in)humanizing interpretations of this biblical figure such as Franz Kafka's »Abraham« (Kafka 1958) and Avital Ronell's »And Sarah Laughed« (Ronell 2003).

29 Instead of focusing on the murderous call or the question if or if not sacrifice has happened, issues which are normally raised in reference to this biblical story, in our reading all we care about is the movement Abraham undergoes and what it effectuates or activates. It seems to us that this is Kierkegaard's genius: in emphasizing the movement that Abraham is capable of enduring, he ultimately allows for a much ›worldlier‹, i.e. immanent, reading of what ultimately does happen. Rather than re-introducing a higher level that supposedly solves the mystery, the movement itself provides a line of flight. Deleuze refers more than once to Kierkegaard as being concerned with a philosophy of difference and repetition, that is, a philosophy of becoming. In *Difference and Repetition*, Deleuze even explicitly names Kierkegaard's *Abraham* as the one »who submits humorously to the law, but finds in that submission precisely the singularity of his only son whom the law commanded him to sacrifice« (DR: 7). He also links this *Abraham* to Nietzsche's *Zarathustra* whose »hatred of the law and *amor fati* (love of fate), aggression and acquiescence are [his] two faces« (ibid).

wards‹ from these heights. In following *his* intellectual tradition — a tradition that in the most general terms could be called a tradition of hereticism — Deleuze problematizes the presupposed one way street of thought and shows that rather than describing a linear process, traceable step by step, it has to be understood as an event that »is in line with other dimensions« (LS: 128). The logic of event that gives thought its structure here always and simultaneously moves in more than one direction, and, thus, it complicates the notion of movement itself, since it always moves paradoxically.[30] This is also why it would be too easy to stop here. Any straight movement downwards still remains purely one-directional and is, thus, in no sense a movement of becoming, not even on the level of thought. Such a movement might be courageous and transgressive, but for Deleuze it is not enough to simply ask to produce such a movement. The much more important question for him is »where… such a descent throw[s] us« (LS: 135). And it is here that the practice of becoming requires so much precision. »To become!« precisely does not mean to be lost in groundlessness but to find, and that is to invent, a way out! It is to become capable of returning to the surface, to become capable of ›surfing‹ this surface as Deleuze defined a movement that no longer has an origin but enters into ›an existing wave‹ and ›puts-into-orbit‹. It is to approach the limit-figure that *a becoming…* can never »reach« but only »forever attain«, as Deleuze and Guattari specify in *A Thousand Plateaus* when they ask the question of »How to produce a Body without Organs«; a question which is precisely only ever adequately understood when taken as an infinite movement of becoming (cf. TP: 150). Although a lot more should be said on this subject of *a becoming-body* that is no longer determined by substance and defined by form, but »is defined only by a longitude and a latitude: in other

30 For another expression of this paradoxical movement, cf. Deleuze's ›definition‹ of becoming as movement ›at once‹ in more than one direction, which he gives at the very beginning of *The Logic of Sense*. He explicates with the example of Lewis Carroll's *Alice* who ›becomes larger‹: »When I say ›Alice becomes larger,‹ I mean that she becomes larger than she was. By the same token, however, she becomes smaller than she is now. Certainly, she is not bigger and smaller at the same time. She is larger now, she was smaller before. But it is at the same moment that one becomes larger than one was and smaller than one becomes. This is the simultaneity of becoming whose characteristic is to elude the present« (LS: 1).

words... the sum total of the intensive affects it is capable of at a given power or degree of potential« (TP: 260), we are here interested in the movement itself. To become capable of re-turning to the surface is to produce the movement of becoming.[31] It is in such a movement that any static subject/object division, as fully present and separated from each other, is overcome and one arrives at the ›event‹ — always eluding the present, ›always yet to (be)come‹. The surface-movement we are encountering here is not another invulnerable subject ›who finally knows it all‹ (this is only the cliché of the wise sage), but rather the very movement of following the event on its very own surface — rejecting both heights and depths, rejecting everything we can think of as ›taking a hold on‹, rejecting all claims of possession. »The event... is not the object as denoted, but the object as expressed or expressible, never present«, Deleuze says (LS: 136). The event ›never is‹ so to speak. All ›there is‹ *is* infinite movement. If there is a task of becoming, the task is to follow a line of flight both without ever objectifying and without ever becoming a fully present subject of this itinerary. It is in this sense that we must remain (in)capable *of* this event. It is ›to affect‹ in such a way that nothing really happens and yet everything has happened (Abraham).[32] It is not to strive for the most outrageous outcome, nor to will simply what occurs but to will ›something *in* that which occurs‹, as Deleuze has said. It is the impossible task, which entails approaching the imperceptible line *in-between* heights and depths — without ever getting something solid in your hands. This also means not ›to be who you are‹ but ›to

---

31 This is similar to what Maurice Blanchot in *The Writing of the Disaster* says about the problem of philosophy as one-directional movement, a problem so substantial because as we here also have elucidated, it is a problem of writing and language itself: »What Plato teaches us about Plato in the myth of the cave is that men in general are deprived of the power or the right to turn, or to turn back« (Blanchot 1995: 34). And in the next fragment, Blanchot continues: »To converse, it seems, is not only to turn away from saying what, thanks to language, *is* — the present of a presence. To converse is also to turn language away from itself, maintaining it outside of all unity, outside even the unity of that which is. To converse is to divert language from itself by letting it differ and defer, answering with an always already to a not yet« (ibid).

32 To come back one more time to the Body without Organs of which Deleuze and Guattari say that it »is what remains when you take everything away« (TP: 151), it is also said that on it »[s]omething will happen. Something is already happening« (TP: 152).

become what one is‹. *Everything* is asked from us in this movement. Because it is literally too much for the ›I‹, the Stoic expertise of *miming*, of which Deleuze so admiringly speaks in his *Logic of Sense*, is much more fundamental in the production of this movement than it seems at first.[33] »To become!« means to produce an effect of something the cause of which one never was and could never be. Such a practice means to become a quasi-cause in the most *serious* sense, which, however, only a *humorous* — (in)capable — submission is ›capable‹ of producing. »Joy is the ethical test that measures degrees of virtualization or implication«: this is important when thinking of a »Deleuzean Ethics« (Goodchild 1997: 41). To become capable of this movement has, thus, nothing to do with tragic heroism. While it remains a question of losing, but more in the sense of ›one loses it‹, it also means ›to have faith in the absurd‹ such as Kierkegaard has said. It is to become capable of a belief ›in this world, as it is‹, a task so impossible that it might make us choke. But a possible result of it, we know now, is laughter — »a transformed, illuminated, *laughing* being« (Z ›On the Vision and the Riddle‹).

It is not a question of recognition, but a »leaping in place of the whole body« (LS: 149) — a passion, a practice, an experiment. This movement of becoming might look stupid, even absurd, and the difference it makes is so difficult to detect that Kierkegaard's wit in the case of his Abraham finds the pettiest bourgeois picture imaginable when he wants to give him a more contemporary face: Abraham the *tax collector*![34] Deleuze is a very fine reader of this irritating gesture

---

33 For Deleuze, ›to mime‹ in the case of the Stoics is precisely not a question of *mimesis* in the representative sense but a true action that yet has nothing to do with a return to authenticity. It means to become capable of a most precision-demanding, yet always paradoxical, movement: to bring the practice of ›miming‹ to its nth power so that it becomes a true *act*.

34 »Here he is. The acquaintance is made, I am introduced to him. The instant I first lay eyes on him, I set him apart at once; I jump back, clap my hands, and say half aloud, ›Good Lord, is this the man, is this really the one — he looks just like a tax collector!‹ But this is indeed the one. I move a little closer to him, watch his slightest movement to see if it reveals a bit of heterogeneous optical telegraphy from the infinite, a glance, a facial expression, a gesture, a sadness, a smile that would betray the infinite in his heterogeneity with the finite. No! I examine his figure from top to toe to see if there may not be a crack through which the infinite would peek. No! He is solid all the way through.« (Kierkegaard 1983: 39)

when he points us to the becoming-imperceptible of this Abraham, which does not mean that he disappears but rather that he becomes »like everybody else« (TP: 279), or in Kierkegaard's own words: »He [Abraham] belongs entirely to the world; no bourgeois philistine [*Spießbürger*] could belong to it more.« (Kierkegaard 1983: 39)

›*What is to Be Done Next!*‹

Becoming breaks open the dualism of active and passive. While I hope to have contributed in my other chapters to a better understanding of the complexity that such a different mode of thinking implies, here I hope to approach convincingly the ethical imperative »to become!« in its complex movement and as such as an always (im)possible demand that requires a most creative response. It is only when the structural paradoxality, the infinitive expression: »to become!« is faced up to in every practice, that it shows its potential to be read in an ethical way. The practical ethical question of such a thought no longer concerns ›What ought to be‹ but rather ›What is to be done‹. It is, as Philip Goodchild says when speaking of the ›Ethics of Immanence‹, the question of how one will »convert shame into joy« (Goodchild 2002: 161), which is but another formulation of Deleuze's belief in the world, as it is, and his demand to continually challenge thought in order to think-otherwise.

And yet, the Capital *E* of an Ethics of Immanence such as Goodchild seems to announce it, cannot be the last word. In order to avoid the danger of again substantializing what defies all robust substance, something ›minor‹ needs to be added to this ethical imperative of ›What is to be done‹, still speaking too much in terms of the general rather than the *singular*.

Instead of finding what is ›good‹ and ›right‹, the ethical force of becoming means to be radically exposed to the much more practical concern of ›what is to be done‹. However, while this conversion from the traditional ›What ought to be‹ to the question of ›What is to be done‹ is essential for a new thought of ethics, it is not yet enough. For »there will never be enough done«—this is the condition of infinite immanence.[35] We thus have to construct the more singular task

---

35 This formulation ›There will never be enough done‹ I take from Leonard Lawlor's most recent discussion of the problem of the worst in Deleuze and Guattari. For reference cf. *There Will Never be Enough Done: an Essay of the*

of ›What is to be done *next*‹ as our ethical claim, such as Abraham in his movement *mimed* for us. »He neither arrived too early nor too late«, Kierkegaard said (1983: 35). He was not only capable of moving ›as such‹, but of ›knowing how to move‹, so that he freed this movement of any lurking transcendence. Only by focusing on the movement itself, do we express the release of the event rather than merely the actions that ›we‹ can trace.[36] In contrast to other ethical imperatives, the movement of becoming as expression of *ethos* is never about regaining the Subject. Whatever *a life*... ›is‹, it will never know once and for all ›What ought to be‹, but only ever — and at its best — *be capable of exposing itself* to ›What is to be done *next*‹. This capacity, as we heard above, is one ›we‹ as Subjects are incapable of. It is a question of radical passivity, of how to be affected, which only through a process of active affirmation might become a capacity to affect. The reference to life — and it is important to emphasize this again at the very end of our discussion — is therefore no reference to some norm inherent to life, even less so to the limited life-form of a Subject. We no longer deal with ethical measures that we are normally used to: the law or *a priori* principles, in which the judgment of good and right, the ›shoulds‹ and ›oughts‹, define a territory safe for ›us‹. Rather, we enter *terra incognita*. We speak of an ethical thought that does not claim to have a *direct* way to ›good conduct‹ by placing itself above its subjects, presenting itself as an unambiguous law. Rather, the ethical thought we speak of here affirms its absolute immanence — there is nothing but this immanence and, thus, there is nothing but *the task to learn how to follow this immanence* — »one step for life, one step for thought«, as Deleuze said (PI: 66).

We speak of a position which not only wants to understand the ethical as an ›art of living‹ but also appreciates thought or philosophy as

---

Worst in Deleuze and Guattari, forthcoming at Columbia University Press.

36 We should remember that the process of becoming is no teleological or result-oriented movement. Like Paola Marrati says in her essay on Deleuze's concept of becoming »L'Animal qui sait fuir. G. Deleuze: Politique du devenir, ontology de l'immanence«: »Le devenir est un processus, mais un processus que ne produit rien d'autre que lui-même. Le devenir est un passage, mais un pur passage, qui trouve sa réalité en lui-même, en ce qui fait ou laisse passer, sans égard pour l'état de depart ou celui d'arrivée« (Marrati-Guénoun 1999: 203).

a life.... Such an art of living cannot simply be acquired or reached. It is the continuous exercise of an *askesis*. It is a technique of measuring where there is no measure (and to say it again: this is not the same as an ›inherent measure‹—to believe in such a measure was already the Neo-Platonic error for Deleuze). It is to dare a thought and practice of singularity without taking from it its daring character by making a new program out of it (which one cannot do without turning the singular again into the particular or the individual). It is a ›know-how to live‹ that has nothing to do with ›learn[ing] to live finally‹, as Jacques Derrida in his last interview pointed out (cf. Derrida 2007). And Deleuze agrees with him on such an attitude of thought to life (and of life to thought—this is *as* important). He gives us more food for thought in relation to this task and in regard to his whole work when—very early in his life and never more *explicitly*—in *The Logic of Sense* he has nothing more to say about ethics but this:

> Either ethics makes no sense at all, or this is what it means and has nothing else to say: not to be unworthy of what happens to us... Nothing more can be said and no more has ever been said: to become worthy of what happens to us, and thus to will and release the event... and to become the offspring of one's events and not of one's actions, for the action is itself produced by the offspring of the event. (LS: 149/150)

Abbreviations

Henri Bergson

CE	*Creative Evolution*
CM	*Creative Mind*
MM	*Matter and Memory*

Gilles Deleuze

B	*Bergsonism*
C2	*Cinema 2. The Time-Image*
EP	*Expressionism in Philosophy: Spinoza*
DR	*Difference and Repetition*
F	*Foucault*
FB	*Francis Bacon. The Logic of Sensation*
LS	*The Logic of Sense*
NP	*Nietzsche and Philosophy*
PI	*Pure Immanence. Essays on A Life*

Gilles Deleuze and Félix Guattari

TP	*A Thousand Plateaus*
WPH	*What is Philosophy?*

Friedrich Nietzsche

BGE	*Beyond Good and Evil*
GM	*On the Genealogy of Morals*
GS	*Gay Science*
WTP	*The Will To Power*
Z	*Thus Spoke Zarathustra*

Baruch de Spinoza

E	*Ethics*

Bibliography

Agamben, Giorgio. (2007) *Profanations*. Trans. Jeff Fort New York/Cambridge: Zone Books/The MIT Press.

— (1999) *Potentialities. Collected Essays in Philosophy*. Ed. and trans. Daniel Heller-Roazen. Stanford: Stanford University Press.

— (1998) *Homo Sacer: Sovereign Power and Bare Life*. Trans. Daniel Heller-Roazen. Stanford: Stanford University Press.

Alliez, Eric. (2004) *The Signature of the World, Or, What is Deleuze and Guattari's Philosophy?* Trans. Eliot Ross Albert and Alberto Toscano. New York/London: Continuum.

Badiou, Alain. (2007) »The Event in Deleuze«. *Parrhesia* 2: 37–44.

— (2001) *Ethics. An Essay on the Understanding of Evil*. Trans. Peter Hallward. London/New York: Verso.

— (2000) *Deleuze. The Clamor of Being*. Trans. Louise Burchill. Minneapolis/London: University of Minnesota Press.

Bell, Jeffrey. (1995) »Philosophizing the Double-Bind. Deleuze reads Nietzsche«. *Philosophy Today* 39/4: 371–390.

Bergson, Henri. (2002) *The Two Sources of Morality and Religion*. Trans. R. Ashley Audra and Cloudesley Brereton. Notre Dame: University of Notre Dame Press.

— (1999) *Duration and Simultaneity, with Reference to Einstein's Theory*. Trans. Leon Jacobson. Manchester: Clinamen Press Ltd.

— (1999) *Matter and Memory*. Trans. Nancy Margaret Paul and W. Scott Palmer. New York: Zone Books.

— (1998) *Creative Evolution*. Trans. Arthur Mitchell. New York: Dover Publications, Inc.

— (1992) *The Creative Mind. An Introduction to Metaphysics*. Trans. Mabelle L. Andison. New York: Carol Publishing Group.

Beistegui, Miguel de. (2005) »The Vertigo of Immanence: Deleuze's Spinozism«. *Research in Phenomenology* 35: 77–100.

Benjamin, Walter. (1968) »The Work of Art in the Age of Mechanical Reproduction«. In Walter Benjamin. *Illuminations. Essays and Reflections*, 217–251. Ed. Hannah Arendt. New York: Schocken Books.

Blanchot, Maurice. (1995) *The Writing of Disaster*. Trans. Ann Smock. Lincoln: University of Nebraska Press.

Boudot, Pierre. ed. (1973) *Nietzsche aujourd'hui?* Vol. 1 and 2. Paris: UGE.

Braidotti, Rosi. (2006) *Transpositions. On Nomadic Ethics*. Cambridge/Malden: Polity Press.

— (2005) *Metamorphoses. Towards a Materialist Theory of Becoming*. Cambridge/Malden: Polity Press.

Colebrook, Claire. (2002a) »The Politics and Potential of Everyday Life«. *New Literary History: A Journal of Theory and Interpretation* 33/4: 687–706.

— (2002b) *Understanding Deleuze*. Crows Nest: Allen & Unwin.

— (2001) »Passive Synthesis and Life«. *Parallax* 7/4: 9–28.

— (1999) »A Grammar of Becoming: Strategy, Subjectivism, and Style«. In Elizabeth Grosz, ed. *Becomings. Explorations in Time, Memory and Future*, 117–140. Ithaca/London: Cornell University Press.

DELANDA, Manuel. (2002) *Intensive Science and Virtual Philosophy*. London/New York: Continuum.

DESCARTES, René. (1993) *Meditations on First Philosophy: in which the existence of God and the distinction of the sould from the body are demonstrated*. Indiana: Hackett Publishing Company.

DELEUZE, Gilles. (2004a) »Bergson, 1859–1941«. In Gilles Deleuze. *Desert Island and Other Texts. 1953–1974*, 22–31. Ed. David Lapoujade, trans. Michael Taormina. Los Angeles/New York: Semiotext(e).

— (2004b) »Bergson's Conception of Difference«. In Gilles Deleuze. *Desert Island and Other Texts. 1953–1974*, 32–51. Ed. David Lapoujade, trans. Michael Taormina. Los Angeles/New York: Semiotext(e).

— (2004c) »The Method of Dramatization«. In Gilles Deleuze. *Desert Island and Other Texts. 1953–1974*, 94–116. Ed. David Lapoujade, trans. Michael Taormina. Los Angeles/New York: Semiotext(e).

— (2004d) »Nomadic Thought«. In Gilles Deleuze. *Desert Island and Other Texts. 1953–1974*, 252–261. Ed. David Lapoujade, trans. Michael Taormina. Los Angeles/New York: Semiotext(e).

— (2004e) »On Nietzsche and the Image of Thought«. In Gilles Deleuze. *Desert Island and Other Texts. 1953–1974*, 135–142. Ed. David Lapoujade, trans. Michael Taormina. Los Angeles/New York: Semiotext(e).

— (2003) *Francis Bacon. The Logic of Sensation*. Trans. Daniel W. Smith. Minneapolis: University of Minnesota Press.

— (2002a) *Bergsonism*. Trans. Hugh Tomlinson and Barbara Habberjam. New York: Zone Books.

— (2002b) *Pure Immanence. Essays on A Life*. Trans. Anne Boyman. New York: Zone Books.

— *Cinema 2. The Time-Image*. Trans. Hugh Tomlinson and Robert Galeta. London: Athlone Press.

— (1998) *Foucault*. Ed. and trans. Seán Hand. Minneapolis/London: University of Minnesota Press.

— (1997) *Expressionism in Philosophy: Spinoza*. Trans. Martin Joughin. New York: Zone Books.

— (1995) *Negotiations. 1972–1990*. Trans. Martin Joughin. New York: Columbia University Press.

— (1994) *Difference and Repetition*. Trans. Paul Patton. New York: Columbia University Press.

— (1993) *The Fold: Leibniz and the Baroque*. Trans. Tom Conley. Minneapolis: University of Minnesota Press.

— (1992) »Ethology: Spinoza and Us«. In Jonathan Crary, Sanford Kwinter, eds. *Zone 6. Incorporations*, 625–633. New York: Zone Books.

— (1990) *The Logic of Sense*. Ed. Constantin V. Boundas, trans. Mark Lester with Charles Stivale. New York: Columbia University Press.

— (1988) *Spinoza: Practical Philosophy*. Trans. Robert Hurley. San Francisco: City Lights.

— (1983) *Nietzsche and Philosophy*. Trans. Hugh Tomlinson. New York: Columbia University Press.

Deleuze, Gilles and Félix Guattari. (2004) *Anti-Oedipus. Capitalism and Schizophrenia*. Trans. Robert Hurley, Mark Seem, and Helen R. Lane. London/New York: Continuum.

— (2000a) *Kafka: toward a minor literature*. Trans. Dana Polan. Minneapolis: University of Minnesota Press.

— (2000b) *A Thousand Plateaus: Capitalism and Schizophrenia*. Trans. Brian Massumi. Minneapolis: University of Minnesota Press.

— (1994) *What is Philosophy?* Trans. Hugh Tomlinson and Graham Burchell. New York: Columbia University Press.

Derrida, Jacques. (2007) *Learning to Live Finally. The Last Interview*. Trans. Pascale-Anne Brault and Michael Naas. Hoboken: Melville House Publishing.

— (2001) »I am Going to Have to Wander All Alone«. In Jacques Derrida. *The Work of Mourning*. Ed. and trans. Pascale-Anne Brault and Michael Naas. Chicago: University of Chicago.

— (1997) *Of Grammatology*. Trans. Gayatri Ch. Spivak. Baltimore: Johns Hopkins University Press.

— (1978) »Violence and Metaphysics: An Essay on the Thought of Emmanuel Levinas.« In Jacques Derrida. *Writing and Difference*, 79–153. Trans. Alan Bass. Chicago: Chicago University Press.

Descombes, Vincent. (1980) *Modern French Philosophy*. Trans. L. Scott-Fox and J.M. Harding. Cambridge: Cambridge University Press.

Diekmann, Stefanie and Thomas Khurana (ed.). (2007) *Latenz. 40 Annäherungen an einen Begriff*. Berlin: Kulturverlag Kadmos.

Foucault, Michel. (2004) »Preface«. In Gilles Deleuze and Félix Guattari. *Anti-Oedipus. Capitalism and Schizophrenia*, xiii-xvi. Trans. Robert Hurley, Mark Seem, and Helen R. Lane. London/New York: Continuum.

— (1998a) »Nietzsche, Freud, Marx«. In Michel Foucault. *Aesthetics, Method, and Epistemology. Essential Works of Foucault 1954–1984*, Vol. 2, 269–278. Ed. James D. Faubion, trans. Robert Hurley et al. New York: The New Press.

— (1998b) »Theatrum Philosophicum«. In Michel Foucault. *Aesthetics, Method, and Epistemology. Essential Works of Foucault 1954–1984*, Vol. 2, 343–368. Ed. James D. Faubion, trans. Robert Hurley et al. New York: The New Press.

— (1998c) »The Thought of the Outside«. In Michel Foucault. *Aesthetics, Method, and Epistemology. Essential Works of Foucault 1954–1984*, Vol. 2, 147–169. Ed. James D. Faubion, trans. Robert Hurley et al. New York: The New Press.

— (1997) »What is Enlightenment?«. In Michel Foucault. *Ethics: Subjectivity and Truth. Essential Works of Foucault 1954–1984*, Vol. 1, 303–319. Ed. Paul Rabinow, trans. Robert Hurley et al. New York: The New Press.

— (1996) »Intellectuals and Power«. In Michel Foucault. *Foucault Live, Collected Interviews, 1961–1984*. Ed. Sylvère Lotringer, trans. Lysa Hochroth and John Johnston. New York: Semiotext(e).

— (1994a) *The Birth of the Clinic. An Archeology of Medical Perception*. New York: Vintage Books.

— (1994b) *The Order of Things. An Archaeology of the Human Sciences*. New York: Vintage.

— (1964) »Nietzsche«. *Cahiers de Royaumont. Philosophie No VI*: 183–192.

GASCHÉ, Rodolphe. (2007) *The Honor of Thinking: Critique, Theory, Philosophy*. Stanford: Stanford University Press.

GOODCHILD, Philip. (2002) *Capitalism and Religion. The Price of Piety*. London/New York: Routledge.

— (2001) »Why is philosophy so compromised with God?«. In Mary Bryden, ed. *Deleuze and Religion*, 156–166. London: Routledge.

— (1997) »Deleuzean Ethics«. *Theory, Culture & Society* 14/2: 39–50.

GROSZ, Elizabeth. (2005) *Time Travels. Feminism, Nature, Power*. Durham/London: Duke University Press.

— (2004) *The Nick of Time. Politics, Evolution, and the Untimely*. Durham/London: Duke University Press.

— ed. (1999) *Becomings. Explorations in Time, Memory and Future*. Ithaca/London: Cornell University Press.

GÜNZEL, Stephan. (2002) »Wille zur Differenz. Gilles Deleuzes Nietzsche-Lektüre«. In Stephan Günzel. *Anteile. Analytik, Hermeneutik, Politik*, 43–64. Weimar: Verlag und Datenbank für Geistewissenschaften.

HALLWARD, Peter. (2006) *Out of this World: Deleuze and the Philosophy of Creation*. London/New York: Verso.

HARDT, Michael. (1995) *Gilles Deleuze. An Apprenticeship in Philosophy*. Minneapolis/London: University of Minnesota Press.

HARDT, Michael and Antonio NEGRI. (2004) *Multitude. War and Democracy in the Age of Empire*. New York: The Penguin Press.

— (2000) *Empire*. Cambridge, MA: Harvard University Press.

HAYDEN, Patrick. (1998) *Multiplicity and Becoming. The Pluralist Empiricism of Gilles Deleuze*. New York: Peter Lang Publishing.

HEGEL, Georg Wilhelm Friedrich. (1995) *Lectures on the History of Philosophy. Medieval and Modern Philosophy*. Vol. 3. Trans. E.S. Haldane and Francis H. Simson. Lincoln/London: University of Nebraska Press.

HEIDEGGER, Martin. (1991a) *Nietzsche*. Vol. I and II. Trans. David Farell Krell. New York: Harper Collins Publishers.

— (1991b) *Nietzsche*. Vol. III and IV. Ed. and trans. David Farell Krell et al. New York: Harper Collins Publishers.

IRIGARAY, Luce. (1993) *An Ethics of Sexual Difference*. Ithaca, NY: Cornell University Press.

JAMES, William. (2003) *Essays in Radical Empiricism*. London/New York: Dover Publications, Inc.

KAFKA, Franz. (1958) *Parables and Paradoxes*. New York: Schocken Books.

KIERKEGAARD, Søren. (1983) *Fear and Trembling* and *Repetition*. Ed. and trans. Howard V. Hong and Edna H. Hong. Princeton: Princeton University Press.

KLOSSOWSKI, Pierre. (2005) *Nietzsche and the Vicious Circle*. Trans. Daniel W. Smith. London/New York: Continuum.

KOLAKOWSKI, Leszek. (2001) *Bergson*. South Bend: St. Augustine's Press.

KUIKEN, Kir. (2005) »Deleuze/Derrida: Towards an almost Imperceptible Difference«. *Research in Phenomenology* 35: 290–308.

LACAN, Jacques. (1997) *The Ethics of Psychoanalysis 1959–1960*. The Seminar of Jacques Lacan, Book VII. Ed. Jacques-Alain Miller, trans. Dennis Porter. New York/London: Norton & Company.

LACLAU, Ernesto and Chantal MOUFFE. (1996) *Hegemony & Socialist Strategy. Towards a Radical Democratic Politics*. London/New York: Verso.

LAWLOR, Leonard. (2007) *This is Not Sufficient. An Essay on Animality and Human Nature in Derrida*. New York: Columbia University Press.

— (2003a) *The Challenge of Bergsonism. Phenomenology, Ontology, Ethics*. London/ New York: Continuum.

— (2003b) *Thinking through French Philosophy. The Being of the Question*. Bloomington: Indiana University Press.

— (2000) »A Nearly Total Affinity: The Deleuzian Virtual Image versus the Derridean Trace«. *Angelaki* 5/2: 59–71.

LEVINAS, Emmanuel. (2003) *On Escape*. Trans. Bettina Bergo. Stanford: Stanford University Press.

— (2000) *Totality and Infinity. An Essay on Exteriority*. Trans. Alphonso Lingis. Pittburgh: Duquesne University Press.

— (1998) *Otherwise than Being: Or Beyond Essence*. Trans. Alphonso Lingis. Pittsburgh: Duquesne University Press.

LYOTARD, Jean-François. (1999) *The Differend*. Trans. Georges Van Den Abbeele. Minneapolis: University of Minnesota Press.

MARRATI, Paola. (2005) »Time, Life, Concepts: The Newness of Bergson«. *MLN* 120: 1099–1111.

— (1999) »L'Animal qui sait fuir. G. Deleuze: Politique du devenir, ontology de l'immanence«. In Marie-Louise Millet. ed. *L'animal autobiographique autour de Jacques Derrida*, 197–214. Paris: Edition Galilée.

MASSUMI, Brian. (2000) »Translator's Foreword: Pleasures of Philosophy«. In Gilles Deleuze, Felix Guattari. *A Thousand Plateaus*, ix-xv. Minneapolis/London: University of Minnesota Press.

MURPHY, Timothy S. (1998) »Quantum Ontology. A Virtual Mechanics of Becoming«. In Eleanor Kaufman, Kevin Heller, eds. *Deleuze and Guattari: New Mappings in Politics and Philosophy, and Culture*, 211–229. Minneapolis/London: University of Minnesota Press.

NESBITT, Nick. (2005) »The Expulsion of the Negative: Deleuze, Adorno, and the Ethics of Internal Difference«. *SubStance* 107, 34/2: 75–97.

NIETZSCHE, Friedrich. (2006a) *The Gay Science*. Ed. Bernard Williams, trans. Josefine Nauckhoff and Adrian del Caro. Cambridge: Cambridge University Press.

— (2006b) *Thus Spoke Zarathustra*. Eds. Adrian del Caro and Robert Pippin, trans. Adrian del Caro. Cambridge: Cambridge University Press.

— (2005) *Beyond Good and Evil*. Eds. Rolf-Peter Horstmann and Judith Norman, trans. Judith Norman. Cambridge: Cambridge University Press.

— (1999a) *Ecce Homo*. In Friedrich Nietzsche. *Nachlaß 1875–1879*, 255–374. Kritische Studienausgabe (KSA), Vol. 6. Eds. Giorgio Colli and Mazzino Montinari. Berlin/New York: Walter de Gruyter.

— (1999b) *Nachlaß 1875–1879*. Kritische Studienausgabe (KSA), Vol. 8. Eds. Giorgio Colli and Mazzino Montinari. Berlin/New York: Walter de Gruyter.

— (1999c) *Nachlaß 1880–1882*. Kritische Studienausgabe (KSA), Vol. 9. Eds. Giorgio Colli and Mazzino Montinari. Berlin/New York: Walter de Gruyter.

— (1999d) *Nachlaß 1882–1884*. Kritische Studienausgabe (KSA), Vol. 10. Eds. Giorgio Colli and Mazzino Montinari. Berlin/New York: Walter de Gruyter.

— (1999e) *Nachlaß 1884–1885*. Kritische Studienausgabe (KSA), Vol. 11. Eds. Giorgio Colli and Mazzino Montinari. Berlin/New York: Walter de Gruyter.

— (1999f) *Nachlaß 1887–1889*. Kritische Studienausgabe (KSA), Vol. 13. Eds. Giorgio Colli and Mazzino Montinari. Berlin/New York: Walter de Gruyter.

— (1995) *On the Genealogy of Morality*. Ed. Keith Ansell Pearson, trans. Carol Diethe. Cambridge: Cambridge University Press.

— (1968) *The Will to Power*. Ed. Walter Kaufmann, trans. Walter Kaufmann and R.J. Hollingdale. New York: Vintage Books.

PARKINSON, G.H.R. (2003) »Editor's Introduction«. In Baruch de Spinoza. *Ethics*, 5–50. Oxford: Oxford University Press.

— (1977) »Hegel, Pantheism, and Spinoza«. *Journal of the History of Ideas* 38/3: 449–459.

PATTON, Paul. (2000) *Deleuze and the Political*. New York/London: Routledge.

PEARSON, Keith Ansell. (2005) »The Eternal Return of the Overhuman: *The Weightiest Knowledge and the Abyss of Light*«. *Journal of Nietzsche Studies* 30: 1–21.

— (2002) *Philosophy and the Adventure of the Virtual. Bergson and the Time of Life*. London/New York: Routledge.

— (2001) »Pure reserve: Deleuze, philosophy, and immanence«. In Mary Bryden, ed. *Deleuze and Religion*, 141–155. London: Routledge.

— (1999) *Germinal Life. The Difference and Repetition of Deleuze*. London/New York: Routledge.

— (1997) *Viroid Life. Perspectives on Nietzsche and the Transhuman Condition*. London/New York: Routledge.

RAJCHMAN, John. (2002) »Introduction«. In Gilles Deleuze, *Pure Immanence. Essays on A Life*, 7–23. Trans. Anne Boyman. New York: Zone Books.

RANCIÈRE, Jacques. (1998) *Disagreement: Politics and Philosophy*. Minneapolis: University of Minnesota Press.

RICCO, John Paul, guest ed. (2005) »Unbecoming«. *Parallax* 35.

RONELL, Avital. (2003) *Stupidity*. Urbana/Chicago: University of Illinois Press.

SIMONDON, Gilbert. (1992) »The Genesis of the Individual«. In Jonathan Crary, Sanford Kwinter, eds. *Zone 6. Incorporations*, 297–319. New York: Zone Books.

SMITH, Daniel W. (2003) »Deleuze and Derrida, Immanence and Transcendence: Two Directions in Recent French Thought«. In Paul Patton, John Protevi, eds. *Between Deleuze and Derrida*, 46–66. London/New York: Continuum.

— (2001) »The Doctrine of Univocity: Deleuze's Ontology of Immanence«. In Mary Bryden, ed. *Deleuze and Religion*, 167–183. London: Routledge.

— (1998) »The Place of Ethics in Deleuze's Philosophy. Three Questions of Immanence«. In Eleanor Kaufman, Kevin Heller, eds. *Deleuze and Guattari: New Mappings in Politics and Philosophy, and Culture*, 251–269. Minneapolis/London: University of Minnesota Press.

SPINOZA, Baruch de. (2003) *Ethics*. Ed. G.H.R. Parkinson. Oxford/New York: Oxford University Press.

ZIAREK, Ewa Płonowska. (2001) *An Ethics of Dissensus. Postmodernity, Feminism, and the Politics of Radical Democracy*. Stanford: Stanford University Press.

ZUPANČIČ, Alenka. (2003) *The Shortest Shadow. Nietzsche's Philosophy of the Two*. Cambridge, Mass.: The MIT Press.